RV Camping
in State Parks

D.J. Davin

Published by:

Roundabout Publications
P.O. Box 19235
Lenexa, KS 66285

800-455-2207

www.TravelBooksUSA.com
www.RVdumps.com
www.RoadNotes.com

Please Note:
Every effort has been made to make this book as complete and as accurate as possible. However, there may be mistakes both typographical and in content. Therefore, this text should be used as a general guide to state parks. Although we regret any inconvenience caused by inaccurate information, the author and Roundabout Publications shall have neither liability nor responsibility to any person or entity with respect to any loss or damage caused, or alleged to be caused, directly or indirectly by the information contained in this book.

Cover photos courtesy Kentucky Department of Parks.
Photos of Cumberland Falls and Jenny Wiley State Resort Parks.

Contents

Introduction

About this Book

Millions of Americans enjoy camping in state parks every year. *RV Camping in State Parks* is designed to make finding RV-friendly state parks easier. In it, you'll find information on more than 1,600 state parks in 49 states (Hawaii is not included) that offer accommodations for RVers.

A summary for each state tells you how many state parks have RV campgrounds and the amenities generally available. You'll also find contact information, including phone number and web site, for each state so you can obtain state park brochures and more information.

Following the summary is a Park Locator Chart, which lists all the state parks alphabetically. The number that follows each park corresponds to the map and the park's listing. This chart is helpful if you already know the name of a state park you'd like to visit.

State maps are provided to aid you in finding state parks with RV facilities. Locations on the map are approximate and are intended to give you the general idea of where parks are located. If you need specific information or directions, it is best to call the state park you are planning to visit.

Details for each state park include location, general directions, and contact information, including each park's phone number. You'll also learn how many RV sites are available, the number of sites that have water and electric hookups, and sites with full hookups. Also provided is each park's season of operation and availability of showers and dump stations.

Camping Fees

We have included a Rate Group guide for each state, which

indicates general camping fees charged throughout the state. These rates do not include any entrance fees, if they are charged by a park. Rates were accurate at press time but are subject to change. We advise you call the park you plan to visit to confirm campsite availability and camping fees. Rates are categorized as follows:

Category	Fee Range
A	$9 to $12 per night
B	$13 to $16 per night
C	$17 and up per night

Abbreviations Used

Below is a list of some of the abbreviations used in this book.

Ave	Avenue	Rd	Road
Blvd	Boulevard	Resv	Reservations
CR	County Road	S	South
Dr	Drive	SE	Southeast
E	East	SP	State Park
Hwy	Highway	SRA	State Recreation Area
I	Interstate Highway	St	Street
N	North	SW	Southwest
NE	Northeast	US	US Highway
NW	Northwest	W	West
Pkwy	Parkway		

About the Author

D.J. Davin is a retired sales and marketing executive. He and his wife of 48 years have been enjoying the RV lifestyle since 2000. In the past four years they have made two cross-country junkets and currently are volunteer campground hosts with Oregon State Parks. They are the parents of four adult children and have ten grandchildren. When not in their RV, D.J. and his wife reside outside the Tucson, Arizona area.

Alabama

Alabama offers 22 state parks for RVers. Two more parks are undergoing renovations that will offer camping facilities. Most parks have dump stations, electric and water at the sites and all have showers. Alabama parks accept MasterCard, Visa and AMEX credit cards. Seniors are eligible for 15% discount, with proof of age. All parks are open year round, weather permitting. If in doubt, call the particular park. Unless noted otherwise, all parks have a sanitary dump station. Rate groups: B and C.

Alabama State Parks
Box 301452
Montgomery, AL 36130
Information and Reservations: (800) 252-7257
Internet: www.dcnr.state.al.us

Alabama Park Locator

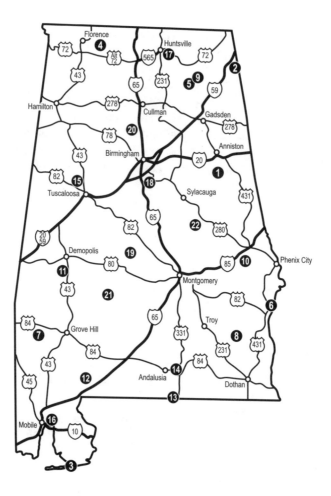

1. Cheaha State Park (Resort), 19644 Hwy 281, Delta, AL 36258. Office: (256) 488-5111. Resort: (800) 846-2654. Located 12 miles south of I-20 off AL 281 near Anniston. 73 sites with water and electric; showers.

2. DeSoto State Park (Resort), 13883 County Rd. 89, Fort Payne, AL 35967. Office: (256) 845-0051. Resort: (800) 568-8840. Located 8 miles NE of Fort Payne near I-59 & US 11. 78 sites with water and electric.

3. Gulf State Park (Resort), 20115 State Hwy 135, Gulf Shores, AL 36542. Campground reservations: (251) 948-6353. Resort: (800) 544-4853. Located in the city of Gulf Shores on the Gulf of Mexico. 200 modern campsites with water and electric; 268 primitive (no facilities) sites.

4. Joe Wheeler State Park (Resort), 201 McLean Dr., Rogersville, AL 35652. Phone: (256) 247-1184. Located 1.5 miles west of Rogersville on US 72. 116 sites with water and electric.

5. Lake Guntersville State Park (Resort), 7966 State Hwy 227, Guntersville, AL 35976. Office: (256) 571-5455. Resort: (800) 548-4553. Located 6 miles NE of Guntersville off Hwy 227. 364 sites with water and electric; showers.

6. Lakepoint Resort State Park (Resort), 104 Lakepoint Dr., Eufaula, AL 39027. Office: (334) 687-6676. Resort: (800) 544-5253. Located 7 miles north of Eufaula on US 431 near Georgia state line. 190 sites with water and electric; showers.

7. Bladon Springs State Park, 3921 Bladon Rd., Bladon Springs, AL 36919. Phone: (251) 754 9207. Located 12 miles west of Coffeeville via US 84 and CR 31. 10 sites with water and electric.

8. Blue Springs State Park, 2595 State Hwy 10, Clio, AL 36017. Phone: (334) 397-4875. Located 6 miles east of Clio on AL 10 about 15 miles west of US 431. 50 sites with water and electric; showers.

9. Buck's Pocket State Park, 393 County Rd. 174, Grove Oak, AL 35975. Phone: (256) 659-2000. Located 2 miles north of Grove Oak. Northbound travelers use exit 205 off I-59 to CR 20 to AL 227. Southbound travelers use exit 218 off I-59 to AL 35 to Rainsville, south on AL 75 to AL 227, follow signs to park. 36 sites with water and electric; laundry; showers.

10. Chewacla State Park, 124 Shell Toomer Pkwy, Auburn, AL 36830. Phone: (334) 887-5621. Located 4 miles south of Auburn off I-85 at exit 51. 36 sites with water and electric; showers.

11. Chickasaw State Park, 26955 US Hwy 43, Gallion, AL 36742. Phone: (334) 295-8230. Located on US 43 about 4 miles north of Linden. 8 sites with water and electric; showers.

12. Claude D. Kelley State Park, 580 H. Kyle Rd., Atmore, AL 36502. Phone: (251) 862-2511. Located 12 miles north of I-65 exit 57 on AL 21. 12 sites with water and electric, showers.

13. Florala State Park, 22738 Azalea Dr., Florala, AL 36442. Phone: (334) 858-6425. Located in the city of Florala on US 331 north of AL/FL state line. 23 sites with water and electric; showers.

14. Frank Jackson State Park, 100 Jerry Adams Dr., Opp, AL 36467. Phone: (334) 493-6988. Located in the town of Opp on US 331 (21 miles north of Florala, see above listing). 26 sites with water and electric; showers.

15. Lake Lurleen State Park, 13226 Lake Lurleen, Coker, AL 35452. Phone: (205) 339-1558. Located 12 miles NW of Tuscaloosa via US 82 and CR 21. 91 sites with water and electric; showers.

16. Meaher State Park, 5200 Battleship Pkwy E., Spanish Fort, AL 36577. Phone: (251) 626-5529. Located on US 90 (Old Spanish Trail) north of I-10 exit 30. 12 sites with water and electric; showers.

17. Monte Sano State Park, 5105 Nolen Ave., Huntsville, AL 35801. Phone: (256) 534-3757. Located in the city of Huntsville, 8 miles southeast of city center on US 431. 89 sites with water and electric; showers.

18. Oak Mountain State Park, 299 Terrace Dr., Pelham, AL 35124. Phone: (205) 620-2527. Reservations: (205) 620-2524. Located east of I-65 exit 246 along AL 119 (15 miles south of Birmingham). 150 sites with water and electric; showers. Largest park in system.

19. Paul M. Grist State Park, 1546 Grist Rd., Selma, AL 36701. Phone: (334) 872-5846. Located 15 miles north of Selma via CR 37. 6 sites with water and electric; showers.

20. Rickwood Caverns State Park, 370 Rickwood Park Rd., Warrior, AL 35180. Phone: (205) 647-9692. Located 4 miles west of I-65 at exit 284 (Warrior). 13 sites with water and electric; showers; pool.

21. Roland Cooper State Park, 285 Deer Run Dr., Camden, AL 35726. Phone: (334) 682-4838. Located 6 miles NE of Camden on AL 41 (about 37 miles SW of Selma). 41 sites with water and electric; showers; laundry; store.

22. Wind Creek State Park, 4325 State Hwy 128, Alexander City, AL 35010. Phone: (256) 329-0845. Located 7 miles SE of Alexander City via AL 63 and AL 128. 642 sites (many waterfront) with water and electric; showers; store.

Alaska

America's largest state also has the most acreage devoted to State Parks, but has only 51 locations suitable for RVs. These locations include State Parks, Recreation Sites and Areas. And they all have two aspects in common: no electrical hook-ups in any location and RVs are limited to 35 feet. Part of the size limitation is because of the access roads being difficult to navigate with larger rigs. These state facilities do not have telephones in the locations so all information about a particular park must come from one of three regional offices (see below.) Several parks have multiple campgrounds in the park and are listed with a single location. Pets are permitted on leashes. All locations have central drinking water facilities. Reservations are not accepted and usually not required. Rate Groups: A and B, depending on park facilities.

Alaska Public Lands Information Center
605 W. 4th Ave., Ste. 105
Anchorage, AK 99501
Information:
Anchorage - (907) 269-8400
Fairbanks - (907) 451-2705
Kenai - (907) 262-5581
Internet: www.alaskastateparks.org

Alaska Park Locator

Alaska Park Locator (*cont.*)

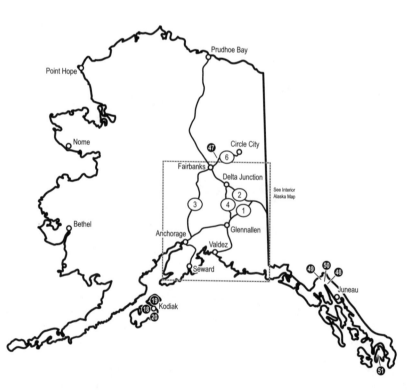

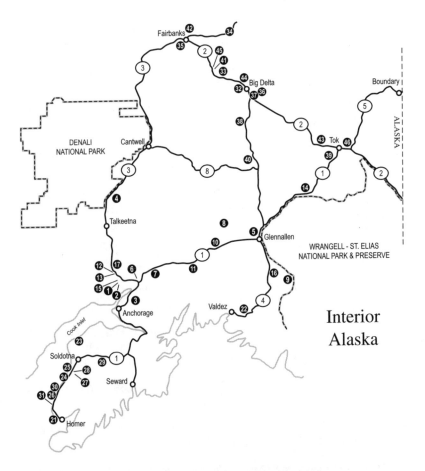

Interior
Alaska

1. Big Lake North State Recreation Site, Big Lake, AK 99652. Located 26 miles west of Wasilla, off AK 3 (Parks Hwy), on North Big Lake Road. 60 sites.

2. Big Lake South State Recreation Site, Big Lake, AK 99652. Located 26 miles west of Wasilla, off AK 3 (Parks Hwy) on South Big Lake Road. 20 sites.

3. Chugach State Park, Eagle River, AK 99577. Located NE of Anchorage off AK 1 (Glenn Hwy) near Eagle River. 3 campgrounds: Eklutna Campground - 50 sites; Eagle River Campground - 57 sites; dump station; Bird Creek Campground - 28 sites (plus 20 overflow sites).

4. Denali State Park, Trapper Creek, AK 99683. Located about 163 miles north of Anchorage on AK 3 (Parks Hwy), next to Denali National Park. 3 campgrounds: Denali View Campground - 20 sites; Byers Lake Campground - 73 sites; Lower Troublesome Creek Campground - 20 sites.

5. Dry Creek State Recreation Site, Glennallen, AK 99588. Located about 125 miles NE of Anchorage, near Glennallen on AK 1 (Glenn Hwy). 58 sites.

6. Finger Lakes State Recreation Site, Palmer, AK 99645. Located on Bogard Road near Palmer, NE of Anchorage, off AK 1 (Glenn Hwy). 41 sites.

7. King Mountain State Recreation Site, Palmer, AK 99645. Located outside Palmer on AK 1 (Glenn Hwy). 22 sites.

8. Lake Louise State Recreation Area, Glennallen, AK 99588. Located off AK 1 (Glenn Hwy) near Glennallen, on Lake Louise. 60 sites.

9. Liberty Falls State Recreation Site, Chitina, AK 99566. Located outside Chitina on AK 10 (Edgerton Hwy), next to Wrangell-Saint Elias National Park. 10 sites.

10. Little Nelchina State Recreation Site, Glennallen, AK 99588. Located on AK 1 (Glenn Hwy) between Chickaloon and Glennallen. 11 sites.

11. Matanuska Glacier State Recreation Site, Palmer, AK 99645. Located NE of Palmer on AK 1 (Glenn Hwy). 12 sites.

12. Nancy Lake State Recreation Area, Willow, AK 99688. Located outside Willow, off AK 3 (Parks Hwy). 2 campgrounds: South Rolly Lake Campgrounds - 98 sites; Tanaina Lake Canoe Trail - 13 sites.

13. Nancy Lake State Recreation Site, Willow, AK 99688. Located outside Willow on AK 3 (Parks Hwy). 30 sites.

14. Porcupine Creek State Recreation Site, Tok, AK 99780. Located about 62 miles south of Tok on AK 1. 12 sites.

15. Rocky Lake State Recreation Site, Big Lake, AK 99652. Located on Big Lake Road, off AK 3, SW of Wasilla. 10 sites.

16. Squirrel Creek State Recreation Site, Copper Center, AK 99573. Located about 35 miles south of Glennallen along AK 4. 23 sites.

17. Willow Creek State Recreation Area, Willow, AK 99688. Located north of Willow on AK 3 (Parks Hwy). 140 sites.

18. Buskin River State Recreation Site*

19. Ft. Abercrombie State Historic Park*

20. Pasagshak State Recreation Site*

   * All 3 are located outside Kodiak on Kodiak Island (accessible only by ferry). 48 total sites.

21. Anchor River State Recreation Area, Homer, AK 99603. Located on Kenai Peninsula, outside Homer on AK 1 (Sterling Hwy). 116 sites.

22. Blueberry Lake State Recreation Site, Valdez, AK 99686. Located on Prince William Sound outside Valdez, on AK 4 (Richardson Hwy). 15 sites.

23. Captain Cook State Recreation Area, Nikiski, AK 99635. Located north of Soldotna, off AK 1. 52 sites.

24. Clam Gulch State Recreation Area, Soldotna, AK 99669. Located SE of Soldotna near Clam Gulch on AK 1 (Sterling Hwy). 116 sites.

25. Crooked Creek State Recreation Site, Soldotna, AK 99669. Located on Cook Inlet outside Soldotna on Coho Loop Rd. 80 sites.

26. Deep Creek State Recreation Area, Homer, AK 99603. Located NE of Homer on Cook Inlet, on AK 1 (Sterling Hwy). 189 sites.

27. Johnson Lake State Recreation Area, Soldotna, AK 99669. Located south of Soldotna on AK 1 (Sterling Hwy). 48 sites.

28. Kasilof River State Recreation Site, Soldotna, AK 99669. Located south of Soldotna on AK 1 (Sterling Hwy). 10 sites.

29. Kenai River Special Management Area, Sterling, AK 99672. Located NW of Soldotna on AK 1 (Sterling Hwy). 4 campgrounds: Bings Landing - 37 sites; Izaak Walton - 26 sites; Morgans Landing - 42 sites; Funny River - 10 sites.

30. Ninilchik State Recreation Area, Homer, AK 99603. Located north of Homer on AK 1 (Sterling Hwy). 117 sites; dump station.

31. Stariski State Recreation Site, Homer, AK 99603. Located north of Homer on AK 1 (Sterling Hwy). 9 sites.

32. Big Delta State Historic Park, Delta Junction, AK 99737. Located 120 miles SE of Fairbanks near Delta Junction on AK 2 (Richardson Hwy). 23 sites.

33. Birch Lake State Recreation Site, Fairbanks, AK. Located near Salcha, SE of Fairbanks, on AK 2 (Richardson Hwy). 20 sites.

34. Chena River State Recreation Area, Fairbanks, AK. Located 57 miles NE of Fairbanks at the end of Chena Hot Springs Road. 3 campgrounds: Rosehip Campground - 37 sites; Tors Trail Campground - 24 sites; Red Squirrel Campground - 5 sites.

35. Chena River State Recreation Site, Fairbanks, AK. Located in Fairbanks on University Avenue. 61 sites; dump station.

36. Clearwater State Recreation Site, Delta Junction, AK 99737. Located outside Delta Junction on AK 2 (Richardson Hwy). 17 sites.

37. Delta State Recreation Site, Delta Junction, AK 99737. Located outside Delta Junction on AK 2 (Richardson Hwy). 25 sites; showers.

38. Donnelly Creek State Recreation Site, Delta Junction, AK 99737. Located south of Delta Junction on AK 4 (Richardson Hwy). 12 sites.

39. Eagle Trail State Recreation Site, Tok, AK 99780. Located south of Tok on Tok Cutoff. 35 sites.

40. Fielding Lake State Recreation Site, Delta Junction, AK 99737. Located south of Delta Junction on AK 4 (Richardson Hwy). 17 sites.

41. Harding Lake State Recreation Area, Fairbanks, AK. Located between Fairbanks and Delta Junction on AK 2 (Richardson Hwy). 78 sites; dump station.

42. Lower Chatanika River State Recreation Area, Fairbanks, AK. Located north of Fairbanks on Elliott Hwy. 12 sites.

43. Moon Lake State Recreation Site, Tok, AK 99780. Located just west of Tok on AK 2 (Richardson Hwy). 15 sites.

44. Quartz Lake State Recreation Area, Delta Junction, AK 99737. Located NW of Delta Junction on AK 2 (Richardson Hwy). 103 sites.

45. Salcha River State Recreation Site, Fairbanks, AK. Located outside Salcha on AK 2 (Richardson Hwy). 6 sites.

46. Tok River State Recreation Site, Tok, AK 99780. Located outside Tok on AK 2 (Richardson Hwy) 43 sites.

47. Upper Chatanika River State Recreation Site, Fairbanks, AK. Located NW of Fairbanks on Steese Hwy, off AK 2. 25 sites.

48. Chilkat State Park, Haines, AK 99827. Located 7 miles south of Haines on AK 7. 32 sites.

49. Mosquito Lake State Recreation Site, Haines, AK 99827. Located 27 miles NW of Haines on AK 7. 13 sites.

50. Chilkoot Lake State Recreation Site, Haines, AK 99827. Located 10 miles north of Haines on Lutak Road, off AK 7. 32 sites.

51. Settlers Cove State Recreation Site, Ketchikan, AK 99903. Located in southeastern Alaska outside Ketchikan off AK 7 on Tongass Road. 14 sites. Note: Ketchikan is accessible only by ferry.

Arizona

Arizona offers the RVer 14 State Parks or Recreation Areas and one special area operated by the Game and Fish Department that has RV facilities (see listing 15). Most of the facilities have electric hook-ups and in-park showers. Some locations accept reservations but you must check with the park or central reservations. Pets are allowed and credit cards are accepted. Rate groups: A and C depending on facilities and park.

Arizona State Parks
1300 West Washington St.
Phoenix, AZ 85007
Information and Reservations: (602) 542-4147
Internet: www.azstateparks.com

Arizona Park Locator

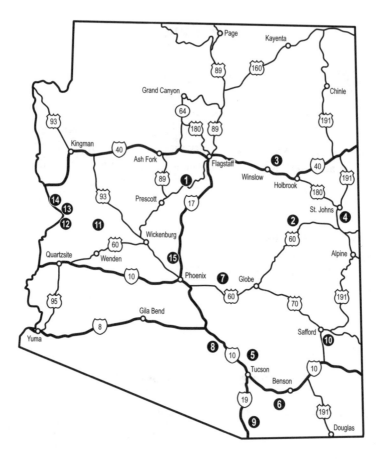

1. Dead Horse Ranch State Park, Cottonwood, AZ 86326. Phone: (928)
    634-5283. Located in northern AZ, 39 miles west of Sedona on AZ 89A.
    104 sites with electric; showers; dump station.

2. Fool Hollow Lake Recreation Area, Show Low, AZ 85901. Phone: (989)
    537-3680. Located in northeastern AZ, 47 miles south of Holbrook. From
    I-40 exit 285 south to Show Low, follow signs. 93 sites with electric;
    showers; dump station.

3. Homolovi Ruins State Park, Winslow, AZ 86047. Phone: (928) 289-4106.
    Located in north-central AZ, 12 miles NE of I-40 exit 257 on AZ 87. 53
    sites with electric; showers; dump station.

4. Lyman Lake State Park, St. Johns, AZ 85936. Phone: (928) 337-4441.
    Located in eastern AZ near NM state line, 15 miles south of St. Johns (I-
    40 exit 339) on US 191. 61 sites with electric; showers; dump station.

5. Catalina State Park, Tucson, AZ 85740. Phone: (520) 628-5798. Located in south-central AZ, 20 miles north of Tucson on AZ 77 at mile marker 81. 48 sites, 24 with electric; showers; dump station.

6. Kartchner Caverns State Park, Benson, AZ 85602. Phone: (520) 586-4100. Reservations: (520) 586-2283. Located in southeastern AZ, 9 miles south of I-10 exit 302 (Benson) on AZ 90. 62 sites with electric, water; showers; dump station. Big tourist attraction park; reservations strongly recommended.

7. Lost Dutchman State Park, Apache Junction, AZ 85219. Phone: (480) 982-4485. Located 50 miles east of Phoenix on AZ 88, off US 60 (Superstition Hwy). 35 sites; showers; dump station.

8. Picacho Peak State Park, Picacho, AZ 85214. Phone: (520) 466-3183. Located northwest of Tucson at I-10 exit 219. 100 sites, 85 with electric, 40 with electric and water; dump station.

9. Patagonia Lake State Park, Patagonia, AZ 85624. Phone: (520) 287-6965. Remote location in southern AZ near Nogales on AZ 82, 35 miles south of I-10 exit 281. 72 sites, 34 with electric and water; showers; dump station. 35 foot limit.

10. Roper Lake State Park, Safford, AZ 85546. Phone: (928) 428-6760. Locate in southeastern AZ, 28 miles north of I-10 exits 352 or 355 on US 191; south of Safford about 6 miles. 71 sites with electric; showers; dump station.

11. Alamo Lake State Park, Wenden, AZ 85357. Phone: (928) 669-2088. Remote location in western AZ on Alamo Dam, 32 miles north of US 60 from Wenden on county roads; follow signs. 250 sites, some with electric and water; dump station. Note: Located in mountains; recommend you call park ranger for directions and site availability.

12. Buckskin Mountain State Park, Parker, AZ 85344. Phone: (928) 667-3231. Located in western AZ, 24 miles NE of Parker on US 95, on Colorado River. 105 sites, 68 with electric; showers; dump station.

13. Cattail Cove State Park, Lake Havasu City, AZ 86405. Phone: (928) 855-1223. Located in western AZ between Parker and Lake Havasu City on US 95, on Colorado River (north of Buckskin Mountain State Park). 61 sites with electric; showers; dump station. Reservations recommended.

14. Lake Havasu State Park, Lake Havasu City, AZ 86403. Phone: (928) 855-2784. Located in western AZ, 6 miles south of Lake Havasu City on US 95. 42 sites with electric; showers; dump station.

15. Ben Avery Shooting Facility, Phoenix, AZ 85086. Phone: (602) 942-3000. Located in central AZ about 16 miles north of Phoenix at I-17 exit 223, off AZ 74. Camping restricted to persons signed to use the shooting range. 99 sites with electric; showers; dump station.

Arkansas

Of the 51 Arkansas state parks, more than half (26) are RV friendly. The sites in these parks range from Premium Class A (water, electric, sewer) to Class B (no hook-ups). Most of the RV parks offer a sanitary dump station and showers. All the listed parks are open year round but some facilities might be limited because of seasonal adjustments. All the state parks accept Visa, MasterCard and Discover credit cards and the Resort Parks accept Amex cards as well. The parks with Class A sites offer 50 amp electric service as an option for a small upcharge. All parks accept reservations (up to 12 months in advance) and reservations are to be made directly with the individual park. Rate groups: A, B, and C depending upon site facilities.

Arkansas Dept. of Parks & Tourism
One Capitol Mall
Little Rock, AR 72201
Information: (888) 287-2757
Internet: www.ArkansasStateParks.com

Arkansas Park Locator

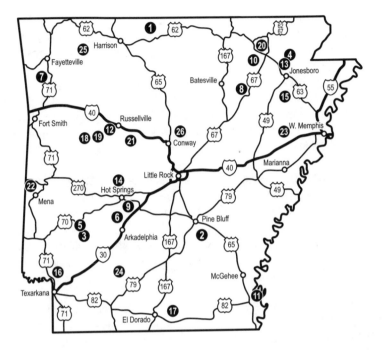

1. Bull Shoals-White River State Park, 129 Bull Shoals Park, Lakeview, AR 72642. Phone: (870) 431-5521. 85 sties (along the river); showers and dump station; store. Located about 9 miles south of AR/MO state line in north-central Arkansas on the White River. From Mountain Home, travel 6 miles north on AR 5 and then 8 miles west on AR 178.

2. Cane Creek State Park, Star City, AR 71667. Phone: (870) 628-4714. 30 Class A/Preferred sites; showers; dump station; store. Located 5 miles east of Star City on AR 293. Star City is located on US 425 about 24 miles SE of Pine Bluff.

3. Crater of Diamonds State Park, 209 State Park Rd., Murfreesboro, AR 71958. Phone: (870) 285-3113. 59 Class A sites; showers; dump station; store. Located on AR 301 about 2 miles SE of Murfreesboro.

4. Crowley's Ridge State Park, 2092 Hwy 168 N, Paragould, AR 72450. Phone: (870) 573-6751. 18 Class A sites; showers; dump station; store. Located in northeastern Arkansas 15 miles north of Jonesboro on AR 141 or 9 miles west of Paragould on US 412, then 2 miles south on AR 168.

5. Daisy State Park, 103 East Park, Kirby, AR 71950. Phone: (870) 398-4487. 96 Class A Premium/Preferred sites; dump station; store (showers nearby). Located 1/4 mile south of Daisy off US 70 near AR 27.

6. DeGray Lake Resort State Park, 2027 State Park Entrance Rd., Bismarck, AR 71929. Phone: (501) 865-2801. 113 Premium/Preferred/Class A sites; showers; dump station; store. Located about 14 miles NW of Arkadelphia on AR 7. Exit I-30 at Caddo Valley/Arkadelphia, exit 78, then 7 miles north on AR 7.

7. Devil's Den State Park, 11333 W Arkansas Hwy 74, West Fork, AR 72774. Phone: (479) 761-3325. 58 Class A/Preferred; 43 sites with water and electric in the Horse Camp; showers, dump station. Located about 25 miles south of Fayetteville. Directions: I-540 S from Fayetteville 8 miles to exit 53 then 17 miles SW on AR 170. From south, on I-540 exit at Winslow, exit 45 then 7 miles west on AR 74. Note: Trailers longer than 26 feet and larger RVs with tow cars should use exit 53.

8. Jacksonport State Park, 205 Avenue St., Newport, AR 72112. Phone: (870) 523-2143. Located in Jacksonport on AR 69, 3 miles north of Newport. 20 Class A sites, all 50-amp; showers; dump station; store.

9. Lake Catherine State Park, 1200 Catherine Park Rd., Hot Springs, AR 71913. Phone: (501) 844-4176. 70 Premium/Preferred/Class A sites; showers; dump station; store. Located southeast of Hot Springs on AR 171 near Malvern. Directions: I-30 exit 97, 12 miles north on AR 171.

10. Lake Charles State Park, 3705 Hwy 25, Powhatan, AR 72458. Phone: (870) 878-6595. 60 Class A/Premium/Preferred Sites. Showers and dump station are seasonal; store. Located in northeastern Arkansas near Hoxie. From Hoxie, 8 miles NW on US 63 then 6 miles south on AR 25.

11. Lake Chicot State Park, 2542 Hwy 257, Lake Village, AR 71653. Phone: (870) 265-5480. 127 sites, including Premium with sewer; Preferred/Class A and Class B. Located on AR 144, 8 miles NE of Lake Village. Exit US 65 at AR 144, east 9 miles to park.

12. Lake Dardanelle State Park, 2428 Marina Rd., Russellville, AR 72802. Phone: (479) 967-5516. This park has 2 areas, 83 sites total. Russellville has Premium sites with sewers, Preferred and Class A. Dardanelle has Class A only; showers, dump station and store. Located near Russellville in north-central AR. Russellville area: I-40 exit 81 (AR 7) south to AR

326, west 4 miles to park. Dardanelle area: 4 miles west of Dardanelle on AR 22.

13. Lake Frierson State Park, 7904 Hwy 141, Jonesboro, AR 72401. Phone: (870) 932-2615. 7 Class B sites. Showers and dump station nearby, not in the park. Located 10 miles north of Jonesboro on AR 141.

14. Lake Ouachita State Park, 5451 Mountain Pine Rd., Mountain Pine, AR 71956. Phone: (501) 767-9366. 117 Premium/Preferred/Class A and Class B sites; showers; dump station; store. Located NW of Hot Springs. Directions: 3 miles west on US 270 then 12 miles north on AR 227.

15. Lake Poinsett State Park, 5752 State Park Lane, Harrisburg, AR 72432. Phone: (870) 578-2064. 30 Class A and Class B sites. Showers, dump station, store. Located near Harrisburg in northeastern Arkansas between US 63 and US 49. Directions: From Harrisburg 1 mile east on AR 14 to AR 163, south 3 miles to park.

16. Millwood State Park, 1564 Hwy 32 E., Ashdown, AR 71822. Phone: (870) 898-2800. 114 Preferred/Class A; 13 Primitive sites. Showers, dump station, store. Located north of Texarkana off US 71. Directions: From Texarkana, north on US 71 to Ashdown (16 miles) east on AR 32 for 9 miles.

17. Moro Bay State Park, 6071 Hwy 600, Jersey, AR 71651. Phone: (870) 463-8555. 20 Class A sites. Showers and dump station operate seasonally; store. Located in southeastern Arkansas between El Dorado and Warren on US 63 (23 miles NE from El Dorado; 29 miles SW from Warren.)

18. Mount Magazine State Park, 16878 Hwy 309 S, Paris, AR 72855. Phone: (479) 963-8502. 18 Premium with sewer sites. Showers, dump station, store. Located on AR 309, 17 miles south of Paris; (exit 37 off I-40, about 35 miles south on AR 309).

19. Mount Nebo State Park, # 1 State Park Drive, Dardanelle, AR 72834. Phone: (479) 229-3655. 24 Class B sites. Showers and dump station operate seasonally; store. Located 7 miles west of Dardanelle on AR 155. Note: AR 155 is a zig-zag road and trailers longer than 24 feet and larger RVs are not recommended.

20. Old Davidsonville State Park, 7953 Hwy 166 S, Pocahontas, AR 72455. Phone: (870) 892-4708. 24 Class A sites. Showers seasonal. Dump station,

store. Located in northeastern Arkansas near Pocahontas and Black Rock. Directions: From Pocahontas, go 2 miles west on US 62 then 9 miles south on AR 166. From Black Rock, take AR 361 north to AR 166.

21. Petit Jean State Park, 1285 Petit Jean Mountain Rd., Morrilton, AR 72110. Phone: (501) 727-5441. 127 Premium/ Preferred/Class A sites. Showers, dump station, store. Located near Morrilton in north-central AR, Directions: From I-40 exit 108 at Morrilton, south 9 miles on AR 9, then 12 miles west on AR 154. From Dardanelle, 7 miles south on AR 7, then 16 miles east on AR 154.

22. Queen Wilhelmina State Park, 3877 Hwy 88 W, Mena, AR 71953. Phone: (479) 394-2863. 41 Class A and Class B (no hook-ups) sites. Showers, dump station, store. Located 13 miles west of Mena on AR 88. Alt. Route: From Mena go 6 miles north on US 71 then 9 miles west on US 270 to AR 272, then 2 miles south to park.

23. Village Creek State Park, 201 County Road 754, Wynne, AR 72396. Phone: (870) 238-9406. 104 Class A sites on lake. Showers seasonal; dump station; store.

24. White Oak Lake State Park, Route 2, Bluff City, AR 71722. Phone: (870) 685-2748. 41 Class A & Preferred sites. Showers, dump station. Located in a state forest southeast of Prescott. From Prescott on I-30 east 20 miles on AR 24 to AR 299, south 100 yards to AR 387, south 2 miles to park.

25. Withrow Springs State Park, 33424 Spur 23, Huntsville, AR 72740. Phone: (479) 559-2593. 16 Class A, 5 Class B sites, showers, dump station. Located on AR 23, 5 miles north of Huntsville.

26. Woolly Hollow State Park, 82 Woolly Hollow Rd., Greenbrier, AR 72058. Phone: (501) 679-2098. 20 Class A, 10 Class B sites. Showers, dump station. Located north of Conway. I-40 exit 125 (Conway), 12 miles north on US 65, 6 miles east on AR 285.

California

RV travelers in The Golden Gate State have their choice of 96 State Parks or Recreation Areas with facilities for recreational vehicles. While services in these locations vary from primitive sites to full hook-ups, a number of parks offer the RVer an "enroute campsite." These sites are usually in the Day Use parking area and available when the regular camping area is full. Users of these *"enroute"* facilities must be fully self-contained and agree they will vacate the area no later than 9am the following day. Parks with this type facility will be designated in the listing by *ER*.

Because of California's administrative assignment of parks to Districts, many parks are not reachable directly by U.S. Mail. Rather, these parks receive mail via the district office. Therefore, in some cases the park's listed address is the city of the district office; in other instances it is the city or town of the park's locale. The park's actual location or nearest city or town is indicated in the "located" section. Many parks have length limits that differ for motor homes and trailers. These differences are indicated in the listings (if different) by *M* for Motorhome and *T* for Trailer.

Most parks hold several sites out of the reservation system for drive-in campers. You should always check the desired location for space availability and direction particulars, if in doubt. Some parks or areas are not included in the State's reservation network. Those that <u>are not</u> have a strict "first come, first served" policy and cannot hold spaces for drive-in visitors. Also, senior citizens (age 62 or older) are entitled to a camping discount. This discount must be requested at check-in and proof of age is necessary. Rate groups: B and C depending on site utilities.

Note: Some of the listed telephone numbers are answered by a central State Park office. You must ask for the desired information by park name. Also, some of these numbers are answered by an automated device. To obtain information, follow the prompts.

State of California
Dept. of Parks and Recreation
Box 942896
Sacramento, CA 94296
Information: (916) 653-6995
Reservations: (800) 444-7275 (Reserve America)
Internet: www.CAescapes.com/camping or www.parks.ca.gov.

California Park Locator

California Park Locator (*cont.*)

1. Anza-Borrego Desert State Park, Borrego Springs, CA 92004. Phone: (760) 767-5311. Remote location in southern CA east of San Diego via CA 78 or 79. 158 sites, 52 with electric, water; dump station. 35 foot limit.

2. Benbow Lake State Recreation Area, Garberville, CA 95542. Phone: (707) 923-3238. Located in northern CA, south of Eureka off US 101, 2 miles south of Garberville. 77 sites with electric, water; showers; dump station. 30 foot limit-M; 24 foot limit-T. ER.

3. Big Basin Redwoods State Park, Boulder Creek, CA 95006. Phone: (831) 874-8368. Located in central CA , 23 miles north of Santa Cruz on CA 236. 150 sites; showers; dump station. 27 foot limit-M; 24 foot limit-T.

4. Bolsa Chica State Beach, San Clemente, CA 92672. Phone: (714) 846-3460. Located in southern CA in Huntington Beach. 57 sites with electric, water; dump station. 40 foot limit. ER.

5. Bothe-Napa Valley State Park, Sonoma, CA 95476. Phone: (707) 942-4575. Located in northern CA, 4 miles north of St. Helena on CA 128. 40 sites; dump station. 31 foot limit-M; 24 foot limit-T.

6. Brannan Island State Recreation Area, Folsom, CA 95630. Phone: (916) 777-6671. Located in central CA, NW of Stockton, 3 miles SE of Rio Vista on CA 160. 135 sites; showers; dump station. 31 foot limit.

7. Butano State Park, Felton, CA 95018. Phone: (650) 879-2040. Located in central CA, SW of San Jose, 7 miles south of Pescadero and east of CA 1. 44 sites. No water. 31 foot limit-M; 24 foot limit-T.

8. Calaveras Big Trees State Park, Stockton, CA 95310. Phone: (209) 795-2334. Located in east-central CA, in foothills of Sierra Nevada Mountains, 4 miles NE of Arnold on CA 4. 106 sites, 47 with electric, water; showers; dump station. 27 foot limit.

9. Carpinteria State Beach, Ventura, CA 93001. Phone: (805) 968-1033. Located on southern CA coast, 12 miles south of Santa Barbara on US 101. 246 sites, 120 with electric, water; dump station. 30 foot limit. ER

10. Castle Crags State Park, Oroville, CA 95966. Phone: (530) 235-2684. Located in northern CA, off I-5, 6 miles SW of Dunsmuir. 60 sites. 27 foot limit-M; 21 foot limit-T. ER

11. Caswell Memorial State Park, Columbia, CA 95310. Phone: (209) 599-3810. Located in central CA, NW of Modesto, 6 miles SW of Ripon on Austin Road. 60 sites. 24 foot limit-M; 21 foot limit-T.

12. China Camp State Park, Duncan Mills, CA 95430. Phone: (415) 456-0766. Located 4 miles east of San Rafael on San Pablo Bay. From US 101, go east on N San Pedro Rd to park. 30 sites; showers. No size limit. ER.

13. Chino Hills State Park, Perris, CA 92571. Phone: (909) 780-6222. Located 10 miles northwest of Corona off CA 71. 10 sites. 28 foot limit.

14. Clear Lake State Park, Oroville, CA 95966. Phone: (707) 279-4293. Located on Clear Lake in northern CA, SE of Ukiah on CA 281. 147 sites; dump station. 35 foot limit.

15. Colonel Allensworth State Historic Park, Earlimart, CA 93219. Phone: (661) 849-3433. Located in south-central CA, NW of Bakersfield and SW of Earlimart on CA 43. 15 sites; showers. 30 foot limit.

16. Colusa-Sacramento River State Recreation Area, Oroville, CA 95966. Phone: (530) 458-4927. Located on Sacramento River in north-central CA, NW of Sacramento in Colusa, 9 miles east of I-5. 12 sites; dump station. 30 foot limit. ER.

17. Cuyamaca Rancho State Park, Descanso, CA 91916. Phone: (760) 765-0755. Located in southern CA on CA 79, NE of San Diego, off I-8 at Descanso. 187 sites, 85 with electric, water; showers; dump station. 30 foot limit-M; 27 foot limit-T.

18. D. L. Bliss State Park, Tahoma, CA 96142. Phone: (530) 525-7277. Located in east-central CA, 15 miles south of Tahoe City on CA 89. 165 sites. 21 foot limit-M; 15 foot limit-T.

19. Del Norte Coast Redwoods State Parks, Crescent City, CA 95531. Phone: (707) 464-6101 ext. 5120. Located in northern coast area on US 101, 7 miles south of Crescent City. 142 sites; showers; dump station. 31 foot limit-M; 27 foot limit-T.

20. Doheny State Beach, Dana Point, CA 92629. Phone: (949) 496-6172. Located in southern CA outside Dana Point, near junction of CA 1 and I-5. 120 sites; showers; dump station. 28 foot limit-M; 24 foot limit-T.

21. Donner Memorial State Park, Tahoma, CA 96142. Phone: (530) 582-7892. Located in east-central CA near Donner Pass, 2 miles west of Truckee, off I-80 at Truckee exit. 140 sites; showers. 28 foot limit-M; 24 foot limit-T.

22. El Capitan State Beach, Ventura, CA 93001. Phone: (805) 968-1033.

Located in southern CA, 17 miles west of Santa Barbara on US 101. 132 sites; dump station. 30 foot limit-M; 27 foot limit-T. ER.

23. Emerald Bay State Park, Tahoma, CA 96142. Phone: (530) 541-3030. Located in east-central CA in Lake Tahoe area, 22 miles south of Tahoe City on CA 89. 120 sites; showers. 24 foot limit-M; 21 foot limit-T.

24. Emma Wood State Beach, Ventura, CA 93001. Phone: (805) 968-1033. Located in southern CA on US 101 in Ventura. 5 sites; showers. 35 foot limit.

25. Folsom Lake State Recreation Area, Folsom, CA 95630. Phone: (916) 988-0295. Located in central CA, NE of Sacramento, outside Folsom off US 50. 150 sites in two campgrounds; showers; dump station. 31 foot limit.

26. Fort Tejon State Historic Park, Columbia, CA 95310. Phone: (661) 248-6692. Located in southern CA, 70 miles NW of Los Angeles, I-5 Fort Tejon exit; (near the "Grapevine"). Open site camping. 36 foot limit-M; 30 foot limit-T.

27. Fremont Peak State Park, Monterey, CA 93940. Phone: (831) 623-4255. Located in central CA, NE of Salinas off US 101. *Narrow, steep road, not easy access.* 25 sites. 27 foot limit-M; 23 foot limit-T.

28. Gaviota State Park, Ventura, CA 93001. Phone: (805) 968-1033. Located 33 miles west of Santa Barbara on US 101. 45 sites; showers. *No water for fill-up.* 28 foot limit-M; 25 foot limit-T.

29. George J. Hatfield State Recreation Area, Columbia, CA 95310. Phone: (209) 632-1852. Located in central CA, on CA 140 between Merced and I-5, Newman exit. 18 sites. 32 foot limit-M; 31 foot limit-T.

30. Grizzly Creek Redwoods State Park, Carlotta, CA 95528. Phone: (707) 777-3683. Located in northern CA, 20 miles SE of Eureka on CA 36 off US 101. 30 sites; showers. 28 foot limit-M; 24 foot limit-T.

31. Grover Hot Springs State Park, Tahoma, CA 96142. Phone: (530) 694-2248. Located in east-central CA, SE of South Lake Tahoe on CA 4, near Markleeville. 76 sites; showers. 27 foot limit-M; 24 foot limit-T.

32. Half Moon Bay State Beach, Felton, CA 95018. Phone: (650) 726-8819. Located in central CA on CA 1, south of San Francisco in Half Moon Bay. 56 sites; showers; dump station. 45 foot limit-M; 40 foot limit-T. ER.

33. Hendy Woods State Park, Mendocino, CA 95460. Phone: (707) 895-3141.

Located in northern CA on CA 128, SW of Ukiah, 8 miles NW of Boonville. 89 sites; showers; dump station. 35 foot limit-M; 24 foot limit-T.

34. Henry Cowell Redwoods State Park, Felton, CA 95018. Phone: (831) 335-4598. Located in central CA, 5 miles north of Santa Cruz on CA 9. 109 sites. 35 foot limit-M; 31 foot limit-T.

35. Henry W. Coe State Park, Morgan Hill, CA 95038. Phone: (408) 779-2728. Remote location in central CA, east of San Jose, 14 miles NE of Morgan Hill on county roads. 20 sites. 26 foot limit-M; 18 foot limit-T.

36. Hollister Hills State Vehicular Recreation Area, Hollister, CA 95023. Phone: (831) 637-3874. Located in central CA, NE of Salinas, 6 miles south of Hollister on CA 25. Open camp sites; showers. 42 foot limit-M; 18 foot limit-T.

37. Humboldt Redwoods State Park, Weott, CA 95571. Phone: (707) 946-2409. Located in northern CA, 45 miles south of Eureka off US 101 and CA 254. 260 sites. 33 foot limit-M; 24 foot limit-T.

38. Indian Grinding Rock State Historic Park, Stockton, CA 95665. Phone: (209) 296-7488. Located in central CA, east of Sacramento, 11 miles NE of Jackson on CA 88. 23 sites with water. 27 foot limit.

39. Jedediah Smith Redwoods State Park, Eureka, CA 95503. Phone: (707) 464-6101. Located in northern CA, 9 miles east of Crescent City on US 199. 105 sites; dump station. 36 foot limit.

40. Lake Oroville State Recreation Area, Oroville, CA 95966. Phone: (530) 538-2200. Located in north-central CA, 7 miles east of Oroville (CA 99). 278 sites in two campgrounds, 74 full hook-up; dump station. 42 foot limit. ER.

41. Lake Perris State Recreation Area, Perris, CA 92571. Phone: (909) 940-5603. Located in southern CA east of Los Angeles, 11 miles SE of Riverside via CA 60 or I-215, follow signs. 596 sites, 265 with electric, water; showers; dump station. 31 foot limit.

42. Leo Carrillo State Park, Calabasas, CA 91302. Phone: (805) 488-1827 or (818) 880-0350. Located in southern CA, 28 miles NW of Santa Monica on CA 1. 136 sites; showers; dump station. 31 foot limit.

43. Limekiln State Park, Big Sur, CA 93920. Phone: (831) 667-2403. Located in southern CA on Pacific Coast between Big Sur and San Simeon on CA 1. 33 sites.

44. MacKerricher State Park, Mendocino, CA 95460. Phone: (707) 964-9112.

Located in northern CA on coast, 3 miles north of Fort Bragg on CA 1. 120 sites; showers; dump station. 35 foot limit.

45. Malakoff Diggins State Historic Park, Tahoma, CA 96142. Phone: (530) 265-2740. Located in east-central CA about 17 miles northeast of Grass Valley on steep, unpaved road, off CA 20. 33 sites. 24 foot limit-M; 18 foot limit-T.

46. Malibu Creek State Park, Calabasas, CA 91302. Phone: (818) 880-0367. Located in southern CA, 4 miles south of US 101 near Calabasas. 63 sites; showers; dump station. 31 foot limit.

47. Manchester State Park, Mendocino, CA 95460. Phone: (707) 937-5804. Located in northern CA on Pacific Coast, 7 miles north of Point Arena on CA 1, outside Manchester. 65 sites; dump station. 32 foot limit-M; 22 foot limit-T.

48. McArthur-Burney Falls Memorial State Park, Oroville, CA 95966. Phone: (530) 335-2777. Located in north-central CA, NE of Redding, on CA 89. 128 sites; dump station. 45 foot limit-M; 32 foot limit-T. ER.

49. McConnell State Recreation Area, Columbia, CA 95310. Phone: (209) 394-7755. Located in central CA on CA 99, SE of Modesto, outside Livingston. 20 sites; showers. 27 foot limit-M; 24 foot limit-T.

50. McGrath State Beach, Ventura, CA 93001. Phone: (805) 968-1033. Located in southern CA just west of Oxnard on CA 1. 168 sites; dump station. 34 foot limit.

51. Millerton Lake State Recreation Area, Columbia, CA 95310. Phone: (559) 822-2332. Located in central CA, 20 miles north of Fresno off CA 145 on Millerton Lake. 133 sites, 28 full hook-up; showers; dump station. 36 foot limit-M; 30 foot limit-T.

52. Montana De Oro State Park, San Simeon, CA 93452. Phone: (805) 528-0513. Located in southern CA on Pacific Coast, 7 miles south of Los Osos off CA 1. 52 sites. 27 foot limit-M; 24 foot limit-T. ER

53. Morro Bay State Park, San Simeon, CA 93452. Phone: (805) 772-7434. Located in southern CA on Pacific Coast, outside Morro Bay on CA 1. 136 sites with electric, water; showers; dump station. 31 foot limit. **Park closed for construction until April, 2005. Call first.**

54. Morro Strand State Beach, San Simeon, CA 93452. Phone: (805) 772-7434. Located in southern CA just north of Morrow Bay on CA 1. 76 sites; 27 foot limit.

55. Mount Diablo State Park, Sonoma, CA 95476. Phone: (925) 837-0904. Located in central CA, NE of Danville, 5 miles east of I-680, east of Oakland. 58 sites; showers. 20 foot limit.

56. Mount San Jacinto State Park, Idyllwild, CA 92549. Phone: (760) 767-5311. Located in south-central CA, SW of Palm Springs, outside Idyllwild via CA 243. 76 sites; showers. 24 foot limit.

57. Mount Tamalpais State Park, Duncan Mills, CA 95430. Phone: (415) 383-1100. Located in central CA, NE of Sausalito on Marin Peninsula, off US 101 on CA 1. 17 sites. No size limits. ER.

58. Navarro River Redwoods State Park, Mendocino, CA 95460. Phone: (707) 895-3141. Located in northern CA off CA 1, near Elk, on CA 128 and Navarro River. 28 sites. No water. 35 foot limit.

59. New Brighton State Beach, Felton, CA 95018. Phone: (831) 429-2850. Located in southern CA, 4 miles south of Santa Cruz on CA 1. 112 sites; dump station. 36 foot limit. ER

60. Oceano Dunes State Vehicle Recreation Area, Arroyo Grande, CA 93420. Phone: (805) 473-7223. Located in southern CA, 3 miles south of Pismo Beach on CA 1. 1000 sites, open camping, no size limit. Sites are on soft sand.

61. Palomar Mountain State Park, Borrego Springs, CA 92004. Phone: (760) 742-3462. Located in southern CA, NE of Oceanside, off CA 76 (off I-15). 31 sites. 30 foot limit-M; 18 foot limit-T.

62. Pfeiffer Big Sur State Park, Monterey, CA 93940. Phone: (831) 667-2315. Located in central CA, 26 miles south of Carmel, in Big Sur, off CA 1. 221 sites; showers; dump station. 32 foot limit-M; 27 foot limit-T. ER.

63. Patrick's Point State Park, Eureka, CA 95503. Phone: (707) 677-3570. Located in northern CA, 25 miles north of Eureka on US 101. 112 sites; showers. 31 foot limit.

64. Picacho State Recreation Area, Borrego Springs, CA 92004. Phone: (760) 393-3052. Remote location in southeast corner of CA, near Yuma, AZ, north of Winterhaven on unpaved road. 54 sites; showers; dump station. 35 foot limit-M; 30 foot limit-T.

65. Pismo State Beach, San Simeon, CA 93452. Phone: (805) 489-2684. Located in southern CA, 2 miles south of Pismo Beach (City) on CA 1. 173 sites, 42 with electric, water; showers. 36 foot limit-M; 31 foot limit-T.

66. Plumas-Eureka State Park, Tahoma, CA 96142. Phone: (530) 836-2380. Located in central CA, 4 miles west of Graeagle, off CA 89 on CR A-14. 67 sites; showers; dump station. 30 foot limit-M; 24 foot limit-T.

67. Point Mugu State Park, Calabasas, CA 91302. Phone: (818) 880-0350. Located in southern CA, 15 miles south of Oxnard on CA 1. 126 sites; dump station. 31 foot limit.

68. Portola Redwoods State Park, Felton, CA 95018. Phone: (650) 948-9098. Located in central CA, west of Saratoga, 6.5 miles west of CA 35. 59 sites; showers. 24 foot limit-M; 18 foot limit-T.

69. Prairie Creek Redwoods State Park, Eureka, CA 95503. Phone: (707) 464-6101. Located in northern CA, 50 miles north of Eureka on US 101, in Redwoods National Park. 63 sites; dump station. 27 foot limit-M; 24 foot limit-T.

70. Providence Mountains State Recreation Area, Perris, CA 92571. Phone: (760) 928-2586. Located in southeastern CA, 40 miles west of Needles, 15 miles NW of I-40 at Essex exit. 6 sites. 32 foot limit.

71. Red Rock Canyon State Park, Perris, CA 92571. Phone: (661) 942-0662. Located in south-central CA, 25 miles north of Mojave on CA 14. 50 sites; dump station. 32 foot limit. ER.

72. Refugio State Beach, Goleta, CA 93117. Phone: (805) 968-1033. Located in southern CA, 23 miles west of Santa Barbara on US 101. 80 sites. 30 foot limit-M; 27 foot limit-T.

73. Richardson Grove State Park, Eureka, CA 95503. Phone: (707) 247-3318. Located in northern CA, 8 miles south of Garberville on US 101. 175 sites; showers. 30 foot limit-M; 24 foot limit-T. ER.

74. Russian Gulch State Park, Mendocino, CA 95460. Phone: (707) 937-5804. Located in northern CA, 2 miles north of Mendocino off CA 1. 28 sites; showers. 27 foot limit-M; 24 foot limit-T.

75. Saddleback Butte State Park, Perris, CA 92571. Phone: (661) 942-0662. Remote location in southern CA, 17 miles east of Lancaster (CA 14). 50 sites; dump station. 30 foot limit.

76. Salt Point State Park, Duncan Mills, CA 95430. Phone: (707) 847-3221. Located in northern CA, 12 miles west of Healdsburg on CA 1. 89 sites. 31 foot limit. ER.

77. Salton Sea State Recreation Area, North Shore, CA 92254. Phone: (760) 393-3059 or 393-3052 (ranger). Located in southern CA, 25 miles SE of Indio (I-10) on CA 111. 18 sites, 4 with electric, water; dump station. 28 foot limit-M; 24 foot limit-T.

78. Samuel P. Taylor State Park, Duncan Mills, CA 94938. Phone: (415) 488-9897. Located in central CA, 15 miles NW of San Rafael, off CA 1. 61 sites; showers; dump station. 30 foot limit.

79. San Clemente State Beach, San Clemente, CA 92672. Phone: (949) 492-3156. Located in southern CA, south end of San Clemente just off I-5. 72 sites with electric, water; showers; dump station. 30 foot limit.

80. San Elijo State Beach, San Diego, CA 92108. Phone: (760) 753-5091. Located in southern CA, north of San Diego, on Old 101, off I-5 Rancho Santa Fe exit. 171 sites; dump station. 35 foot limit.

81. San Luis Reservoir State Recreation Area, Columbia, CA 95310. Phone: (209) 826-1197. Located in central CA, SE of San Jose, 12 miles west of Los Banos on CA 152. 132 sites, 70 with electric, water; showers; dump station. 37 foot limit. Note: *Lake level and wind affect accessibility. Call ahead.*

82. San Onofre State Beach, San Clemente, CA 92672. Phone: (949) 492-4872. Located in southern CA, off I-5 south of San Clemente. 334 sites (includes San Mateo campground), 67 with electric, water; showers; dump station. 30 foot limit.

83. San Simeon State Park, San Simeon, CA 93452. Phone: (805) 927-2020. Located in southern CA, 5 miles south of San Simeon on CA 1. 203 sites; showers; dump station. 35 foot limit.

84. Seacliff State Beach, Felton, CA 95018. Phone: (831) 685-6500. Located in central CA, 5.5 miles south of Santa Cruz on CA 1. 26 sites with electric, water; showers. 40 foot limit-M; 36 foot limit-T.

85. Silverwood Lake State Recreation Area, Perris, CA 92571. Phone: (760) 389-2881. Located in southern CA, north of San Bernardino, 12 miles off I-15 on CA 138. 258 sites; showers; dump station. 34 foot limit-M; 31 foot limit-T.

86. Sonoma Coast State Beach, Duncan Mills, CA 95430. Phone: (707) 875-3483. Located in northern CA on Pacific Coast, SW of Santa Rosa, north of Bodega Bay. 119 sites in four campgrounds; showers in one campground. RV limits vary by campground. Call for details, site assignments.

87. South Carlsbad State Beach, Carlsbad, CA 92008. Phone: (760) 438-3143. Located in southern CA, 3 miles south of Carlsbad off I-5. 222 sites; showers; dump station. 35 foot limit.

88. Standish-Hickey State Recreation Area, Eureka, CA 95503. Phone: (707) 925-6482. Located in northern CA, 2 miles north of Leggett on CA 1. 161 sites; showers. 27 foot limit-M; 24 foot limit-T.

89. Sugar Pine Point State Park, Tahoma, CA 96142. Phone: (530) 525-7982. Located in east-central CA, 10 miles south of Tahoe City on Lake Tahoe. 100 sites; dump station. 32 foot limit-M; 26 foot limit-T.

90. Sugarloaf Ridge State Park, Sonoma, CA 95476. Phone: (707) 833-5712. Located in central CA, 7 miles east of Santa Rosa off CA 12 on Adobe Canyon Road. 47 sites. 27 foot limit-M; 24 foot limit-T.

91. Sunset State Beach, Felton, CA 95018. Phone: (831) 763-7063. Located in central CA just south of Watsonville off CA 1. 90 sites. 31 foot limit.

92. Tahoe State Recreation Area, Tahoma, CA 96142. Phone: (530) 583-3074. Located in east-central CA on Lake Tahoe, 1/4 mile east of Tahoe City. 28 sites. 21 foot limit-M; 15 foot limit-T. No camping from September 30 to Memorial Day.

93. Turlock Lake State Recreation Area, LaGrange, CA 95329. Phone: (209) 874-2056. Located in central CA, 22 miles east of Modesto off CA 132. 66 sites. 27 foot limit-M; 24 foot limit-T.

94. Van Damme State Park, Mendocino, CA 95460. Phone: (707) 937-5804. Located in northern CA on Pacific Coast, 3 miles south of Mendocino on CA 1. 84 sites; showers; dump station. 35 foot limit. ER.

95. Westport-Union Landing State Beach, Mendocino, CA 95460. Phone: (707) 937-5804. Located in northern CA on Pacific Coast, 1.5 miles north of Westport on CA 1. Open camping; no size limits.

96. Woodson Bridge State Recreation Area, Oroville, CA 95966. Phone: (530) 839-2112. Located in central CA, 6 miles east of I-5 Corning exit. 37 sites; showers. 31 foot limit.

Colorado

Twenty-four of Colorado's 28 RV-friendly State Parks are located west of I-25. Many locations are near or on major roadways. While these are open year round, some of the facilities are curtailed in winter months. Reservations are available through the state-wide system but sites are also available on a drive-in basis. It is important to check with the particular park for site availability. Pets are permitted but must be on leashes. There are some "primitive" (no facilities) sites available, but most sites are developed and offer upgraded amenities. Rate groups: B and C.

Colorado State Parks
1313 Sherman St., Room 618
Denver, CO 80203
Information: (303) 866-3437 / Reservations: (800) 678-2267
Internet: www.parks.state.co.us

ColoradoPark Locator

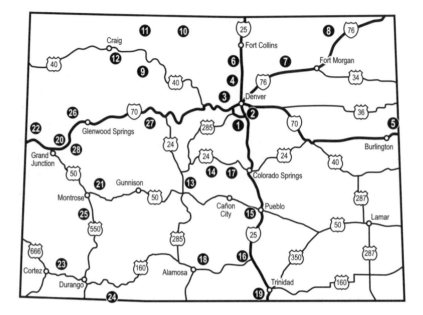

1. Chatfield State Park, 11500 N Roxborough Park Rd., Littleton, CO 80125. Phone: (303) 791-7275. Located south of Denver off CO 470 along CO 121. 163 sites, 51 with electric; showers; dump station.

2. Cherry Creek State Park, 4201 S Parker Rd., Aurora, CO 80014. Phone: (303) 699-3860. Located in Aurora south of I-225 exit 4. 102 sites, 42 with electric; showers; dump station.

3. Golden Gate State Park, 3873 Hwy 46, Golden, CO 80403. Phone: (303) 582-3707. Located NW of Golden via CR 70 and CO 46. 155 sites, 59 with electric; showers; dump station.

4. Barbour Ponds State Park, 4995 Weld County Rd. 24½, Longmont, CO 80504. Phone: (303) 678- 9402. Located near Longmont just west of I-25 exit 240. 60 sites; dump station.

5. Bonny Lake State Park, 30010 Road 3, Idalia, CO 80735. Phone: (970) 354-7306. Located in eastern Colorado, 24 miles north of Burlington off US 385. 190 sites; showers; dump station.

6. Boyd Lake State Park, 3720 N County Rd. 11-C, Loveland, CO 80538. Phone: (970) 669-1739. Located 1 mile east of Loveland off US 34 (I-25 exit 257). 148 sites, 84 with electric; showers; dump station.

7. Jackson Lake State Park, 26363 County Rd. 3, Orchard, CO 80649. Phone: (970) 645-2551. Located about 11 miles from US 34/I-76 interchange via CO 39 through Goodrich. 260 sites, 54 with electric; showers; dump station.

8. North Sterling State Park, 24005 County Rd. 330, Sterling, CO 80751. Phone: (970) 522-3657. Located in northeastern Colorado, 12 miles north of Sterling (I-76 exit 125) via CR 39 and CR 37. 141 sites, 97 with electric; showers; dump station.

9. Stagecoach State Park, Oak Creek, CO 80467. Phone: (970) 736-2436. Remote location off CO 131 about 43 miles north of I-70 exit 157. 92 sites; showers; dump station.

10. State Forest State Park, 2746 Jackson County Rd. 41, Walden, CO 80480. Phone: (970) 723-8366. Remote location in northern Colorado, 75 miles west of Fort Collins off CO 14. 158 sites; dump station.

11. Steamboat Lake State Park, Clark, CO 80428. Phone: (970) 879-3922. Remote location about 28 miles NW of Steamboat Springs off CR 129. 198 sites, 83 with electric; showers; dump station.

12. Yampa River State Park, Headquarters, Hayden, CO 81639. Phone: (970) 276-2061. Located between Craig and Hayden off US 40. 45 sites, some with electric; showers; dump station. Note: some RV sites are also available at the Yampa River location and at Yampa/Elkhead. Both areas are accessible off US 40. Check with park rangers.

13. Arkansas Headwaters State Park, 307 W Sackett Ave., Salida, CO 81201. Phone: (719) 539-7289. Located NW of Salida near junction of CO 291 and US 24. 86 sites; no drinking water.

14. Eleven Mile State Park, 4229 County Road 92, Lake George, CO 80827. Phone: (719) 748-3401. Remote location about 45 miles west of Colorado Springs via US 24 and CR 90. 349 sites, 51 with electric; showers; (dry) dump station.

15. Lake Pueblo State Park, 640 Pueblo Reservoir Rd., Pueblo, CO 81005. Phone: (719) 561-9320. Located west of Pueblo (I-25 exit 102) via US 50; follow signs. 401 sites; showers; dump station.

16. Lathrop State Park, 70 County Road 502, Walsenburg, CO 81089. Phone: (719) 738-2376. Located off US 160, 3 miles west of Walsenburg (I-25 exit 49). 100 sites; showers; dump station.

17. Mueller State Park, Divide, CO 80814. Phone: (719) 687-2366. Located

3.5 miles south of Divide, 25 miles west of Colorado Springs, via US 24. 132 sites; showers; dump station.

18. San Luis Lakes State Park, Mosca, CO 81146. Phone: (719) 378-2020. Located about 17 miles NE of Alamosa between CO 17 and CO 150 on Six Mile Lane. 51 sites; showers; dump station.

19. Trinidad Lake State Park, 32610 Hwy 12, Trinidad, CO 81082. Phone: (719) 846-6951. Located 3 miles west of Trinidad (I-25 exit 13) on CO 12. 62 sites; showers; dump station.

20. Colorado River, Clifton, CO 81520. Phone: (970) 434-3388. Two areas:
    a. Island Acres: Located off I-70 exit 47. 80 sites with electric, sewers; showers; laundry; dump station.
    b. Fruita: Located off I-70 exit 19, south on CO 340. 63 sites with electric, sewers; showers; laundry; dump station.

21. Crawford State Park, Crawford, CO 81415. Phone: (970) 921-5721. Located on CO 92 about 25 miles east of Delta (US 550 & 50). 66 sites; showers.

22. Highline Lake State Park, 1800 11.8 Rd., Loma, CO 81524. Phone: (970) 858-7208. Located north of Loma (I-70 exit 15) off CO 139 and Q Road. 28 sites; showers; laundry; dump station.

23. Mancos State Park, Mancos, CO 81121. Phone: (970) 883-2208 (Navajo State Park). Located NW of Durango in southwestern Colorado; north of Mancos off US 160 and CO 184; follow signs. 31 sites; dump station.

24. Navajo State Park, Arboles, CO 81121. Phone: (970) 883-2208. Located near New Mexico state line southwest of Pagosa Springs (US 160) off CO 151 south. 115 sites with electric, sewers; showers; laundry; dump station.

25. Ridgway State Park, 28555 Hwy 550, Ridgway, CO 81432. Phone: (970) 626-5822. Located 20 miles south of Montrose on US 550. 280 sites with electric; showers; dump station.

26. Rifle Falls State Park, 50 County Rd. 219, Rifle, CO 81650. Phone: (970) 625-1607. Located north of Rifle (I-70 exit 90) on CO 325, off CO 13. 20 sites.

27. Sylvan Lake State Park, Eagle, CO 81631. Phone: (970) 625-1607. Located 18 miles south of I-70 exit 147 (Eagle) off Brush Creek Road. 46 sites; showers; dump station.

28. Vega State Park, Collbran, CO 81624. Phone: (970) 487-3407. Located 29 miles east of I-70 exit 49 via CO 65 and CO 330. 108 sites; showers; dump station.

Connecticut

Connecticut has 13 State Parks or Forests with RV campgrounds. Only one park, Salt Lake, has utilities at the sites. The other locations have facilities on the grounds but the sites are "dry camp" sites. Some of the parks are alcohol-free. Check listings below. Only Salt Rock Campground and the two State Forest areas allow pets. Most of the locations are open mid-April through September 30. Some are open through October and one, Housatonic State Park, is open mid-April until December 31. RVs cannot exceed 35 feet in any state campground. Reservation service is available but requires 48 hours advance request. Rate groups: A and B; Salt Rock State Park: C

Bureau of Outdoor Recreation
State Parks Division
Dept. of Environmental Protection
79 Elm St.
Hartford, CT 06106
Information: (860) 424-3200 / Reservations: (877) 668-2267
Internet: www.ct.gov / Reservations: www.reserveamerica.com

Connecticut Park Locator

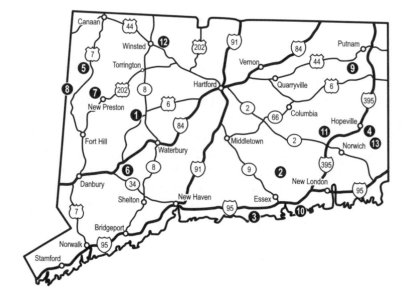

1. Black Rock State Park, Route 6, Thomaston, CT 06787. Phone: (860) 283-8088. Located on US 6 off CT 8 exit 38 SW of Thomaston. 96 sites; showers; dump station. No alcohol.

2. Devil's Hopyard State Park, 366 Hopyard Rd., East Haddam, CT 06423. Phone: (860) 873-8566. Located NE of East Haddam off CT 11 exit 5; remote location. 21 sites.

3. Hammonasset Beach State Park, 1288 Boston Post Rd., (US 1), Madison, CT 06443. Phone: (203) 245-1871. Located on Long Island Sound on US 1 between New Haven and New London. 558 sites; showers; dump station.

4. Hopeville Pond State Park, 193 Roode Rd., Jewett City, CT 06351. Phone: (860) 376-2920. Located west of Pachaug State Forest off CT 201 (I-395 exit 86). 95 sites; showers; dump station.

5. Housatonic Meadows State Park, Route 7, Cornwall Bridge, CT 06754. Phone: (860) 672-6772. Located on US 7 in northwestern CT between Cornwall Bridge and West Cornwall. 95 sites; showers; dump station. No alcohol.

6. Kettletown State Park, 1400 Georges Hill Rd., Southbury, CT 06488. Phone: (203) 264-5678. Located on the Housatonic River SE of I-84 exit 14. 68 sites; showers; dump station. 26 foot limit.

7. Lake Waramaug State Park, 30 Lake Waramaug Rd., New Preston, CT 06777. Phone: (860) 868-0220. Located off CT 478 NW of New Preston (US 202). 78 sites; showers; dump station.

8. Macedonia Brook State Park, 159 Macedonia Brook Rd., Kent, CT 06757. Phone: (860) 927-4100. Located in northwestern Connecticut off CT 41, west of US 7. 51 sites. No alcohol.

9. Mashamoquet Brook State Park, Route 44, Pomfret Center, CT 06259. Phone: (860) 928-6121. Located on US 44, SW of Putnam. 55 sites (two campgrounds); showers, Wolf Den Campground only; dump stations.

10. Rocky Neck State Park, Route 156, Niantic, CT 06357. Phone: (860) 739-1339. Located on CT 156 off I-95 exits 71 or 72. 160 sites; showers; dump station.

11. Salt Rock State Park, 173 Scotland Rd., Baltic, CT 06330. Phone: (860) 822-0884. Located 2 miles north of Baltic on CT 97. 71 sites, some with full hook-ups; showers; dump station.

12. American Legion State Forest, West River Road, Pleasant Valley, CT 06063. Phone: (860) 379-0922. Located in northwestern Connecticut near the junction of US 44 and CT 318. 30 sites; showers; dump station.

13. Pachaug State Forest, Voluntown, CT 06384. Phone: (860) 376-4075. Green Falls Campground located on CT 138, 3 miles east of Voluntown. 18 sites. Mt. Misery Campground, located 1 mile north of Voluntown on CT 49. 22 sites. No reservations.

Delaware

Although Delaware has only five state parks with RV facilities, there are more than 800 sites available, most of which have at least electric hook-ups. All the parks have dump stations and drinking water in the park, if not at the particular site. All the parks accept reservations, which can be executed in as little as 24 hours. Pet policies can vary by park, so it is wise to call ahead for particulars. All the parks are on water; two on the Atlantic Ocean. Rate Group: C+

Delaware Division of Parks & Recreation
89 Kings Highway
Box 1401
Dover, DE 19903
Information: (302) 739-4702 / Reservations: (877) 987-2757
Internet: www.destateparks.com

Delaware Park Locator

1. Cape Henlopen State Park, 42 Cape Henlopen Dr., Lewes, DE 19958. Phone: (302) 645-2103. Located in Lewes and east end of US 9 on the Atlantic Ocean. 139 sites with water; 17 no hook-ups; showers; dump station. Seasonal.

2. Delaware Seashore State Park, Inlet 850, Rehoboth Beach, DE 19971. Phone: (302) 539-7202. Located along DE 1 south of Dewey Beach on the Atlantic Ocean. 145 full hook-up sites; 133 no hook-ups; 156 "overflow" sites (self-contained units only); showers; dump station.

3. Killens Pond State Park, 5025 Killens Pond Rd., Felton, DE 19943. Phone: (302) 284-3412. Located south of Felton one mile east of US 13. 59 sites with water and electric; showers; dump station.

4. Lums Pond State Park, 1068 Howell School Rd., Bear, DE 19701. Phone: 877 - 987 - 2757 (302) 368-6989. Located on DE 71 south of Newark, off DE 896. 6 sites with electric; 62 sites no hook-ups; showers; dump station.

5. Trap Pond State Park, 33587 Baldcypress Lane, Laurel, DE 19956. Phone: (302) 875-5153. Located on DE 24 about 4 miles east of Laurel. 130 sites with full hook-ups; showers; dump station.

Florida

There are 46 State Parks or Recreation Areas in Florida with RV accommodations. The facilities in these parks all include water and electric hook-ups and at least one dump station at the park. Some parks do not allow pets, as noted by park. All parks have showers. Reservations require a minimum of 24 hours advance notice and depending upon the park, could require 48 hours. It is imperative you call the particular park to verify space, especially in the Spring through Summer months. All parks are open year round. Senior discounts are available but you must ask. Rate groups: B and C depending upon the season.

Florida Dept. of Environmental Protection
Division of Recreation and Parks MS 536
3900 Commonwealth Blvd.
Tallahassee, FL 32399
Information: (850) 488-9872 or (850) 245-2157
Reservations: (800) 326-3521 (Reserve America)
Internet: www.FloridaStateParks.org

Florida Park Locator

Florida Park Locator (*cont.*)

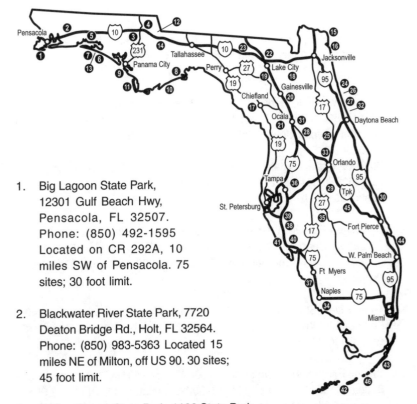

1. Big Lagoon State Park,
    12301 Gulf Beach Hwy,
    Pensacola, FL 32507.
    Phone: (850) 492-1595
    Located on CR 292A, 10
    miles SW of Pensacola. 75
    sites; 30 foot limit.

2. Blackwater River State Park, 7720
    Deaton Bridge Rd., Holt, FL 32564.
    Phone: (850) 983-5363 Located 15
    miles NE of Milton, off US 90. 30 sites;
    45 foot limit.

3. Falling Waters State Park, 1130 State Park
    Rd., Chipley, FL 32428. Phone: (850) 638-6130. Located 3 miles south of
    Chipley, off FL 77A. 24 sites; 35 foot limit.

4. Florida Caverns State Park, 3345 Caverns Rd., Marianna, FL 32446.
    Phone: (850) 482-9598. Located 3 miles north of Marianna on FL 166. 38
    sites; 40 foot limit.

5. Fred Gannon Rocky Bayou State Park, 4281 State Route 20, Niceville, FL 32578. Phone: (805) 833-9144. Located on FL 20, 5 miles east of Hwy 85. 42 sites; 35 foot limit.

6. Grayton Beach State Park, 357 Main Park Rd., Santa Rosa, FL 32459. Phone: (805) 231-4210. Located on FL 30A near Grayton Beach, south of US 98. 37 sites; 40 foot limit. No pets.

7. Henderson Beach State Park, 17000 Emerald Coast Pkwy, Destin, FL 32541. Phone: (850) 837-7550. Located on US 98, east of Destin. 60 sites; 45 foot limit.

8. Ochlockonee River State Park, Sopchoppy, FL 32358. Phone: (850) 962-2771. Located 4 miles south of Sopchoppy on US 319. 30 sites; 30 foot limit.

9. St. Andrews State Park, 4607 State Park Lane, Panama City, FL 32408. Phone: (850) 233-5140. Located 3 miles east of Panama City Beach off FL 392 (Thomas Drive). 176 sites; 40 foot limit. No pets.

10. St. George Island State Park, 1900 E Gulf Beach Dr., St. George Island, FL 32328. (850) 927-2111. Located on St. George Island 10 miles SE of Eastpoint, off US 98. 60 sites; 43 foot limit.

11. St. Joseph Peninsula State Park, 8899 Cape San Blas Rd., Port St. Joe, FL 32456. Phone: (850) 227-1327. Located between Port St. Joe and Apalachicola on Cape San Blas Road, off CR 30. 119 sites; 38 foot limit. No pets.

12. Three Rivers State Park, 7908 Three Rivers Park Rd., Sneads, FL 32460. Phone: (850) 482-9006. Located on FL 271, 2 miles north of Sneads. 30 sites; 40 foot limit.

13. Topsail Hill Preserve State Park, 7525 W Scenic Hwy 30A, Santa Rosa Beach, FL 32459. Phone: (850) 267-0299. Located in Santa Rosa Beach on US 98. 156 sites; 55 foot limit. Special Reservation Number: 877-232-2478.

14. Torreya State Park, Bristol, FL 32321. Phone: (850) 643-2674. Located 12 miles north of Bristol, off FL 12 on CR 1641. 30 sites; 30 foot limit. No pets.

15. Fort Clinch State Park, 2601 Atlantic Ave., Fernandina Beach, FL 32034. Phone: (904) 277-7274. Located near Fernandina Beach off FL A1A (I-95 exit 373). 62 sites; 30 foot limit.

16. Little Talbot Island State Park, 12157 Heckscher Dr., Jacksonville, FL 32226. Phone: (904) 251-2320. Located 17 miles NE of Jacksonville on FL A1A. 40 sites; 30 foot limit.

17. Manatee Springs State Park, 11650 NW 115th St., Chiefland, FL 32626. Phone: (352) 493-6072. Located at the end of FL 320, off US 98, 6 miles west of Chiefland. 92 sites; 30 foot limit.

18. Mike Roess Gold Head Branch State Park, 6239 State Route 21, Keystone Heights, FL 32656. Phone: (352) 473-4701. Located 6 miles NE of Keystone Heights on FL 21, between US 301 & 17. 72 sites; 45 foot limit.

19. O'Leno State Park, High Springs, FL 32643. Phone: (386) 454-1853. Located north of High Springs on US 41/441, off I-75 exits 414 or 404. 61 sites. 76 foot limit. No pets.

20. Paynes Prairie Preserve State Park, 100 Savannah Blvd., Micanopy, FL 32667. Phone: (352) 466-3397. South of Gainesville between I-75 exits 374 and 382. 50 sites; 30 foot limit. No pets.

21. Rainbow Springs State Park, 18185 SW 94th St., Dunnellon, FL 34432. Phone: (352) 465-8550. Located 3 miles north of Dunnellon on US 41. Camping Entrance: 2 miles north of CR 484 off SW 180th Avenue. 105 sites; 40 foot maximum. Special Reservation Number: (352) 489-5201.

22. Stephan Foster Folk Culture Center State Park, White Springs, FL 32096. Phone: (386) 397-2733. Located in White Springs off US 41 north. 45 sites. 100 foot limit.

23. Suwannee River State Park, Live Oak, FL 32060. Phone: (386) 362-2746. Located 13 miles west of Live Oak, off US 90. 27 sites. 94 foot limit.

24. Anastasia State Park, St. Augustine, FL 32080. Phone: (904) 461-2033. Located near Saint Augustine on FL A1A, 1/2 mile north of FL 312. 139 sites. 40 foot limit.

25. Blue Springs State Park, Orange City, FL 32763. Phone: (386) 775-3663. Located in Orange City (US 17), 2 miles west on French Avenue. 51 sites. 30 foot limit.

26. Faver-Dykes State Park, St. Augustine, FL 32086. Phone: (904) 794-0997. Located 15 miles south of St. Augustine near intersection of I-95 and US 1. 30 sites. 30 foot limit. No pets.

27. Gamble Rogers Memorial State Recreation Area, Flagler Beach, FL 32136. Phone: (386) 517-2086. Located south of Flagler Beach along FL A1A. 34 sites. 40 foot limit.

28. Lake Griffin State Park, Fruitland Park, FL 34731. Phone: (352) 360-6760. Located 3 miles north of Leesburg and 30 miles SE of Ocala on US 27/441. 40 sites. 40 foot limit.

29. Lake Kissimmee State Park, Lake Wales, FL 33853. Phone: (863) 696-1112. Located off FL 60, 15 miles east of Lake Wales (US 27 and FL 60). 60 sites. 30 foot limit.

30. Sebastian Inlet State Park, Melbourne Beach, FL 32951. Phone: (321) 984-4852. Located on FL A1A, 15 miles south of Melbourne Beach. 51 sites. 40 foot limit.

31. Silver River State Park, Ocala, FL 34470. Phone: (352) 236-7148. Located NE of Ocala, 1 mile south of FL 40 on FL 35. 59 sites. 50 foot limit.

32. Tomoka State Park, Ormond Beach, FL 32174. Phone: (386) 676-4050. Located 3 miles north of Ormond Beach on North Beach Street. 100 sites. 34 foot limit.

33. Wekiwa Springs State Park, Apopka, FL 32712. Phone: (407) 884-2008. Located on Wekiwa Springs Road, off FL 434 or FL 436, west of I-4. 60 sites. 50 foot limit.

34. Collier-Seminole State Park, Naples, FL 34114. Phone: (239) 394-3397. Located on US 41, 17 miles south of Naples on Tamiami Trail. 118 sites. 30 foot limit. Also 19 "small" rig sites.

35. Highlands Hammock State Park, Sebring, FL 33872. Phone: (863) 386-6094. Located on CR 634, 4 miles west of Sebring, off US 27. 154 sites. 30 foot limit.

36. Hillsborough River State Park, Thonotosassa, FL 33592. Phone: (813) 987-6771. Located 12 miles north of Tampa and 6 miles south of Zephyrhills, on US 301. 108 sites. 50 foot limit.

37. Koreshan State Historic Site, Estero, FL 33928. Phone: (239) 992-0311. Located in Estero on US 41 at Corkscrew Road (I-75 exit 123). 48 sites. 30 foot limit.

38. Lake Manatee State Park, Bradenton, FL 34202. Phone: (941) 741-3028. Located 15 miles east of Bradenton on FL 54. 60 sites. 65 foot limit.

39. Little Manatee River State Park, Wimauma, FL 33598. Phone: (813) 671-5005. Located 5 miles south of Sun City, off US 301 on Lightfoot Road. 34 sites. 68 foot limit.

40. Myakka River State Park, Sarasota, FL 34241. Phone: (941) 361-6511. Located 9 miles east of Sarasota on FL 72. 76 sites. 34 foot limit.

41. Oscar Scherer State Park, Osprey, FL 34229. Phone: (941) 483-5956. Located on US 41, 2 miles south of Osprey on Tamiami Trail. 104 sites. 35 foot limit.

42. Bahia Honda State Park, Big Pine Key, FL 33043. Phone: (305) 872-2353. Located 12 miles south of Marathon in Florida Keys, on US 1. 80 sites. 40 foot limit.

43. John Pennekamp Coral Reef State Park, Key Largo, FL 33037. Phone: (305) 451-1202. Located on US 1 at mile marker 102.5, north of Key Largo. 47 sites. 45 foot limit. No pets.

44. Jonathan Dickinson State Park, Hobe Sound, FL 33455. Phone: (772) 546-2771. Located 12 miles south of Stuart on US 1. 135 sites. 30 foot limit.

45. Kissimmee Prairie Preserve State Park, Okeechobee, FL 34972. Phone: (863) 462-5360. Located 25 miles NW of Okeechobee via US 441 and CR 724. 20 sites. 30 foot limit. No pets.

46. Long Key State Park, Long Key, FL 33001. Phone: (305) 664-4815. Located on US 1 at mile marker 67.5 in Florida Keys, between Key Largo and Marathon. 60 sites. 45 foot limit. No pets.

Georgia

Georgia is unique in that all its state parks with RV sites (41) all have water and electric hookups at each site. All parks with camping sites also have shower facilities and dump stations. Several parks offer cable TV hook-ups. Georgia has a state-wide reservation network (48-hour lead time) and requires a two-night minimum stay on weekends only. All parks offer drive-in space, depending upon availability. You should call to verify space. Many parks have pull-through sites and most have laundry facilities. All parks are open year round and offer discounts to seniors (62 and older; 20 percent off published fees) and senior disabled veterans receive an extra discount. Pets are allowed in campgrounds. Rate groups: B and C.

Georgia State Parks & Historic Sites
205 Butler Street
Floyd Tower East
Atlanta, GA 30334
Information and Reservations: (800) 864-7275
Internet: www.gastateparks.org

Georgia Park Locator

Georgia Park Locator (*cont.*)

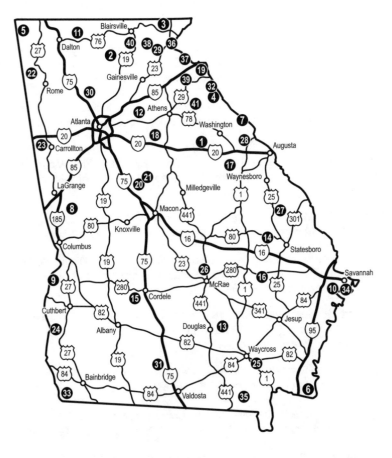

1. A.H. Stephens State Park, Crawfordville, GA 30631. Phone: (706) 456-2602. Located 3 miles north of I-20 exit 148 via GA 22. 25 sites.

2. Amicalola Falls State Park, 240 Amicalola Falls State Park Rd., Dawsonville, GA 30534. Phone: (706) 265-4703. Located 15 miles NW of Dawsonville on GA 52. 20 sites.

3. Black Rock Mountain State Park, Mountain City, GA 30562. Phone: (706) 746-2141. Located 3 miles north of Clayton off US 441 on Black Rock Mountain Pkwy; follow signs from Mountain City. 48 sites.

4. Bobby Brown State Park, 2509 Bobby Brown State Park Rd., Elberton, GA 30635. Located 21 miles SE of Elberton off GA 72. 61 sites.

5. Cloudland Canyon State Park, 122 Cloudland Canyon Park Rd., Rising Fawn, GA 30738. Phone: (706) 657-4050. Located 8 miles east of Trenton and I-59 exit 11 on GA 136. 73 sites.

6. Crooked River State Park, 6222 Charlie Smith Sr. Hwy, St. Mary's GA 31558. Phone: (912) 882-5256. Located 7 miles north of St. Mary's on GA Spur 40; 8 miles east of I-95 exit 3. 60 sites.

7. Elijah Clark State Park, 2959 McCormick Hwy, Lincolnton, GA 30817. Phone: (706) 359-3458. Located 7 miles NE of Lincolnton on US 378. 165 sites.

8. F. D. Roosevelt State Park, 2970 State Hwy 190, Pine Mountain, GA 31822. Phone: (706) 663-4858. Located on GA 190 off I-85 exits 34 or 42, west of Warm Springs. 140 sites.

9. Florence Marina State Park, Omaha, GA 31821. Phone: (229) 838-6870. Located 16 miles west of Lumpkin at end of GA 39C. 43 sites.

10. Fort McAllister State Park, 3894 Fort McAllister Rd., Richmond Hill, GA 31324. Phone: (912) 727-2339. Located 10 miles east of I-95 exits 87 or 90 to GA Spur 144. 65 sites.

11. Fort Mountain State Park, 181 Fort Mountain Park Rd., Chatsworth, GA 30705. Phone: (706) 695-2621. Located 8 miles east of Chatsworth via GA 52 (I-75 exit 333) to GA 411. 70 sites.

12. Fort Yargo State Park, Winder, GA 30680. Phone: (770) 867-3489. Located 1 mile south of Winder on GA 81. 40 sites.

13. General Coffee State Park, 46 John Coffee Rd., Nicholls, GA 31554. Phone: (912) 384-7082. Located 6 miles east of Douglas on GA 32. 50 sites.

14. George L. Smith State Park, 371 George L. Smith State Park Rd., Twin City, GA 39471. Phone: (478) 763-2759. Located between Metter and Twin City off GA 23. (I-16 exit 104). 25 sites.

15. Georgia Veterans Memorial State Park, 2459-A US Hwy 280 West, Cordele, GA 31015. Phone: (229) 276-2371. Located 9 miles west of I-75 exit 10 on US 280. 77 sites.

16. Gordonia-Alatamaha State Park, Reidsville, GA 30453. Phone: (912) 557-7744. Located in Reidsville off US 280. 26 sites.

17. Hamburg State Park, 6071 Hamburg State Park Rd., Mitchell, GA 30820. Phone: (478) 552-2393. Located 20 miles north of Sandersville via GA 15, GA 102, and GA 248. 30 sites.

18. Hard Labor Creek State Park, Rutledge, GA 30663. Phone: (706) 557-3001. Located 3 miles north of Rutledge (I-20 exit 105) on Fairplay Road. 51 sites.

19. Hart State Park, 330 Hart State Park Rd., Hartwell, GA 30643. Phone: (706) 376-8756. Located just north of Hartwell off US 29 via Ridge Road. 78 sites.

20. High Falls State Park, 76 High Falls Park Dr., Jackson, GA 30233. Phone: (478) 993-3053. Located 1.8 miles east of I-75 exit 198. 112 sites.

21. Indian Springs State Park, 678 Lake Clark Rd., Flovilla, GA 30216. Phone: (770) 504-2277. Located off GA 42 about 15 miles from I-75 exits 188 or 205. 88 sites.

22. James H. "Sloppy" Floyd State Park, 2800 "Sloppy" Floyd Lake Rd., Summerville, GA 30747. Phone: (706) 857-0826. Located 3 miles south of Summerville to park road via US 27. 25 sites.

23. John Tanner State Park, 354 Tanner's Beach Rd., Carrollton, GA 30117. Phone: (770) 830-2222. Located 6 miles west of Carrollton off GA 16. 32 sites.

24. Kolomoki Mounds State Park, 205 Indian Mounds Rd., Blakely, GA 39823. Phone: (228) 724-2150. Located 6 miles north of Blakely off US 27. 43 sites.

25. Laura S. Walker State Park, 5633 Laura Walker Rd., Waycross, GA 31503. Phone: (912) 287-4900. Located 9 miles SE of Waycross on GA 177. 44 sites.

26. Little Ocmulgee State Park, McRae, GA 31055. Phone: (229) 868-7474. Located 2 miles north of McRae off US 319. 55 sites.

27. Magnolia Springs State Park, 1053 Magnolia Springs Dr., Millen, GA 30442. Phone: (478) 982-1660. Located 5 miles north of Millen on US 25. 26 sites.

28. Mistletoe State Park, 3723 Mistletoe Rd., Appling, GA 30802. Phone: (706) 541-0321. Located 10 miles north of I-20 exit 175 via GA 150 and Mistletoe Road. 92 sites.

29. Moccasin Creek State Park, 3655 State Hwy 197, Clarkesville, GA 30523. Phone: (706) 947-3194. Located 20 miles north of Clarkesville on GA 197. 54 sites.

30. Red Top Mountain State Park, 50 Lodge Rd., Cartersville, GA 30121. Phone: (770) 975-0055. Located near Cartersville, 1.5 miles east of I-75 exit 285. 92 sites.

31. Reed Bingham State Park, Adel, GA 31620. Phone: (229) 896-3551. Located 6 miles west of Adel (I-75 exit 39) and 14 miles east of Moultrie on GA 37. 46 sites.

32. Richard B. Russell State Park, 2650 Russell State Park Rd., Elberton, GA 30635. Phone: (706) 213-2045. Located 8 miles NE of Elberton via GA 77 and GA 368; follow signs. 28 sites.

33. Seminole State Park, 7870 State Park Rd., Donalsonville, GA 39845. Phone: (229) 861-3137. Located in southwest corner of Georgia, 16 miles south of Donaldsonville via GA 39. 50 sites.

34. Skidaway Island State Park, 52 Diamond Causeway, Savannah, GA 31411. Phone: (912) 598-2300. Located 6 miles SE of Savannah. Use I-16 exit 164A to DeRenne Avenue, Waters Avenue to Causeway; follow signs. 88 sites.

35. Stephen C. Foster State Park, Fargo, GA 31631. Phone: (912) 637-5274. Located in Okefenokee Swamp; remote location. 18 miles NE of Fargo via GA 177 to end. 66 sites.

36. Tallulah Gorge State Park, Tallulah Falls, GA 30573. Phone: (706) 754-7970. Located on US 441 in northeast corner of state. 50 sites.

37. Tugaloo State Park, 1763 Tugaloo State Park Rd., Lavonia, GA 30553. Phone: (706) 356-4362. Located off GA 328 via I-85 exit 173, GA 17. Follow signs. 108 sites.

38. Unicoi State Park, Helen, GA 30545. Phone: (706) 878-2201. Located 2 miles NE of Helen via GA 356. 84 sites.

39. Victoria Bryant State Park, 1105 Bryant Park Rd., Royston, GA 30662. Phone: (706) 245-6270. Located 2 miles north of Franklin Springs on GA 327; I-85, exit 160, follow signs. 25 sites.

40. Vogel State Park, 7485 Vogel State Park Rd., Blairsville, GA 30512. Phone: (706) 745-2628. Located 11 miles south of Blairsville off US 19/129. 85 sites.

41. Watson Mill Bridge State Park, 650 Watson Mill Rd., Comer, GA 30629. Phone: (706) 783-5349. Located 3 miles south of Comer off GA 22. 21 sites.

Idaho

There are 16 State Parks in The Gem State with RV camping spaces but very few have site facilities. Most parks do offer centralized drinking water. Lake Cascade State Park, located north of Boise on the Cascade Reservoir, has 10 different camping locations around the "lake" but only two locations have any desired facilities. (See listing under Lake Cascade.) Despite Idaho's mountainous terrain, most of the parks are open year round, but you should check with the particular park before proceeding to it. One park, Dworshak State Park near Orofino, has a 10 percent downgrade approach road and is not recommended for larger RVs. Reservations are accepted at some parks by contacting the park but all locations operate on a "first-come" basis. Credit cards are accepted and pets are OK but must be leashed. Rate groups: A, B, and C depending on facilities. Daily admission fee extra.

Idaho Dept. of Commerce
700 W. State St. / Statehouse Mall
Boise, ID 83720
Information: (208) 334-4199
Internet (also reservations): www.idahoparks.org

Idaho Park Locator

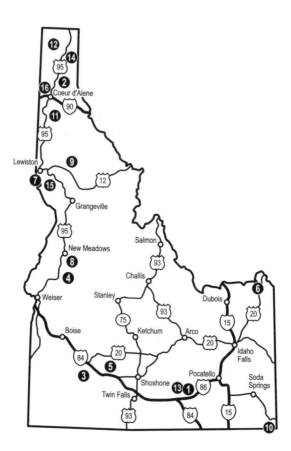

1. Massacre Rocks State Park, 3592 N Park Lane, American Falls, ID 83211. Phone: (208) 548-2672. Located 12 miles west of American Falls just off I-86 exit 28. 43 sites; dump station; pull-thrus. 55 foot limit.

2. Farragut State Park, 13400 E Ranger Rd., Athol, ID 83801. Phone: (208) 683-2425. Located in northern Idaho along ID 54, 4 miles east of Athol and US 95. 108 sites; showers; dump station; pull-thrus. 31 foot limit.

3. Bruneau Dunes State Park, Mountain Home, ID 83647. Phone: (208) 366-7919. Located 18 miles south of I-84 exit 95 via ID 51. 73 sites, some with full hook-ups; showers; dump station. 70 foot limit.

4. Lake Cascade State Park, Cascade, ID 83611. Phone: (208) 382-6544, telephone number for all Cascade Park units. All units located along

Cascade Reservoir, starting at main park about 70 miles north of Boise on ID 55. All units have 32 foot limit and most are seasonal.

a) Big Sage - 100 primitive sites
b) Blue Heron - 10 sites
c) Buttercup - 28 sites
d) Crown Point - 31 sites; some pull-thrus
e) Huckleberry - 28 sites; some pull-thrus
f) Poison Creek - 18 primitive sites; (open year round)
g) Sugarloaf - 45 sites
h) Van Wyck Central - 40 primitive sites
i) Van Wyck Main - 22 primitive sites; dump station
j) West Mountain - 26 primitive sites; dump station

5. Three Island Crossing State Park, 1083 S Three Island Fork Dr., Glenns Ferry, ID 83623. Phone: (208) 366-2395. Located in Glenns Ferry on Madison Street about 2 miles from I-84 exit 121. 101 sites with electric; showers; dump station. 60 foot limit.

6. Henry's Lake State Park, 3917 E 5100 N, Island Park, ID 83429. Phone: (208) 558-7532. Located near Yellowstone National Park on US 20 mile post 401, 45 miles north of Ashton. 45 sites; dump station. 40 foot limit.

7. Hells Gate State Park, 4832 Hells Gate Rd., Lewiston, ID 83501. Phone: (208) 799-5015. Located 4 miles south of Lewiston on Snake River Avenue. 93 sites with full hook-ups, some pull-thrus; showers. 60 foot limit.

8. Ponderosa State Park, McCall, ID 83668. Phone: (208) 634-2164. Located 2 miles NE of McCall off ID 55, north of Boise. 170 sites with electric, water, some pull-thrus; showers; dump station. 35 foot limit.

9. Dworshak State Park, Orofino, ID 83544. Phone: (208) 476-5994. Remote location on Snake River about 6 miles north of Orofino on county roads. NOTE: 10 percent downgrade on entrance road. 105 sites; showers; dump station. 50 foot limit.

10. Bear Lake State Park, Paris, ID 83261. Phone: (208) 847-1045. Located 11 miles east of Paris (southeastern corner of Idaho) off US 89, on Bear Lake. 48 sites with hook-ups, some pull-thrus. 60 foot limit.

11. Heyburn State Park, 1291 Chatcolet Rd., Plummer, ID 83851. Phone: (208) 686-1308. Located between Plummer and St. Maries, southeast of Coeur d'Alene, along ID 5. 132 sites with electric; showers; dump station. 55 foot limit.

12. Priest Lake State Park, 314 Indian Creek Park Rd., Coolin, ID 83821. Phone: (208) 443-2200. Three units; remote location in northern Idaho on Priest Lake. 151 sites with hook-ups; showers; dump station.
    a) Dickensheet - located 4 miles south of Coolin
    b) Indian Creek - 11 miles north of Coolin
    c) Lionhead - 23 miles north of Coolin

13. Lake Walcott State Park, 959 E Minidoka Dam, Rupert, ID 83350. Phone: (208) 436-1258. Located 13 miles NE of Rupert, I-84 exit 211, in southern ID. 22 sites; dump station 35 foot limit.

14. Round Lake State Park, Sagle, ID 83860. Phone: (208) 263-3489. Located on US 95, 10 miles south of Sandpoint in Idaho Panhandle. 53 sites; showers; dump station. 35 foot limit.

15. Winchester Lake State Park, Winchester, ID 83555. Phone: (208) 924-7653. Located SE of Lewiston on US 95, west of Winchester. 70 sites with electric; showers; dump station. 40 foot limit.

16. Mary M. McCrosky State Park, 2750 Kathleen Ave., Coeur d'Alene, ID 83815. Phone: (208) 666-6711 ext 344. Located in Coeur d'Alene. 35 primitive sites. Not good for large RVs (over 26 foot).

Illinois

Sixty-two State Parks or Recreational Areas have RV sites in Illinois. The state classifies these areas as A, B, and C (see list below) and the charges for these sites vary as to facilities available. All patrons of these campgrounds must pay a basic entrance fee plus a fee for site use. Many of the parks are self-register and it is imperative that all users check in at the park office to obtain a camping permit. Some parks or facilities in a park are seasonal so it is wise to call ahead. Some parks accept or require reservations, which are handled at the particular park. Most parks, however, are on a first-come, first-served basis. Rate groups: A and B.

Site classifications:
Class A: electric, showers in campground.
Class B/E: electric.
Class B/S: showers in campground
Class C: vehicle access; showers nearby.

Illinois Dept. of Natural Resources
Office of Land Management and Education
One Natural Resources Way
Springfield, IL 62707
Information: (217) 782-6752
Internet: www.dnr.state.il.us

Illinois Park Locator

1. Argyle Lake State Park,
    640 Argyle Park Rd.,
    Colchester, IL 62326. Phone:
    (309) 776-3422. Located off
    US 136 near Colchester.
    86 A; 24 B; 18 C sites.
    Dump station.

2. Apple River Canyon
    State Park, 8763 E
    Canyon Rd., Apple
    River, IL 61001.
    Phone: (815)
    745-3302.
    Located in the
    northwestern
    corner of state near
    Apple River between
    US 20 and IL 78. 47 C
    sites. Dump station.

3. Big River State Forest,
    Keithsburg, IL 61442.
    Phone: (309) 374-2496.
    Located on Mississippi River
    south of Keithsburg off IL 94. 65
    C sites. Dump station.

4. Delabar State Park, Oquawka, IL 61469.
    Phone: (309) 374-2496. Located on
    Mississippi River about 1.5 miles north of
    Oquawka off IL 164; follow signs. 54 B/E sites. Dump station.

5. Green River State Wildlife Area, 375 Game Rd., Harmon, IL 61042. Phone:
    (815) 379-2324. Located 6 miles NW of Ohio (IL) off IL 26. Open camping
    (dry). Dump station.

6. Illini State Park, 2660 E. 2350th Rd., Marseilles, IL 61341. Phone: (815)
    795-2448. Located on Illinois River near Marseilles on US 6. 50 A; 50 B/
    S sites. Dump station.

7. Johnson-Sauk Trail State Recreation Area, 27500 N. 1200 Ave., Kewanee,
    IL 61443. Phone: (309) 853-5589. Located 5 miles north of Kewanee off
    IL 78. 68 A sites. Dump station.

8. Jubilee College State Park, 13921 W Route 150, Brimfield, IL 61517. Phone: (309) 446-3758. Located 15 miles NW of Peoria near Kickapoo on US 150. 107 A; 40 B/S sites. Dump station.

9. Lake Le-Aqua-Na State Recreation Area, 8542 N Lake Rd., Lena, IL 61048. Phone: (815) 369-4282. Located near Lena, 10 miles north of US 20, off IL 73. 112 A sites. Dump station.

10. Lowden State Park, 1411 N River Rd. Oregon, IL 61061. Phone: (815) 732-6828. Located near Oregon (IL 2 & 64); follow signs. 80 A sites. Dump station.

11. Marshall State Fish and Wildlife Area; 236 State Route 26, Lacon, IL 61540. Phone: (309) 246-8351. Located off IL 26 about 27 miles NE of Peoria. 22 B/E; 6 C sites. Dump station.

12. Mississippi Palisades State Park, 16327 A Route 84, Savanna, IL 61074. Phone: (815) 273-2731. Located about 4 miles north of Savanna on IL 84. 241 A & B sites. Dump station.

13. Morrison-Rockwood State Park, 18750 Lake Rd., Morrison, IL 61270. Phone: (815) 772-4708. Located north of Morrison (US 30 & IL 78) on IL 78. 92 A sites. Dump station.

14. Prophetstown State Recreation Area, Riverside Drive & Park Avenue, Prophetstown, IL 61277. Phone: (815) 537-2926. Located on northeast edge of Prophetstown on IL 78, on the Rock River. 44 A; 42 B/E sites; showers. Dump station.

15. Rice Lake State Fish and Wildlife Area, 19721 N US 24, Canton, IL 61520. Phone: (309) 647-9184. Located 15 miles north of Havana on US 24. 34 B/E sites. Dump station.

16. Rock Cut State Park, 7318 Harlem Rd., Loves Park, IL 61111. Phone: (815) 885-3311. Located 1.5 miles north of Riverside Boulevard exit from I-90, follow signs. 208 A, 60 B/E sites. Dump station.

17. Shabbona Lake State Recreation Area, 4201 Shabbona Grove Rd., Shabbona, IL 60550. Phone: (815) 436-1258. Located off US 30, between DeKalb and LaSalle-Peru. 150 A sites. Dump station.

18. Spring Lake State Fish and Wildlife Area, 7982 S Park Rd., Manito, IL 61546. Phone: (309) 968-7135. Located 25 miles SW of Peoria on the Illinois River. Access via US 136 & IL 29, follow signs. 70 C sites. Dump station.

19. Starved Rock State Park, Routes 178 and 71, Utica, IL 61373. Phone: (815) 667-4726. Located 1 mile south of Utica off US 6, midway between Ottawa and LaSalle-Peru. 133 A sites. Dump station.

20. White Pines Forest State Park, 6712 West Pines Rd., Mt. Morris, IL 61054. Phone: (815) 946-3717. Located about 9 miles SW of Mt. Morris (IL 64). 103 B/S sites. Dump station.

21. Woodford State Fish and Wildlife Area, Low Point, IL 61545. Phone: (309) 822-8861. Located NE of Peoria on the Illinois River, off IL 26. 40 C sites. Dump station.

22. Chain O'Lakes State Park, 8916 Wilmot Rd., Spring Grove, IL 60081. Phone: (847) 587-5512. Located near Wisconsin state line off US 12. 151 A sites. Dump station.

23. Des Plaines State Fish and Wildlife Area, 24621 North River Rd., Wilmington, IL 60481. Phone: (815) 423-5326. Located just west of I-55 exit 241 near Wilmington. 20 C sites. Dump station.

24. Illinois Beach State Park, Lake Front, Zion, IL 60099. Phone: (847) 662-4828. Located on Lake Michigan near Waukegan. 249 A sites. Dump station. NOTE: this park is especially busy in summer months. It would be wise to telephone first. Reservations are recommended, if possible. Weekends are especially crowded.

25. Kankakee River State Park, 5314 W Route 102, Bourbonnais, IL 60914. Phone: (815) 933-1383. Located on IL 102 about 5 miles NW of Bourbonnais. 110 A; 150 B sites. Dump station. (Two campgrounds). Busy weekend park. Call ahead.

26. Clinton Lake State Recreation Area, 725 1900 E, DeWitt, IL 61735. Phone: (217) 935-8722. Located about 10 miles NE of Clinton (US 51 & IL 54) on IL 54. 211 A; 97 B sites; showers. Dump station.

27. Eagle Creek State Park, Findlay, IL 62534. Phone: (217) 756-8260. Located on Lake Shelbyville off IL 128 between Effingham and Decatur. 35 A; 24 B/E sites; showers.

28. Fox Ridge State Park, 18175 State Park Rd., Charleston, IL 61920. Phone: (217) 345-6416. Located on IL 130 about 7 miles south of Charleston. 43 A sites. Dump station.

29. Kickapoo State Park, 10906 Kickapoo Park Rd., Oakwood, IL 61858.

Phone: (217) 442-4915. Located off I-74 exit 206 west of Danville. 108 A; 109 B/S sites. Dump station.

30. Lincoln Trail State Park, 16985 E 1350th Rd., Marshall, IL 62441. Phone: (217) 826-2222. Located 2 miles south of Marshall off IL 1. 173 A; 6 C sites (two campgrounds).

31. Moraine View State Park, 27374 Moraine View Park Rd., Le Roy, IL 61752. Phone: (309) 724-8032. Located SE of Bloomington off US 150 via County Road 36. 137 A; 65 B/E sites. Dump station.

32. Walnut Point State Park, 2331 E Country Road 370 N, Oakland, IL 61943. Phone: (217) 346-3336. Located NE of Charleston off IL 133. 34 A; 5 B/S sites. Dump station.

33. Weldon Springs State Recreation Area, 1159 500 N, Clinton, IL 61727. Phone: (217) 935-2644. Located 3 miles SE of Clinton off US 51. 77 A (5 pull-thru) sites. Dump station.

34. Wolf Creek State Park, Windsor, IL 61957. Phone: (217) 459-2831. Located on Lake Shelbyville, NW of Windsor, off IL 16. 304 A; 140 B/E sites.

35. Beaver Dam State Park, 14548 Beaver Dam Lane, Plainview, IL 62685. Phone: (217) 854-8020. Located SW of Carlinville off IL 111. 64 A sites; showers.

36. Eldon Hazlet State Recreation Area, Hazlet Park Road, Carlyle, IL 62231. Phone: (618) 594-3015. Located on Carlyle Lake north of Carlyle (US 50), off IL 127. 328 A sites; store. Dump station.

37. Horseshoe Lake State Fish and Wildlife Area (Madison Co.), 3321 Hwy 111, Granite City, IL 60240. Phone: (618) 931-0270. Located on IL 111 east of St. Louis, MO. 48 C sites; showers. Dump station.

38. Jim Edgar Panther Creek State Fish and Wildlife Area, 10149 Hwy 11, Chandlerville, IL 62627. Phone: (217) 452-7741. Located on IL 78, NE of Virginia. 16 AA (with sewer hookups); 64 A sites. Dump station.

39. Nauvoo State Park, Nauvoo, IL 62354. Phone: (217) 453-2512. Located on IL 96 about 8 miles north of Hamilton and US 136. 150 A & B/S sites. Dump station.

40. Pere Marquette State Park, Route 100 W, Grafton, IL 62037. Phone:

(618) 786-3323. Located NW of St. Louis, MO on IL 100 near Grafton. 80 A & B/S sites. Dump station.

41. Randolph County State Recreation Area, 4301 S Lake Dr., Chester, IL 62233. Phone: (618) 826-2706. Located 5 miles north of Chester on IL 150. 95 C sites. Dump station.

42. Sand Ridge State Forest, 25799 E County Road 2300, North Forest City, IL 61532. Phone: (309) 597-2212. Located 25 miles SW of Peoria; access via US 136 from Chatauqua Park, follow signs. 27 C sites. Dump station.

43. Sangchris Lake State Recreation Area, 9898 Cascade Rd., Rochester, IL 62563. Phone: (217) 498-9208. Located SE of Springfield via IL 29 and CR 20. 80 A; 40 B/S sites. Dump station.

44. Siloam Springs State Park, 938 E 3003rd Lane, Clayton, IL 62324. Phone: (217) 894-6205. Located SW of Mt. Sterling off US 24 or north of IL 104; follow signs. 98 A; 84 B/S sites. Dump station.

45. South Shore State Park, 20100 Hazlet Park Rd., Carlyle, IL 62231. Phone: (618) 594-3015. Located on Carlyle Lake (south shore) off US 50. 33 C sites. Dump station.

46. Weinberg-King State Park, Augusta, IL 62311. Phone: (217) 392-2345. Located NE of Augusta on IL 101. 60 C sites. Dump station.

47. Beall Woods State Park, 9285 Beall Woods Ave., Mt. Carmel, IL 62863. Phone: (618) 298-2442. Located 6 miles south of Mount Carmel on IL 1.

48. Cave-in-Rock State Park, #1 New State Park Rd., Cave-in-Rock, IL 62919. Phone: (618) 289-4325. Located on the Ohio River on IL 1 near junction of IL 146. 34 A; 25 B/S sites. Dump station.

49. Dixon Springs State Park, Route 146, Golconda, IL 62938. Phone: (618) 949-3304. Located in Dixon Springs on IL 146 in southern Illinois. 38 B/E sites. Dump station.

50. Fort Massac State Park, 1308 E Fifth St., Metropolis, IL 62960. Phone: (618) 524-4712. Located on the Ohio River at junction of US 45 & IL 145. 50 A sites. Dump station.

51. Giant City State Park, 460 Giant City Lodge Rd., Makanda, IL 62958. Phone: (618) 457-4836. Located south of Carbondale off US 51; follow signs. 85 A sites. Dump station.

52. Hamilton County State Fish and Wildlife Area - Dolan Lake, McLeansboro, IL 62859. Phone: (618) 773-4340. Located off IL 14 near US 45, outside McLeansboro. 81 A sites. Dump station.

53. Horseshoe Lake State Fish and Wildlife Area (Alexander), Miller City, IL 62962. Phone: (618) 776-5689. Located on IL 3 near junction of IL 127, NW of Cairo. 38 A; 40 B/E; 10 C sites. Dump station.

54. Lake Murphysboro State Park, 52 Cinder Hill Dr., Murphysboro, IL 62966. Phone: (618) 684-2867. Located west of Murphysboro off IL 149.

55. Pyramid State Park, 1562 Pyramid Park Rd., Pinckneyville, IL 62274. Phone: (618) 357-2574. Located 5 miles south of Pinckneyville off IL 127/13. 10 C sites. Dump station.

56. Ramsey Lake State Park, Ramsey, IL 62080. Phone: (618) 423-2215. Located 1 mile NW of Ramsey off US 51. 90 A sites. Dump station.

57. Red Hills State Park, 1100N & 400E, Route 2, Sumner, IL 62466. Phone: (618) 936-2469. Located on US 50 between Olney and Lawrenceville. 103 A sites (some pull-thru & 50-amp electric). Dump station.

58. Saline County State Fish and Wildlife Area, 85 Glen O. Jones Rd., Equality, IL 62934. Phone: (618) 276-4405. Located 5 miles SW of Equality near Shawnee National Forest, off IL 13 & 142. 8 C sites. Dump station.

59. Sam Dale Lake State Fish and Wildlife Area, Johnsonville, IL 62850. Phone: (618) 835-2292. Located 1 mile NW of Johnsonville off CR 16. 68 B/E sites. Dump station.

60. Sam Parr State Fish and Wildlife Area, 13225 E State Hwy 23, Newton, IL 63448. Phone: (618) 783-2661. Located 3 miles NE of Newton at junction of IL 30 & 133. 16 B/E; 18 C sites. Dump station.

61. Stephen A. Forbes State Recreation Area, 6924 Omega Rd., Kinmundy, IL 62854. Phone: (618) 547-3381. Located off IL 37, NE of Salem (US 50 & I-57). 115 A sites. Dump station.

62. Wayne Fitzgerrell State Recreation Area, 11094 Ranger Rd., Whittington, IL 62897. Phone: (618) 629-2320. Located on Rend Lake west of I-57 exit 77 and south of Mount Vernon. 243 A sites. Dump station.

Indiana

Twenty of Indiana's State Parks are RV friendly. All the parks have basic amenities; some offer full hook-ups. RV sites are classified AA, for full hook-ups to Class C for primitive. Camping fees for each reflect these classifications. Some parks offer seasonal "specials" and you have to ask about these offers when calling. Indiana residents are eligible for senior discounts. However, there are senior discounts (60 years or older) available to all, Sunday through Wednesday in April and May and again in September and October when the parks are less busy. It is always wise to call ahead because most of the parks do not accept reservations. Rate groups: B and C depending on type of site.

Indiana Dept. of Natural Resources
402 West Washington St., Room W298
Indianapolis, IN 46204
Information: (574) 656-8186
Internet: www.camp.in.gov

Indiana Park Locator

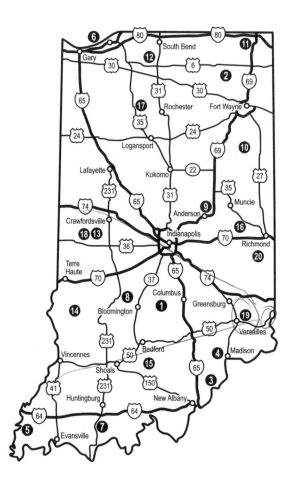

1. Brown County State Park, Hwy 46, Nashville, IN 47448. Phone: (812)
    988-6406. Located on IN 46 between Bloomington and Columbus. 401
    sites with electric; 28 non-electric. Dump station.

2. Chain O'Lakes State Park, 2355 E 75 South, Albion, IN 46701. Phone:
    (260) 636-2654. Located SW of Kendallville on IN 9. 331 sites with electric;
    49 non-electric; 33 primitive. Dump station.

3. Charlestown State Park, Charlestown, IN 47111. Phone: (812) 256-5600.
    Located in Charlestown in Southern Indiana near KY state line at Junction
    of IN 62 & 160. 61 sites with full hook-ups; 131 sites with electric; showers.
    Dump station.

4. Clifty Falls State Park, 222 N Clifty St., Madison, IN 47250. Phone: (812) 273-8885. Located in southeastern Indiana near junction of IN 256 & 7. 106 sites; electric, showers; 59 primitive sites. Dump station.

5. Harmonie State Park, 3451 Harmonie State Park Rd., New Harmony, IN 47631. Phone: (812) 682-4821. Located on Wabash River, 25 miles NW of Evansville, off IN 69. 200 sites; electric; showers. Dump station; store.

6. Indiana Dunes State Park, 1600 N 25 E, Chesterton, IN 46304. Phone: (219) 926-1952. Located north of Chesterton, off US 12, on Lake Michigan. *Campground under reconstruction for 2004 season - closed until late May 2005.* Call for information. Upon reopening: about 75 sites with electric; 115 non-electric; showers. Dump station.

7. Lincoln State Park, Hwy 162, Lincoln City, IN 47552. Phone: (812) 937-4710. Located in southern Indiana on US 231 near junction with IN 162; I-64 exit 57. 150 sites with electric; showers; 120 primitive sites. Dump station.

8. McCormick's Creek State Park, State Road 46 E, Spencer, IN 47460. Phone: (812) 829-2235. Located outside Spencer near junction of US 231 & IN 46. 189 sites with electric; showers. 100 non-electric. Dump station.

9. Mounds State Park, 4306 Mounds Rd., Anderson, IN 46017. Phone: (765) 642-6627. Located east of Anderson, I-69 & IN 32. 75 sites, electric; showers. Dump station.

10. Ouabache State Park, 4930 E State Road 201, Bluffton, IN 46714. Phone: (260) 824-0926. Located on the Wabash River, outside Bluffton. 77 sites with electric; showers; 47 non-electric. Dump station.

11. Pokagon State Park, 450 Lane 100 Lake James, Angola, IN 46703. Phone: (260) 833-2012. Located on Lake James near Angola, I-69 & IN 727. 200 sites with electric; showers; 73 non-electric. Dump station.

12. Potato Creek State Park, 25601 State Road 4, North Liberty, IN 46554. Phone: (574) 656-8186. Located 12 miles SW of South Bend on IN 4, off US 31. 287 sites, electric; showers. Dump station.

13. Shades State Park, Waveland, IN 47989. Phone: (765) 435-2810. Located 17 miles SW of Crawfordsville on IN 234. 195 sites, non-electric; showers. Dump station.

14. Shakamak State Park, 6265 W State Road 48, Jasonville, IN 47438. Phone: (812) 665-2158. Located about 10 miles east of US 41/150 from Shelburn. 122 sites with electric; 62 primitive sites; showers. Dump station.

15. Spring Mill State Park, 3333 State Road 600 E, Mitchell, IN 47446. Phone: (812) 849-4129. Located east of Mitchell, off IN 37. 187 sites with electric; 36 primitive sites; showers. Dump station.

16. Summit Lake State Park, 5993 N Messick Rd., New Castle, IN 47362. Phone: (765) 766-5873. Located on US 36, NE of New Castle. 125 sites, electric; showers. Dump station.

17. Tippecanoe River State Park, 4200 N US 35, Winamac, IN 46996. Phone: (574) 946-3213. Located on US 35, 6 miles north of Winamac. 112 sites, electric; showers. Dump station.

18. Turkey Run State Park, 8121 E Park Rd., Marshall, IN 47859. Phone: (765) 597-2635. Located SW of Crawfordsville on IN 47, east of US 41. 213 sites; electric; showers. Dump station.

19. Versailles State Park, US 50, Versailles, IN 47042. Phone: (812) 689-6424. Located near Versailles on US 50 near Junction of US 421. 226 sites; electric; showers. Dump station.

20. Whitewater Memorial State Park, 1418 S State Road 101, Liberty, IN 47353. Phone: (765) 458-5565. Located east of Connorsville, near junction of IN 101 & 44. 236 sites with electric; showers; 45 non-electric. Dump station.

Iowa

Of Iowa's State Park and Recreation Areas, 54 locations have RV facilities. These locations have two categories of sites: Modern (M) - showers in the park and Non-modern (NM) - no facilities nearby. Most locations have electric at the site; some have sewer hookups. Most locations have dump stations. Iowa's parks are on a first-come, first-served basis for campsites. Unless noted, there are no rig size limitations. All the parks have direction signs from major highways and Interstates. Rate groups: A and B depending on site utilities.

Iowa Department of Natural Resources
Wallace State Office Bldg.
502 E 9th Street
Des Moines, IA 50319
Information: (515) 281-8368
Internet: www.exploreiowaparks.com

Iowa Park Locator

Iowa Park Locator (*cont.*)

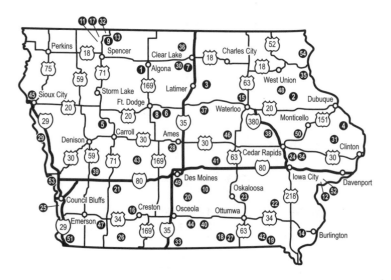

1. Ambrose A. Call State Park, Algona, IA (641) 581-4835. Located in north-central IA, 1.5 miles SW of Algona, off US 169. 16 sites, 13 with electric; NM.

2. Backbone State Park, Dundee. IA 52038. Phone: (536) 924-2527. Located in northeastern IA, 4 miles SW of Strawberry Point on IA 410, near IA 3. 126 sites, 40 with electric; showers; dump station. M & NM.

3. Beeds Lake State Park, Hampton, IA 50441. Phone: (641) 456-2047. Located in north-central IA, 3 miles NW of Hampton (US 65 & IA 3) on CR 134. 144 sites, 70 with electric; showers; dump station. M.

4. Bellevue State Park, Bellevue, IA 52031. Phone: (563) 872-4019. Located in eastern IA, 2.5 miles south of Bellevue on US 52; near Mississippi River. 39 sites, 22 with electric; showers; dump station. M.

5. Black Hawk State Park, Lake View, IA 51450. Phone: (712) 657-8712. Located in west-central IA in Lake View near US 71 & IA 175. 176 sites, 68 with electric; showers; dump station. M.

6. Brushy Creek State Recreation Area, Lehigh, IA 50557. Phone: (515) 543-8298. Located in central IA, 4 miles south of Duncombe on CR P-73, off US 20. 202 sites, 120 with electric; showers; dump station. M.

7. Clear Lake State Park, Clear Lake, IA 50428. Phone: (641) 357-4212. Located in north-central IA west of Mason City, 2 miles south of Clear Lake on IA 107, near US 18 and I-35. 200 sites, 95 with electric; showers; dump station. M.

8. Dolliver Memorial State Park, Lehigh, IA 50557. Phone: (515) 359-2539. Located in central IA south of Fort Dodge, 3 miles NW of Lehigh on IA 50, off US 169. 33 sites, 19 with electric; showers; dump station. M.

9. Elinor Bedell State Park, Milford, IA 51351. Phone: (712) 337-3211. Located in northwestern IA near MN state line, 2 miles west of Spirit Lake on 250th Ave, off US 71. 8 sites with electric; showers. M.

10. Elk Rock (Red Rock) State Park, Knoxville, IA 50138. Phone: (641) 842-6008. Located in south-central IA, SE of DesMoines, 7 miles north of Knoxville on IA 14, on Red Rock Lake. 90 sites, 36 with electric; showers; dump station. M.

11. Emerson Bay & Lighthouse State Park, Milford, IA 51351. Phone: (712) 337-3211. Located in northwestern IA near MN state line, 2.5 miles north of Milford on IA 86, off US 71. 117 sites, 60 with electric; showers; dump station. M.

12. Fairport State Recreation Area, Muscatine, IA 52761. Phone: (563) 263-3197. Located on Mississippi River in southeastern IA, 5 miles east of Muscatine on IA 22. 42 sites with electric; showers; dump station. M.

13. Fort Defiance State Park, Milford, IA 51351. Phone: (712) 362-2078. Located in northwestern IA near MN state line, 1 mile west of Estherville (IA 9 & 4) on IA 9. 16 sites. NM.

14. Geode State Park, Danville, IA 52623. Phone: (319) 392-4601. Located in southeastern IA, 4 miles SW of Danville (NW of Burlington), off IA 79. 186 sites, 96 with electric; showers; dump station. M.

15. George Wyth Memorial State Park, Waterloo, IA 50703. Phone: (319) 232-5505. Located in east-central IA, NW of Waterloo, east of Cedar Falls. 66 sites, 46 with electric; showers; dump station. M.

16. Green Valley State Park, Creston, IA 50801. Phone: (641) 782-5131. Located in southwestern IA, NW of Creston, on IA 186, off US 34. 143 sites, 88 with electric; showers; dump station. M.

17. Gull Point State Park, Milford, IA 51351. Phone: (712) 337-3211. Located in northwestern IA, near MN state line, 3.5 miles north of Milford via US 71 and IA 86. 112 sites, 60 with electric; showers; dump station. M.

18. Honey Creek State Park, Moravia, IA 52571. Phone: (641) 724-3739. Located on Rathbun Lake in south-central IA, 9.5 miles west of Moravia on IA 142. 153 sites, 94 with electric; showers; dump station. M.

19. Lacey-Keosauqua State Park, Keosauqua, IA 52565. Phone: (319) 293-3502. Located in southeastern IA near MO state line, 5 miles south of Keosauqua on IA 15. 113 sites, 45 with electric; showers; dump station. M.

20. Lake Ahquabi State Park, Indianola, IA 50125. Phone: (515) 961-7101. Located about 20 miles south of DesMoines via US 69 and IA 349. 161 sites, 85 with electric; showers; dump station. M.

21. Lake Anita State Park, Anita, IA 50020. Phone: (712) 762-3564. Located in southwestern IA, 5 miles south of Anita on IA 83, off I-80 exit 70. 145 sites, 76 with electric; showers; dump station. M.

22. Lake Darling State Park, Brighton, IA 52540. Phone: (319) 694-2323. Located in southeastern IA, 3 miles west of Brighton (SW of Washington), off IA 78. 118 sites, 81 with electric; showers; dump station. M.

23. Lake Keomah State Park, Oskaloosa, IA 52577. Phone: (641) 673-6975. Located in southeastern IA, 5 miles east of Oskaloosa via IA 92. 88 sites, 52 with electric; showers; dump station. M.

24. Lake McBride State Park, Solon, IA 52333. Phone: (319) 624-2200. Located in eastern IA, 4 miles NW of Solon (SE of Cedar Rapids), on IA 88. 122 sites, 60 with electric; showers; dump station. M.

25. Lake Manawa State Park, Council Bluffs, IA 51501. Phone: (712) 366-1220. Located in southwestern IA, 1 mile south of IA 92 (I-29 exit 47), south of Council Bluffs. 68 sites, 35 with electric; showers; dump station. M.

26. Lake of Three Fires State Park, Bedford, IA 50833. Phone: (712) 523-2700. Located in southwestern IA, 3 miles north of Bedford on IA 49. 122 sites, 30 with electric; showers; dump station. M.

27. Lake Wapello, Drakesville, IA. Phone: (641) 722-3371. Located in southeastern IA, 6 miles west of Drakesville on IA 273, off US 63. 82 sites, 42 with electric; showers; dump station. M.

28. Ledges State Park, Madrid, IA 50156. Phone: (515) 432-1852. Located in central IA west of Ames, 6 miles south of Boone, off US 30 on IA 164. 94 sites, 40 with electric; showers; dump station. M.

29. Lewis and Clark State Park, Onawa, IA 51040. Phone: (712) 423-2829. Located in western IA near NE state line, 3 miles west of Onawa, off IA 175 & I-29 exit 112; follow signs. 82 sites with electric; showers; dump station. M.

30. McIntosh Woods State Park, Ventura, IA 50482. Phone: (641) 829-3847. Located in north-central IA about 8 miles west of Clear Lake on US 18. 49 sites, 45 with electric; showers; dump station. M.

31. Maquoketa Caves State Park, Maquoketa, IA 52060. Phone: (563) 652-5833. Located in eastern IA, 7 miles NW of Maquoketa (US 61 & IA 64). 29 sites, 17 with electric; showers; dump station. M.

32. Marble Beach State Park, Milford, IA 51351. Phone: (712) 337-3211. Located in northwestern IA near MN state line, 2 miles NW of Orleans, off US 71 & IA 276. 224 sites, 103 with electric; showers; dump station. M.

33. Nine Eagles State Park, Davis City, IA 50065. Phone: (641) 442-2855. Located in southern IA near MO state line, 6 miles SE of Davis City (I-35 exit 4) on county road. 62 sites, 40 with electric; showers; dump station. M.

34. Palisades-Kepler State Park, Mt. Vernon, IA 52314. Phone: (319) 895-6039. Located in eastern IA, SE of Cedar Rapids, 3.5 miles west of Mt. Vernon on US 30. 44 sites, 26 with electric; showers; dump station. M.

35. Pikes Peak State Park, McGregor, IA 52157. Phone: (563) 873-2341.

Located in northeastern IA, 3 miles SE of McGregor (US 18/52, IA 340), on Mississippi River. 80 sites, 60 with electric; showers; dump station. M.

36. Pilot Knob State Park, Forest City, IA 50436. Phone: (641) 581-4835. Located in north-central IA, NW of Mason City, 4 miles east of Forest City on IA 9. 60 sites, 48 with electric; showers; dump station. M.

37. Pine Lake State Park, Eldora, IA 50627. Phone: (641) 858-5832. Located in central IA next to Eldora, off IA 14/175 on CR 556. 128 sites, 75 with electric; showers; dump station. M.

38. Pleasant Creek State Recreation Area, Palo, IA 52324. Phone: (319) 436-7716. Located in east-central IA, NW of Cedar Rapids, off I-380 exit 35. 69 sites, 43 with electric; showers; dump station. M.

39. Prairie Rose State Park, Harlan, IA 51537. Phone: (712) 773-2701. Located 9 miles southeast of Harlan via IA 44 and Road M47. 97 sites, 61 with electric; showers; dump station. M.

40. Red Haw State Park, Chariton, IA 50049. Phone: (641) 774-5632. Located in south-central IA, 1 mile south of Chariton, off US 34. 80 sites, 60 with electric; showers; dump station. M.

41. Rock Creek State Park, Kellogg, IA 50135. Phone: (641) 236-3722. Located in central IA between Newton and Grinnell, 6 miles NE of Kellogg via county roads. 196 sites, 103 with electric; showers; dump station. M.

42. Shimek State Forest Campground, Farmington, IA 52626. Phone: (319) 878-3811. Located in southeastern IA, 1 mile east of Farmington on IA 2. 56 sites. NM.

43. Springbrook State Park, Guthrie Center, IA 50115. Phone: (641) 747-3591. Located in west-central IA, 8 miles NE of Guthrie Center on IA 384, off IA 25. 120 sites, 81 with electric; showers; dump station. M.

44. Stephens State Forest, Chariton, IA 50049. Phone: (641) 774-5632. Located in south-central IA, 2.5 miles south of Lucas on US 65. 85 sites. NM. (Equestrian park).

45. Stone State Park, Sioux City, IA 51103. Phone: (712) 255-4698. Located in western IA, 8 miles NW of Sioux City on IA 12. 30 sites, 9 with electric. NM.

46. Union Grove State Park, Gladbrook, IA 50635. Phone: (641) 473-2556. Located in central IA, NE of Marshalltown, 4 miles south of Gladbrook via CR T47. 25 sites, 7 with electric. NM.

47. Viking Lake State Park, Stanton, IA 51573. Phone: (712) 829-2235. Located in southwestern IA, SE of Red Oak off US 34 on CR 115. 115 sites, 94 with electric; showers; dump station. M.

48. Volga River State Recreation Area, Fayette, IA 52142. Phone: (563) 425-4161. Located in northeastern IA, 4 miles NE of Fayette on IA 150. 50 sites. NM.

49. Walnut Woods State Park, West DesMoines, IA 50265. Phone: (515) 285-4502. Located in south-central IA, 4 miles SW of DesMoines on IA 5, near I-35. 24 sites. NM.

50. Wapsipinicon State Park, Anamosa, IA 52205. Phone: (712) 382-2786. Located about 15 miles northeast of Cedar Rapids via US 51. 30 sites, 15 with electric; showers; dump station. M.

51. Waubonsie State Park, Hamburg, IA 51640. Phone: (712) 382-2786. Located in southwest corner of IA, south of Sidney, off I-29 exits 1 or 10, on IA 239 at IA 2. 95 sites, 22 with electric; showers; dump station. M.

52. Wildcat Den State Park, Muscatine, IA 52761. Phone: (563) 263-4337. Located in southeastern IA, 10 miles east of Muscatine on IA 22. 27 sites NM.

53. Wilson Island State Park, Missouri Valley, IA 51555. Phone: (712) 642-2069. Located in southwestern IA, 5 miles west of Loveland, off I-29 exit 72 on IA 362. 131 sites, 61 with electric; showers; dump station. M.

54. Yellow River State Forest, Harpers Ferry, IA 52146. Phone: (563) 873-2341. Located in northeastern IA, 14 miles SE of Waukon, off IA 76, near junction IA 360. 152 sites. NM.

Kansas

There are 22 State Parks with RV facilities in Kansas. They range from full hook-ups to electric only sites. In most cases the electric service is 50 amps at all campgrounds. All parks require a daily or annual usage fee ($5 per vehicle for 2004) plus an additional fee for utility sites. Reservations are accepted at some parks, as listed. Visa and MasterCard accepted. Rate groups: B and C depending upon site facilities.

Kansas Dept. of Commerce
Travel & Tourism Development Division
1000 SW Jackson St., Ste. 100
Topeka, KS 66612
Information: (620) 672-5911 / Reservations: (877) 444-6777
Internet: www.kdwp.state.ks.us

Kansas Park Locator

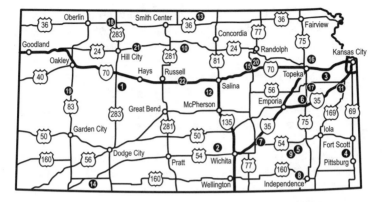

1. Cedar Bluff State Park, Ellis, KS 67637. Phone: (785) 726-3212. Located on Cedar Bluff Reservoir on KS 147 south of I-70 exit 135. 10 full hookup, 91 water & electric, 20 electric and 300 non-utility sites; showers, dump station(s). All 50-amp electric. Reservable sites available.

2. Cheney State Park, 16000 NE 50th St., Cheney, KS 67025. Phone: (316) 542-3664. Located on Cheney Reservoir about 28 miles west of Wichita off US 54. 185 water & electric, 245 non-utility sites; showers, dump station(s). All 50-amp electric. Reservable sites available

3. Clinton State Park, 798 N 1415 Rd., Lawrence, KS 66049. Phone: (785) 842-8562. Located off Kansas Turnpike exit 197 & US 40, on Clinton Lake west of Lawrence. 240 water & electric, 220 non-utility sites; showers; dump station(s). Reservable sites available.

4. Crawford State Park, 1 Lake Rd., Farlington, KS 66734. Phone: (620) 362-3671. Located off KS 7 west of US 69 between Pittsburg and Fort Scott. 48 water & electric, 27 electric, some non-utility sites; showers, dump station.

5. Cross Timbers State Park, 144 Hwy 105, Toronto, KS 66777. Phone: (620) 637-2213. Located on Toronto Lake about 13 miles west of Yates Center (US 75 & 54) on KS 105. 15 full hook-ups, 37 water & electric, 10 electric, 180 non-utility sites; showers, dump station. Reservable sites available.

6. Eisenhower State Park, 29810 S. Fairlawn Rd., Osage City, KS 66523. Phone: (785) 528-4102. Located SW of Lyndon off KS 278, on Melvern

Lake. Use I-35 exit 155 and then proceed north on US 75 to KS 278. 25 full hook-ups, 38 water & electric, 127 electric, some non-utility sites; showers, dump station(s). Reservable sites available.

7. El Dorado State Park, 618 NE Bluestem Rd., El Dorado, KS 67042. Phone: (316) 321-7180. Located on El Dorado Lake NE of Wichita at Kansas Turnpike exit 76. 128 full hook-ups, 352 water & electric, 566 non-utility sites; showers, dump station(s). Reservable sites available.

8. Elk City State Park, 4825 Squaw Creek Rd., Independence, KS 67301. Phone: (620)331-6295. Located on Elk City Lake, NW of Independence off US 75. 11 full hook-ups, 84 water & electric, 70 non-utility sites; showers; dump station(s).

9. Fall River State Park, 144 Hwy 105, Toronto, KS 66777. Phone: (620) 637-2213. Located on Fall River Lake about 14 miles northwest of Fredonia via US 400. 45 water & electric, 100 non-utility sites; showers; dump station.

10. Glen Elder State Park, RR 1, Glen Elder, KS 67446. Phone: (785) 545-3345. Located in north-central KS along US 24 about 26 miles east of Osborne. 112 water & electric, 8 electric, 240 non-utility sites; showers, dump station(s). Reservable sites available.

11. Hillsdale State Park, 26001 W 255th St., Paola, KS 66071. Phone: (913) 546-2565. Located about 16 miles east of Ottawa (I-35 exit 187) on KS 68. 160 water & electric, 40 non-utility sites; showers, dump station.

12. Kanopolis State Park, 200 Horsethief Rd., Marquette, KS 67464. Phone: (785) 753-4971. Located on Kanopolis Reservoir about 18 miles west of Lindsborg (I-135 exit 72 or 78) via KS 4 and KS 141. 16 full hook-ups, 31 water & electric, 200 electric, some non-utility sites; showers, dump station(s). Reservable sites available.

13. Lovewell State Park, RR 1, Webber, KS 66970. Phone: (785) 753-4971. Located in north-central KS on Lovewell Reservoir about 18 miles northeast of Mankato via US 36 and KS 14. 23 full hook-ups, 13 water & electric, 82 electric, 306 non-utility sites; showers, dump station(s).

14. Meade State Park, 13051 V Rd., Meade, KS 67864. Phone: (620) 873-2572. Located in southwestern Kansas on KS 14, off US 54 near Meade. 42 water & electric, 150 non-utility sites; showers, dump station.

15. Milford State Park, 8811 State Park Rd., Milford, KS 66514. Phone: (785) 238-3014. Located on Milford Lake near Junction City; I-70 exit 295 N on US 77 to KS 57. 31 full hook-ups, 92 water & electric, 10 non-utility sites; showers, dump station(s).

16. Perry State Park, 5441 W Lake Rd., Ozawkie, KS 66070. Phone: (785) 246-3449. Located NE of Topeka on Perry Lake; US 24 east to KS 237, north to park. 124 water & electric, 200 non-utility sites; showers, dump station(s).

17. Pomona State Park, 22900 S Hwy 368, Vassar, KS 66543. Phone: (785)828-4933. Located about 20 miles northeast of I-35 exit 155 via US 75 and KS 268. 47 full hook-ups, 97 water & electric, 200 non-utility sites; showers, sump station(s). Reservable sites available.

18. Prairie Dog State Park, Norton, KS 67654. Phone: (785)877-2953. Located SW of Norton off US 36 on KS 383. 40 water & electric, 18 electric, 125 non-utility sites; showers, dump station(s). Reservable sites available.

19. Scott State Park, 529 W Scott Lake Dr., Scott City, KS 67871. Phone: (620) 872-2061. Located in western KS, north of Scott City, off US 83 on KS 95. 25 water & electric, 35 electric, 170 non-utility sites; showers, dump station.

20. Tuttle Creek State Park, 5800 A River Pond Rd., Manhattan, KS 66502. Phone: (785) 539-7941. Located near Manhattan on Tuttle Creek Lake about 16 miles north of I-70 exit 313. 104 water & electric, 12 electric, 500 non–utility sites; showers, dump station(s). Reservable sites available.

21. Webster State Park, 1210 Nine Rd., Stockton, KS 67669. Phone: (785) 425-6775. Located 8 miles west of Stockton via US 24. 66 water & electric, 8 electric, 100 non-utility sites; showers, dump station. Reservable sites available.

22. Wilson State Park, RR 1, Sylvan Grove, KS 67481. Phone: (785) 658-2465. Located on Wilson Lake about 5 miles north of I-70 exit 206 via KS 232. 99 water & electric, 36 electric, 100 non-utility sites; showers, dump station(s). Reservable sites available.

Kentucky

Kentucky is very rich in state parks with RV facilities. There are 32 state parks with facilities and all offer water and electricity, although some parks are seasonal, as listed. Seasonal parks are open April 1 through October 31. And all parks have a dump station and showers. All parks except Breaks Interstate Park have laundry facilities. Reservations are not accepted at state parks but are recommended at the state-run resorts. Resort telephone numbers are listed with each park. Rate groups: B and C.

Kentucky State Parks
500 Mero Street
Frankfort, KY 40601
Information: (800) 255-7275
Internet: www.kystateparks.com

Kentucky Park Locator

Barren River Lake SRP 10
Big Bone Lick SP 18
Blue Licks Battlefield SRP 20
Breaks InterSP 32
Carr Creek SP 25
Carter Caves SRP 27
Columbus-Belmont SP 1
Cumberland Falls SRP 23
Dale Hollow Lake SRP 11
Fort Boonesborough SP 21
General Burnside Island SP 14
General Butler SRP 17
Grayson Lake SP 26
Green River Lake SP 12
Greenbo Lake SRP 28
Jenny Wiley SRP 31
John James Audubon SP 6
Kenlake SRP 3
Kentucky Dam Village SRP 2
Kincaid Lake SP 19
Lake Barkley SRP 4
Lake Cumberland SRP 13
Lake Malone SP 7
Levi Jackson Wilderness Rd SP . 24
My Old Kentucky Home SP 15
Natural Bridge SRP 22
Nolin Lake SP 9
Paintsville Lake SP 30
Pennyrile Forest SRP 5
Rough River Dam SRP 8
Taylorsville Lake SP 16
Yatesville Lake SP 29

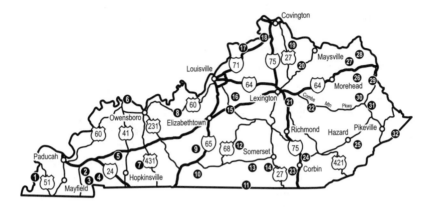

1. Columbus-Belmont State Park, 350 Park Rd., Columbus, KY 42032. Phone: (270) 677-2327. Located 36 miles SW of Paducah on KY 80; use KY 123, KY 58 or KY 80. 38 sites; seasonal.

2. Kentucky Dam Village State Resort Park, 113 Administration Dr., Gilbertsville, KY 42044. Resort: (800) 325-0146. Located on Kentucky Lake 21 miles SE of Paducah. Exit 27 off I-24 to US 62 to US 641, east to Resort. 221 sites, year round.

3. Kenlake State Resort Park, 542 Kenlake Rd., Hardin, KY 42048. Resort: (800) 325-0143. Located 40 miles SE of Paducah. From Paducah take I-24 east to Purchase Pkwy (exit 25), south to US 68 (exit 47) to Resort. From I-24 West, exit US 68/KY 80 (exit 65) west to Resort. 90 sites, seasonal.

4. Lake Barkley State Resort Park, 3500 State Park Rd., Cadiz, KY 42211. Resort: (800) 325-1708. Located 29 miles west of Hopkinsville. From I-24 exit 65, follow US 68 west to park. 78 sites, seasonal.

5. Pennyrile Forest State Resort Park, 20781 Pennyrile Lodge Rd., Dawson Springs, KY 42408. Resort: (800) 325-1711. Located 20 miles NW of Hopkinsville and 5 miles south of Western Kentucky Parkway exit 24, on KY 109. 68 sites, seasonal.

6. John James Audubon State Park, 3100 US Hwy 41 N, Henderson, KY 42419. Phone: (270) 826-2247. Located in Henderson on the Ohio River about 10 miles south of Evansville, Indiana. 71 sites, year round.

7. Lake Malone State Park, 331 State Route Road 8001, Dunmore, KY
    42339. Phone: (270) 657-2111. Located about 20 miles south of Central
    City and Western Kentcuky Parkway exit 58 via US 431 and KY 973. 19
    sites, seasonal.

8. Rough River Dam State Resort Park, 450 Lodge Rd., Falls of Rough, KY
    40119. Resort: (800) 325-1713. From Western Kentucky Parkway exit 94
    (Caneyville), follow KY 79 north about 17 miles. 66 sites, seasonal.

9. Nolin Lake State Park, Bee Spring, KY 42207. Located 7 miles north of
    Mammoth Cave National Park via KY 728 & KY 1827. From I-65 exit 53,
    follow KY 70 to KY 259 and then north to KY 728. From Western Kentucky
    Parkway exit 107, follow KY 259 south to KY 728. 32 sites, seasonal.

10. Barren River Lake State Resort Park, 1149 State Park Rd., Lucas, KY
    42156. Resort: (800) 325-0057. Located about 14 miles SW of Glasgow
    and Cumberland Parkway exit 11 via US 31E. 99 sites, seasonal.

11. Dale Hollow Lake State Resort Park, 6371 State Park Rd., Burkesville,
    KY 42717. Resort: (800) 325-2282. Located SE of Bowling Green on KY/
    TN state line. From Bowling Green, I-65 exit 43 (Cumberland Pkwy), take
    KY 90 east to KY 449 south to park. 144 sites, seasonal.

12. Green River Lake State Park, 179 Park Office Rd., Campbellsville, KY
    42718. Phone: (270) 465-8255. Located about 4 miles south of
    Campbellsville on KY 55. 156 sites, seasonal.

13. Lake Cumberland State Resort Park, 5465 State Park Rd., Jamestown,
    KY 42629. Resort: (800) 325-1709. Located between Glasgow and
    Somerset, south of Cumberland Pkwy on Lake Cumberland. From I-65
    exit 43, Cumberland Pkwy, east to US 127, south about 8 miles. From I-
    75 exit 41 (KY 80) west to Somerset & Cumberland Pkwy to US 127,
    south to Resort. 147 sites, seasonal.

14. General Burnside Island State Park, 8801 S Hwy 27, Burnside, KY 42519.
    Phone: (606) 561-4104. Located 8 miles south of Somerset on US 27. 94
    sites, seasonal.

15. My Old Kentucky Home State Park, 501 E Stephen Foster Ave.,
    Bardstown, KY 40004. Phone: (502) 348-3502. Located in Bardstown on
    US 150. 39 sites, seasonal.

16. Taylorsville Lake State Park, 1320 Park Rd., Taylorsville, KY 40071. Phone: (502) 477-0086. Located 20 miles SE of I-64 exit 32. From I-64 south on KY 55 to KY 44 east to KY 248 then south to park. 45 sites, seasonal.

17. General Butler State Resort Park, 1608 Hwy 227, Carrollton, KY 41008. Resort: (866) 462-8853. Located 44 miles NE of Louisville, I-71 exit 44, north to Carrollton, follow signs. 111 sites, year round.

18. Big Bone Lick State Park, 3380 Beaver Rd., Union, KY 41091. Phone: (859) 384-3522. Located on KY 338 west of I-75 exit 175. 62 sites, open year round.

19. Kincaid Lake State Park, 565 Kincaid Park Rd., Falmouth, KY 41040. Phone: (859) 654-3531. Located 48 miles SE of Covington and 61 miles NE of Lexington. From Covington or Lexington, US 27 to Falmouth then KY 159 to park. 84 sites, seasonal.

20. Blue Licks Battlefield State Resort Park, Hwy 68, Mount Olivet, KY 41064. Resort: (800) 443-7008. Located 48 miles NE of Lexington on US 68, near junction of KY 165. 51 sites, open year round.

21. Fort Boonesborough State Park, 4375 Boonesborough Rd., Richmond, KY 40475. Phone: (859) 527-3131. Located about 38 miles SE of Lexington on KY 627. From I- 75, use exit 75. From I-64, use Winchester exits 94 or 96. 167 sites, open year round.

22. Natural Bridge State Resort Park, 2135 Natural Bridge Rd., Slade, KY 40376. Resort: (800) 325-1710. Located 52 miles SE of Lexington off Combs Mountain Pkwy, on KY 11. Exit 33 off Mountain Pkwy (KY 402) at KY 11, south about 3 miles. 95 sites, seasonal.

23. Cumberland Falls State Resort Park, 7351 Hwy 90, Corbin, KY 40701. Resort: (800) 325-0063. Located in southeastern Kentucky. From I-75 exit 25 (Corbin) US 25W to KY 90, west to park. 50 sites, seasonal.

24. Levi Jackson Wilderness Road State Park, 998 Levi Jackson Mill Rd., London, KY 40744. Phone: (606) 878-8000. Located about 7 miles SE of London. I-75 exit 36, east on KY 80 to park. 146 sites, open year round.

25. Carr Creek State Park, Sassafras, KY 41759. Phone: (606) 642-4050. Located 15 miles SE of Hazard in southeastern Kentucky on KY 15 S. From Daniel Boone Pkwy, exit at Hazard (exit 59) to KY 15 S; about 15 miles to park. 39 sites, seasonal.

26. Grayson Lake State Park, 314 Grayson Lake Park Rd., Olive Hill, KY 41164. Phone: (606) 474-9727. Located 25 miles SW of Ashland. From I-64 exit 172 (KY 7) south about 16 miles to park. 71 sites, seasonal.

27. Carter Caves State Resort Park, 344 Caveland Dr., Olive Hill, KY 41164. Phone: (800) 325-0059. Located 30 miles west of Ashland. From I-64 exit 161, KY 182 north about 5 miles. 89 sites, open year round.

28. Greenbo Lake State Resort Park, HC 60, Greenup, KY 41144. Resort: (800) 325-0083. From I-64 exit 172 (Grayson) north 18 miles to park. 64 sites, seasonal.

29. Yatesville Lake State Park, Hwy 1185 Yatesville Marina, Louisa, KY 41230. Phone: (606) 673-1490. Located about 30 miles south of Ashland in eastern KY. From US 23, exit at Louisa (KY 3) west 3 miles to park. 27 sites, seasonal.

30. Paintsville Lake State Park, Staffordsville, KY 41256. Phone: (606) 297-8488. Located 4 miles west of Paintsville on KY 172, from US 460 and KY 40. 32 sites, seasonal.

31. Jenny Wiley State Resort Park, 75 Theater Court, Prestonsburg, KY 41653. Resort: (606) 886-2711. Located on KY 3 off US 23/460 in Prestonsburg. 117 sites, seasonal.

32. Breaks Interstate Park, Breaks, VA (540) 865-4413. Resort: (800) 982-5122. Located on KY-VA border, 30 miles SE of Pikesville on KY/VA 80. 122 sites, seasonal.

Louisiana

Louisiana maintains 16 state parks with RV facilities. Most of these parks (14) have "improved" campsites which are a designated site with water and electricity on site and toilet and shower facilities nearby. "Unimproved" sites are not designated spaces, have no utilities but may have toilet and shower facilities in the area. All Louisiana parks are open year round. Holders of Golden Age or Golden Access Passports from the U.S. National Park Service are entitled to a 50 percent discount on camping fees in the state park system. There is a state reservation system (see below) but Drive-Up users are welcome. Rate group: A

Louisiana Dept. of Culture, Recreation and Tourism
Office of State Parks
Box 44426
Baton Rouge, LA 70804
Information: (888) 677-1400 / Reservations: (877) 226-7652
Internet: www.lastateparks.com

Louisiana Park Locator

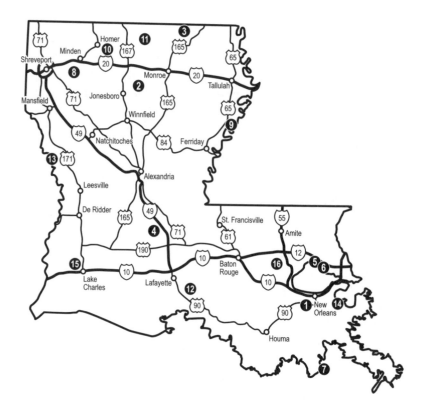

1.   Bayou Segnette State Park, 7777 Westbank Expwy., Westwego, LA 70094.
     Phone: (504) 736-7140 or (888) 677-2296. Located in Westwego off the
     Westbank Expwy (Bus. 90 E). I-10 east from New Orleans, across Greater
     New Orleans Bridge to the Westbank Expwy, west to Westwego. From
     east I-10 to US 90 south, cross the Huey P. Long Bridge to Westbank
     Expwy. 98 improved sites; dump station, laundry.

2.   Jimmie Davis State Park (was Caney Creek Lake State Park), State Road
     1209, Chatham, LA 71226. Phone: (318) 249-2595 or (888) 677-2263.
     Located 12 miles east of Jonesboro off LA 4. From LA 4 take Lakeshore
     Drive to LA 1209. 73 improved sites; dump station; laundry.

3.   Chemin-A-Haut State Park, 14656 Loop Park Rd., Bastrop, LA 71220.
     Phone: (318) 283-0812 or (888) 677-2436. Located 10 miles north of
     Bastrop. From I-20 take US 165 north from Monroe to Bastrop then US
     425 10 miles north to LA 2229 (Loop Park Rd.) 26 improved sites; dump
     station; laundry.

4. Chicot State Park, 3469 Chicot Park Rd., Ville Platte, LA 70586. Phone: (337) 363-2403 or (888) 677-2442. Located 7 miles north of Ville Platte (US 167 & LA 10) on LA 3042. From Ville Platte, 7 miles north on LA 3042. From I-49 exit 46 to LA 106 south 6 miles to LA 3042. 200 improved sites; dump station; laundry.

5. Fairview-Riverside State Park, Madisonville, LA 70447. Phone: (985) 845-318 or (888) 677-3247. Located 2 miles east of Madisonville on LA 22; 4 miles from I-12 at LA 21 to LA 22. 81 improved sites; dump station; laundry.

6. Fontainebleau State Park, Mandeville, LA 70470. Phone: (985) 624-4443 or (888) 677-3668. Located on US 190, SE of Mandeville. I-12 exit at LA 434 to US 190. 123 improved and 37 unimproved sites; dump station; laundry.

7. Grand Isle State Park, Grand Isle, LA 70358. Phone: (985) 787-2559 or (888) 787-2559. Located on the Gulf of Mexico on Grand Island, end of LA 1 (off US 90 at Matthews LA). 40 improved and 66 unimproved sites; dump station.

8. Lake Bistineau State Park, 103 State Park Rd., Doyline, LA 71023. Phone: (318) 745-3503 or (888) 677-2478. Located 7 miles south of Doyline on LA 163. From I-20, exit at Minden and take US 371 south to Sibley, then LA 164 west to Doyline and LA 163 south to park. 67 improved sites; dump station.

9. Lake Bruin State Park, Route 1, St. Joseph, LA 71366. Phone: (318) 766-3530 or (888) 677- 2784. Located east of US 65, NE of St. Joseph via LA 128, 605 & 604. 25 improved sites; dump station; laundry.

10. Lake Claiborne State Park, Homer, LA 71040. Phone: (318) 927-2976 or (888) 677-2524. Located 7 miles SE of Homer (US 79 & LA 2) on LA 146. 87 improved sites; dump station; laundry.

11. Lake D'Arbonne State Park, Farmerville, LA 71241. Phone: (318) 368-2086 or (888) 677-5200. Located 5 miles west of Farmerville (LA 15 & 2) off LA 2. 65 improved sites; dump station; laundry.

12. Lake Fausse Pointe State Park, 5400 Levee Rd., St. Martinville, LA 70582. Phone: (337) 229-4764 or (888) 677-7200. Located about 18 miles SE of St. Martinsville (LA 31 & 96,off US 90) Rural road access - West Atchafalaya Protection Levee Rd. 50 improved sites; dump station; laundry.

13. North Toledo Bend State Park, Zwolle, LA 71486. Phone: (318) 645-4715. Located 9 miles SW of Zwolle near Texas state line, off LA 3229 and US 171. 63 improved sites; dump station; laundry.

14. Saint Bernard State Park, 501 Saint Bernard Pkwy, Braithwaite, LA 70040. Phone: (504) 682-2101 or (888) 677-7823. Located on LA 39 south, 18 miles SE of New Orleans. 51 improved sites; dump station; laundry.

15. Sam Houston Jones State Park, 107 Sutherland Rd., Lake Charles, LA 70611. Phone: (337) 855-2665 or (888) 677-7264. Located 12 miles north of Lake Charles (I-10 & US 171) on LA 378. 73 improved sites; dump station.

16. Tickfaw State Park, 27225 Patterson Rd., Springfield, LA 70462. Phone: (225) 294-5020 or (888) 981-2020. Located 32 miles east of Baton Rouge (southeast of I-12 & I-55 junction) off I-12 exit 32, south on LA 43 to LA 42 to LA 1037 (W) to Patterson Road, south to park. 30 improved sites; dump station; laundry.

Maine

Of Maine's 32 State Parks, 11 offer RV sites. All campgrounds have potable water but there are no hook-ups at the campsites; neither water or electricity. Only one, Bradbury Mountain, of the listed parks is open all year. The "season" for the other parks varies from May 1 through October 1, depending upon the park. You should call the particular park to verify opening and space availability. Maine does not charge a day-use fee in addition to the site fee. Reservation requests require a 48-hour advance notice. Visa, MasterCard and Discover cards are accepted. There are no rig size limitations. Rate groups: A, B, and C depending on site facilities. Non-resident fees are higher.

Maine Bureau of Parks & Lands
Dept. of Conservation
22 State House Station
Augusta, ME 04333
Information: (207) 287-2209 / Reservations: (207) 287-3824 (M-F) out of state; (800) 332-1501 in state
Internet: www.CampWithMe.com

Maine Park Locator

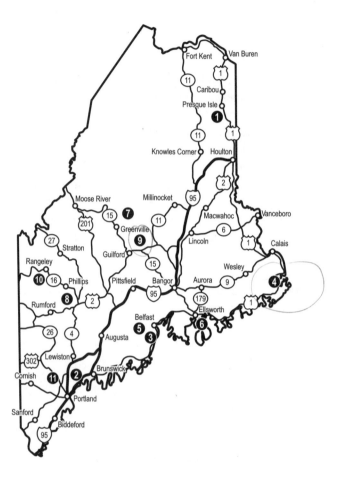

1. Aroostook State Park, Presque Isle, ME 04769. Phone: (207) 768-8341. Located off US 1 near Presque Isle (northeast tip of state). 30 sites; showers.

2. Bradbury Mountain State Park, Pownal, ME 04069. Phone: (207) 688-4712. Located off ME 9, I-95 at Freeport exit. 43 sites.

3. Camden Hills State Park, Camden, ME 04843. Phone: (207) 236-3109. Located 1 mile north of Camden on the Atlantic Coast on US 1. 107 sites; showers; dump station.

4. Cobscook Bay State Park, Dennysville, ME 04628. Phone: (207) 726-4412. Located on US 1 between Lubec and Calais. 106 sites; showers; dump station.

5. Lake St. George State Park, Liberty, ME 04949. Phone: (207) 589-4255. Located on ME 3 between Augusta (20 miles) and Belfast on Lake St. George. 38 sites; showers; dump station.

6. Lamoine State Park, Lamoine, ME 04605. Phone: (207) 667-4778. Located on ME 184, off US 1 between Ellsworth and Bar Harbor on the Atlantic Coast. 62 sites; showers.

7. Lilly Bay State Park, Greenville, ME 04441. Phone: (207) 695-2700. Located on Moosehead Lake on Lily Bay Road, off ME 6 & 15; 8 miles NE of Greenville. 90 sites; dump station.

8. Mount Blue State Park, (Weld) Farmington, ME 04938. Phone: (207) 585-2347. Located on ME 156, off US 2 at Farmington. 136 sites; showers; dump station.

9. Peaks-Kenny State Park, Dover-Foxcroft, ME 04426. Phone: (207) 564-2003. Located on ME 153 at Sebec Lake. 56 sites; showers; dump station.

10. Rangeley Lake State Park, Rangeley, ME 04970. Phone: (207) 864-3858. Located on Rangeley Lake, 30 miles NW of Rumford (US 2 & ME 17). 50 sites; showers; dump station.

11. Sebago Lake State Park, Naples, ME 04055. Phone: (207) 693-6613. Located on Sebago Lake on US 302, 30 miles NE of Portland. 249 sites; showers; dump station.

Maryland

Fifteen of Maryland's 58 State Parks have RV facilities. Most of the parks feature sites with electric hook-ups but few have water at the site. However, all the parks have drinking water available and you can fill holding tanks. All the parks have reservable sites but several hold some spaces for a "first-come" basis. You can verify availability by calling the particular park. Most of the parks are open for camping seasonally. Rate Group: C, depending on site facilities.

Department of Natural Resources
State Forest & Park Service
580 Taylor Ave., E-3
Annapolis, MD 21401
Information: (800) 830-3974 or (410) 260-8186
Reservations: (888) 432-2267
Internet: www.dnr.state.md.us

Maryland Park Locator

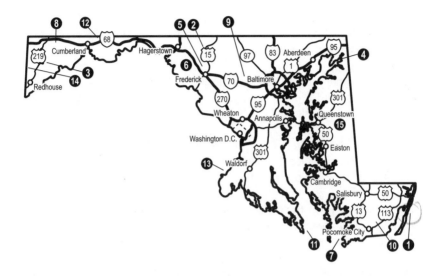

1. Assateague State Park, Berlin, MD, 21811. Phone: (410) 641-2120. Located on the Atlantic Ocean about 9 miles south of Ocean City, via US 50 and MD 611. 350 sites with electric; showers; dump station.

2. Cunningham Falls State Park, Thrumont, MD 21788. Phone: (301) 271-7574. Located 15 miles north of Frederick on US 15. 176 sites with electric; showers; dump station.

3. Deep Creek Lake State Park, National Resource Management Area, Swanton, MD 21561. Phone: (301) 387-5563. Located 10 miles NE of Oakland on Deep Creek Lake, off US 219. 109 sites with electric; showers; dump station.

4. Elk Neck State Park, North East, MD 21901. Phone: (410) 287-5333. Located 9 miles SW of North East (US 40) on MD 272. 236 sites, most with full hook-ups; showers; dump station.

5. Gambrill State Park Thrumont, MD 21702. Phone: (301) 271-7574. Located 6 miles NW of Frederick off I-70 exit 48. 34 sites; showers; dump station.

6. Greenbrier State Park, Boonsboro, MD 21713. Phone: (301) 791-4767. Located 10 miles SE of Hagerstown on US 40. 165 sites with electric; showers; dump station.

7. Janes Island State Park, Crisfield, MD 21817. Phone: (410) 968-1565. Located on Chesapeake Bay near Crisfield, off MD 413. 57 sites; electric; showers; dump station.

8. New Germany State Park, Grantsville, MD 21536. Phone: (301) 895-5453. Located 5 miles south of Grantsville off I-68 exit 22. 39 sites; showers; dump station.

9. Patapsco Valley State Park, Ellicott City, MD 21228. Phone: (410) 461-5005. Five areas located west of Baltimore off I-70 exit 83. 84 sites with electric; showers; dump station. Call park for campground locations.

10. Pocomoke River State Park, Snow Hill, MD 21863. Phone: (410) 632-2566. Two areas located SW of Snow Hill off US 113. 230 sites with electric; showers; dump station. Call park for campground locations.

11. Point Lookout State Park, Scotland, MD 20687. Phone: (301) 872-5688. Located SE of St. Mary's City on MD 5 where the Potomac River meets Chesapeake Bay. 117 sites; most with full hook ups; showers; dump station.

12. Rocky Gap State Park Lodge & Golf Resort, Flintstone, MD 21530. Phone: (301) 777-2139. Located NE of Cumberland off I-68 exit 50. 278 sites with electric; showers. Dump station.

13. Smallwood State Park, Marbury, MD 20640. Phone: (800) 784-5380. Located west of St. Charles off MD 224, near Potomac River. 16 sites with electric; showers.

14. Swallow Falls State Park, Oakland, MD 21550. Phone: (301) 334-9180. Located near West Virginia state line, NW of Oakland on Swallow Falls Road (follow signs from Oakland). 57 sites with electric; showers; dump station.

15. Tuckahoe State Park, Queen Anne, MD 21657. Phone: (410) 820-1688. Located 6 miles north of Queen Anne (west of Denton) off MD 404 via MD 480. 51 sites with electric; showers, dump station.

Massachusetts

The Bay State has 13 State Parks or Recreation Areas with RV sites; most do not have in-site facilities. Alcoholic beverages are not permitted in state lands but pets on leashes are OK. Most of the facilities are seasonal and heavily used in summer months. It is advisable to call the particular park to check conditions, facilities and availability. Reservations require a 48-hour lead time. No camping discounts. Rig limits are not a problem. Rate groups: B and C

Massachusetts Dept. of Environmental Management
251 Causeway St., Ste 600 - 700
Boston, MA 02114
Information: (617) 626-1250 / Reservations: (877) 422-6762
Internet: www.massparks.org / Reservations: www.ReserveAmerica.com

Massachusetts Park Locator

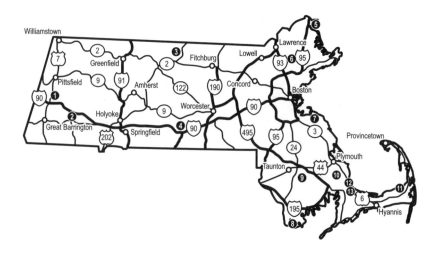

1. Mountain State Forest, Woodland Road, Lee, MA 01238. Phone: (413) 243-1778. Located north of Stockbridge (I-90 exit 2) to US 20 west, follow signs. 46 sites; showers; dump station.

2. Tolland State Forest, Tolland Road, Otis, MA 01253. Phone: (413) 269-6002. Located south of I-90 between exits 2 & 3, in southwestern MA off MA 23 or MA 8; follow signs. 92 sites; showers; dump station.

3. Lake Dennison Recreation Area, Route 202, Winchendon, MA 01029. Phone: (978) 939-8962 (Otter River State Forest). Located north of Baldwinville off MA 2 & US 202 near Otter River State Forest. 151 sites; showers; dump station.

4. Wells State Park, Route 49, Sturbridge, MA 01379. Phone: (508) 347-9257. Located on MA 49 just north of I-90 exit 9 and Sturbridge Village; follow signs from MA 49 & US 20 junction. 60 sites; showers; dump station.

5. Salisbury Beach State Reservation, Reservation Road, Salisbury, MA 01952. Phone: (978) 462-4481. Located in far northeastern MA on the Atlantic Ocean, off I-95 exit 58A to US 1 & MA 110. 484 sites, 324 with electric; showers; dump station.

6. Harold Parker State Forest, 1951 Turnpike Rd., North Andover, MA 05501. Phone: (978) 686-3391. Located on MA 114 between I-95 & 495, north of Boston. 90 sites; showers; dump station.

7. Wompatuck State Park, Union Street, Hingham, MA 02043. Phone: (781) 749-7160. Located SE of Boston off I-93 and MA 228. 450 sites, 140 with electric; showers; dump station.

8. Horseneck Beach State Reservation, Route 88, Westport Point, MA 02791. Phone: (508) 636-8816. Located at south end of MA 88, south of Fall River (I-195) on Rhode Island Sound. 100 sites; showers; dump station.

9. Massasoit State Park, 1361 Middleboro Ave. E, Taunton, MA 02718. Phone: (508) 822-7405. Located east of Taunton off I-495 exit 5 (MA 18). 108 sites, 77 with electric; showers; dump station.

10. Myles Standish State Forest, 194 Cranberry Rd. S, Carver, MA 02366. Phone: (508) 866-2526. Located between MA 3 exit 5 & I-495 exit 2, SW of Plymouth off MA 58. 475 sites; showers; dump station.

11. Nickerson State Park, Route 6A, (Main Street), Brewster, MA 02631. Phone: (508) 896-3491. Located at east end of Cape Cod on MA 6A, east of Brewster. 418 sites; showers; dump station.

12. Scusset Beach State Reservation, 140 Scusset Beach Rd., Sandwich, MA 02562. Phone: (508) 888-0859. Located on the Atlantic Ocean, SE of Plymouth off MA 3 at Sagamore Bridge. 103 sites, 98 with electric; showers; dump station.

13. Shawme-Crowell State Forest, Route 130, Sandwich, MA 02563. Phone: (508) 888-0351. Located off US 6 exit 2 (MA 130), follow signs. 285 sites; showers; dump station.

Michigan

Michigan offers the traveling RVer 68 State Parks or Recreation Areas with facilities. While most of these locations have electric hook-ups, showers and dump stations, three parks (Holland, Hartwick Pines and Sterling state parks) have full hook-up facilities. Michigan has a unique definition method to classify its parks and area sites:

F - Full Hookup Camping: electric, (20, 30 or 50-amp), water, sewer at site.

M - Modern Campground: electric, showers and dump station

R - Rustic Campground: primitive sites, no showers, water is by hand pump

Se - Semi-modern Campground: electric; no showers

Pets on leashes are permitted in all locations. Alcoholic beverages are prohibited in some parks, as listed. If in doubt you should call the destination park. Some parks/areas have reservable sites, others accept reservations directly at the park. Nearly all the parks host an annual Harvest Festival sometime in the Autumn months. These events usually fill the respective park so you will need to call ahead to check if you're a Fall traveler. All parks require an admission fee in addition to the camping charges. Note: Some parks are open in the winter but the locations change each year. You have to call the particular park. Plowing in these parks is "iffy." Rate groups: A, B and C depending on site facilities.

Michigan Dept. of Natural Resources
Parks and Recreation
Box 30257
Lansing, MI 48909
Information: (517) 373-9900 / Reservations: (800) 447-2757
Internet: www.michigan.gov/dnr

Michigan Park Locator

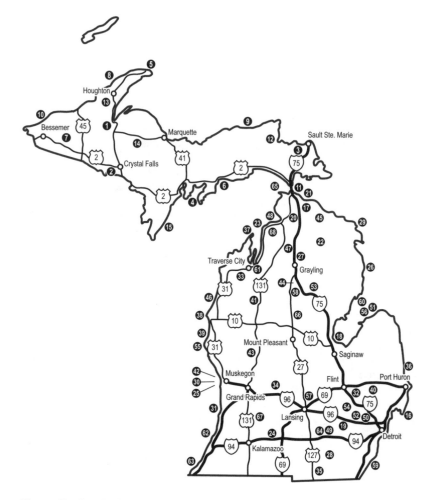

Upper Peninsula Parks

1. Baraga State Park, Baraga, MI 49908. Phone: (906) 353-6558. Located 1/2 mile south of Baraga on US 41. 188 M sites.

2. Bewabic State Park, Crystal Falls, MI 49920. Phone: (906) 875-3324. Located on southern edge of Peninsula, next to WI state line, 4 miles west of Crystal Falls on US 2. 144 M sites.

3. Brimley State Park, Brimley, MI 49715. Phone: (906) 248-3422. Located in eastern portion of Peninsula near Canadian border, SW of Sault Ste. Marie; I-75 exit 386 to MI 28, west 7 miles, follow signs. 270 M sites.

4. Fayette Historic State Park, Garden, MI 49835. Phone: (906) 644-2603. Located in southern portion of Peninsula, 18 miles south of Garden Corners (US 2) on MI 183. 61 Se sites.

5. Fort Wilkins Historic State Park, Copper, MI 49918. Phone: (906) 289-4215. Located in far northern tip of Peninsula, at end of US 41, outside Copper Harbor; on Lake Superior. 165 M sites.

6. Indian Lake State Park, Manistique, MI 49854. Phone: (906) 341-2355. Located in southern portion of Peninsula, west of Manistique via CR 442. 302 M and Se sites.

7. Lake Gogebic State Park, Marenisco, MI 49947. Phone: (906) 842-3341. Located in western portion of Peninsula, south of Merriweather, on MI 64 between US 2 and MI 28. 127 M and Se sites.

8. F.J. McLain State Park, Hancock, MI 49930. Phone: (906) 482-0278. Located on northwestern arm of Peninsula, north of Houghton, off US 41, 9 miles north on MI 209. 103 M sites.

9. Muskallonge Lake State Park, Newberry, MI 49868. Phone: (906) 658-3338. Located 28 miles north of Newberry via MI 123 and CR 407. 171 M sites.

10. Porcupine Mountains Wilderness State Park, Ontonagon, MI 49953. Phone: (906) 885-5275. Located about 20 miles west of Ontonagon via MI 64 and MI 107. 201 M sites.

11. Straits State Park, St.Ignace, MI 49781. Phone: (906) 643-8620. Located at southern tip of Peninsula, off I-75 exit 344 (north of Mackinac Bridge) off US 2. 275 M sites.

12. Tahquamenon Falls State Park, Paradise, MI 49768. Phone: (906) 492-3415. Located in northeast portion of Peninsula between Paradise and Eckerman on MI 123, on Lake Superior Whitefish Bay. 277 M sites in three campgrounds.

13. Twin Lakes State Park, Toivola, MI 49965. Phone: (906) 288-3321. Located in northwestern portion of Peninsula, 26 miles SW of Houghton on MI 26. 62 M sites.

14. Van Riper State Park, Champion, MI 49814. Phone: (906) 339-4461.

Located in northwestern portion of Peninsula, 3 miles NW of Champion off US 41. 188 M and R sites.

15. J.W. Wells State Park, Cedar River, MI 49813. Phone: (906) 863-9747. Located in southwestern portion of Peninsula, 35 miles SW of Escanaba on MI 35, on Lake Michigan. 150 M sites.

Lower Peninsula Parks

16. Algonac State Park, Marine City, MI 48039. Phone: (810) 765-5605. Located NE of Detroit, 19 miles from I-94 exit 243; follow signs. 296 M sites.

17. Aloha State Park, Cheboygan, MI 49721. Phone: (231) 625-2522. Located in northern MI, 5 miles south of Cheboygan on MI 33. 287 M sites.

18. Bay City Recreation Area, Bay City, MI 48706. Phone: (989) 684-3020. Located in east-central MI outside Bay City, 5 miles east of I-75 exit 168. 193 M sites.

19. Brighton Recreation Area, Howell, MI 48843. Phone: (810) 229-6566. Located in southeastern MI, 4 miles west of Brighton, off I-96 exit 147; follow signs from Brighton. 215 M & R sites.

20. Burt Lake State Park, Indian River, MI 49749. Phone: (906) 238-9392. Located in northern MI just west of I-75 exit 310; on Burt Lake. 300 M sites.

21. Cheboygan State Park, Cheboygan, MI 49721. Phone: (231) 627-2811. Located at northern tip of MI on Lake Huron, 18 miles NE of I-75 exit 313, via MI 27; follow signs. 76 M sites.

22. Clear Lake State Park, Atlanta, MI 49709. Phone: (989) 785-4388. Located in northern MI, 10 miles north of Atlanta, 20 miles east of I-75 exit 290 (Vanderbilt) via county road. 200 M sites.

23. Fisherman's Island State Park, Charlevoix, MI 49720. Phone: (231) 547-6641. Located in northwestern MI at mouth of Grand Traverse Bay on Lake Michigan, on US 31, SW of Petoskey. 81 R sites.

24. Fort Custer Recreation Area, Augusta, MI 49012. Phone: (616) 731-4200. Located in southwestern MI, 16 miles east of Kalamazoo, on MI 96, off I-94 exit 92. 217 M sites.

25. Grand Haven State Park, Grand Haven, MI 49417. Located in southwestern MI just south of Grand Haven on US 31, on Lake Michigan. 174 M sites.

26. Harrisville State Park, Harrisville, MI 48740. Phone: (989) 724-5126. Located in northeastern MI in Harrisville on US 23, on Lake Huron. 195 M sites.

27. Hartwick Pines State Park, Grayling, MI 49738. Phone: (989) 348-7068. Located in north-central MI, north of Grayling off I-75 exit 259. 100 sites, some full hookup, some M.

28. Walter J. Hayes State Park, Onsted, MI 49265. Phone: (517) 467-7401. Located in southeastern MI, 9 miles west of Clinton on US 12 and MI 124. 185 M sites.

29. P.H. Hoeft State Park, Rogers City, MI 49779. Phone: (989) 734-2543. Located in northern MI on Lake Huron, NW of Rogers City on US 23. 142 M sites.

30. P.J. Hoffmaster State Park, Muskegon, MI 49441. Phone: (231) 789-3711. Located in western MI on Lake Michigan, 10 miles south of Muskegon on US 31; off I-96 exit 4, follow signs. 293 M sites. No alcohol.

31. Holland State Park, Holland, MI 49424. Phone: (616) 399-9390. Located in western MI, 7 miles NW of Holland, off US 31; follow signs. 309 sites; some full hookup, some M. No alcohol.

32. Holly Recreation Area, Holly, MI 48442. Phone: (248) 634-8811. Located in southeastern MI, 14 miles SE of Flint, near I-75 exit 101; follow signs. 159 M sites. No alcohol.

33. Interlochen State Park, Interlochen, MI 49643. Phone: (231) 276-9511. Located in northwestern MI, 15 miles SW of Traverse City on MI 137, via US 31. 490 R and M sites.

34. Ionia Recreation Area, Ionia, MI 48846. Phone: (616) 527-3750. Located in west-central MI, 28 miles east of Grand Rapids, north of I-96 exit 67 and MI 66; follow signs. 149 M sites.

35. Lake Hudson Recreation Area, Clayton, MI 49235. Phone: (517) 445-2265. Located in southeastern MI, 8 miles east of Hudson, off MI 34 on MI 156. 50 Se sites.

36. Lakeport State Park, Lakeport, MI 48059. Phone: (810) 327-6224. Located in eastern MI, 10 miles north of Port Huron on MI 25, on Lake Huron. 284 M sites.

37. Leelanau State Park, Northport, MI 49670. Phone: (231) 386-5422. Located in northwestern MI at end of MI 201, north of Traverse City. 52 R sites.

38. Ludington State Park, Ludington, MI 49431. Phone: (231) 843-8671. Located just north of Ludington (US 10/31) on Hamlin Lake. 344 M sites.

39. Charles Mears State Park, Pentwater, MI 49449. Phone: (231) 869-2051. Located in western MI, 12 miles south of Ludington off US 31, on Lake Michigan. 179 M sites.

40. Metamora-Hadley Recreation Area, Metamora, MI 48455. Phone: (810) 797-4439. Located north of Detroit off I-69 exit 155, off MI 24; follow signs. 214 M sites. No alcohol.

41. William Mitchell State Park, Cadillac, MI 49601. Phone: (231) 775-7911. Located in northwestern MI, just outside Cadillac, north on MI 115, off US 131. 215 M sites.

42. Muskegon State Park, Muskegon, MI 49445. Phone: (231) 744-3480. Located in western MI on Lake Michigan, off US 31, north of Muskegon; follow signs. 247 M sites.

43. Newaygo State Park, Newaygo, MI 49337. Phone: (231) 856-4452. Located in west-central MI south of Big Rapids, off US 131 exit 125; follow signs. 99 R sites.

44. N. Higgens Lake State Park, Roscommon, MI. Phone: (989) 733-8279. Located in north-central MI between US 27 and I-75 exit 244 on Higgens Lake. 175 M sites.

45. Onaway State Park, Onaway, MI 49765. Phone: (989) 733-8279. Remote location in northern MI, 6 miles north of Onaway on MI 211, on Black Lake. 85 M sites.

46. Orchard Beach State Park, Manistee, MI 49660. Phone: (231) 723-7422. Located in northwestern MI off US 31, 4 miles north of Manistee, on Lake Michigan. 210 M sites.

47. Otsego Lake State Park. Gaylord, MI 49462. Phone: (989) 732-5485. Located in north-central MI on Old MI 27, off I-75 exit 270, north of Waters. 155 M sites.

48. Petoskey State Park, Petoskey, MI 49712. Phone: (231) 347-2311. Located in northwestern MI on MI 119, off US 31, outside Petoskey. 170 M sites.

49. Pinckney Recreation Area, Pinckney, MI 48169. Phone: (734) 426-4913. Located in southeastern MI, northwest of Ann Arbor, 11 miles west of US 23 exit 49; follow signs. 205 R and M sites. No alcohol.

50. Pontiac Lake Recreation Area, Waterford, MI 48327. Phone: (248) 666-1020. Located NW of Greater Detroit off I-75 at MI 59, west 11 miles. 176 M sites. No alcohol.

51. Port Crescent State Park, Port Austin, MI 48467. Phone: (989) 738-8663. Remote location in eastern MI on Lake Huron near Saginaw Bay, 5 miles SW of Port Austin on MI 25. 137 M sites.

52. Proud Lake Recreation Area, Commerce Township, MI 48382. Phone: (248) 685-2433. Located in southeastern MI, 7 miles north of I-96 exit 155. 130 M sites.

53. Rifle River Recreation Area, Lupton, MI 48635. Phone: (989) 473-2258. Located in northeastern MI, 4.5 miles east of Rose City, off MI 33, 20 miles north of I-75 exit 202. 174 M and R sites.

54. Seven Lakes State Park, Fenton, MI 48430. Phone: (248) 634-7271. Located south of Flint in southeastern MI about 5 miles west of I-75 exit 101. 71 M sites. No alcohol.

55. Silver Lake State Park, Mears, MI 48436. Phone: (231) 873-3083. Located in western MI off US 31 at Shelby or Hart exits; follow signs. 196 M sites. No alcohol.

56. Albert E. Sleeper State Park, Caseville, MI 48725. Phone: (989) 856-4411. Remote location in eastern MI at the mouth of Saginaw Bay on Lake Huron; 5 miles east of Caseville and 55 miles east of I-75 exit 161 (Bay City). 223 M sites.

57. Sleepy Hollow State Park, Laingsburg, MI 48848. Phone: (517) 651-6217. Located in south-central MI, 5.5 miles east of US 27, Price Road exit. 181 M sites.

58. S. Higgins Lake State Park, Roscommon, MI 48653. Phone: (989) 821-6374. Located in north-central MI south of Roscommon on CR 100, off I-75 exit 239 and MI 18. 400 M sites.

59. Sterling State Park, Monroe, MI 48162. Phone: (734) 289-2715. Located on Lake Erie in southeastern MI, 3 miles NE of Monroe, off I-75 exit 15. 288 sites; some full hookup, some M sites.

60. Tawas Point State Park, East Tawas, MI 48730. Phone: (989) 362-5041. Located in northeastern MI off US 23 in East Tawas. 195 M sites.

61. Traverse City State Park, Traverse City, MI 49686. Phone: (231) 922-5270. Located in northwestern MI outside Traverse City east off US 31, at south end of Grand Traverse Bay. 343 M sites.

62. Van Buren State Park, South Haven, MI 49090. Phone: (269) 637-2788. Located in southwestern MI on US 31 between Benton Harbor and South Haven on Lake Michigan. 220 M sites. No alcohol.

63. Warren Dunes State Park, Sawyer, MI 49125. Phone: (616) 426-4013. Located in southwestern MI just north of IN state line, 2 miles south of I-94 exit 16, on Lake Michigan. 185 M and R sites. No alcohol.

64. Waterloo Recreation Area, Chelsea, MI 48118. Phone: (734) 475-8307. Located in southeastern MI, NW of Ann Arbor, near Chelsea. Four Camping areas: I-94 exits 150, 153 and 157. *Contact Park office for directions, site assignment.* 323 M and R sites. No alcohol.

65. Wilderness State Park, Carp Lake, MI 49718. Phone: (231) 436-5381. Located in northern MI, 11 miles west of Mackinac City, I-75 exit 339. 250 M sites.

66. Wilson State Park, Harrison, MI 48625. Phone: (989) 539-3021. Located in north-central MI, 3.5 miles east of US 27, Harrison exit. 160 M sites.

67. Yankee Springs Recreation Area, Middleville, MI 49333. Phone: (269) 795-9081. Located in southwestern MI off MI 179 (US 131 exit 61, east 3.5 miles). 345 R and M sites. No alcohol.

68. Young State Park, Boyne City, MI 49712. Phone: (231) 582-7523. Located in northern MI, 7 miles NW of Boyne City, off US 131 on CR 56. 240 M sites.

Minnesota

The Gopher State has 59 parks or recreation areas with RV facilities; more than 4,000 sites are available and only two parks, Carley State Park and Franz Jevne, have 30 foot maximum length limits. The remaining 57 locations will accept big rigs easily. While all the locations are open year round, some of the facilities (i.e. showers and flush toilets) are shut down after Labor Day. Reservations are not required but are recommended during the summer season. About 1/3 of the state's sites are on a first-come basis and no reservations are needed from November through April. Pets are permitted in the campgrounds. Red River Recreation Area in northwestern Minnesota has recently been renovated (after the floods of late 90s) and is the only park in the system with full hook-ups. Showers are to be operational in late 2004. Rate groups: B and C

Minnesota Department of Natural Resources
500 Lafayette Road
Saint Paul, MN 55155
Information: (888) 646-6367 / Reservations: (866) 857-2757
Internet: www.dnr.state.mn.us / Reservations: www.stayatmnparks.com

Minnesota Park Locator

Minnesota Park Locator (*cont.*)

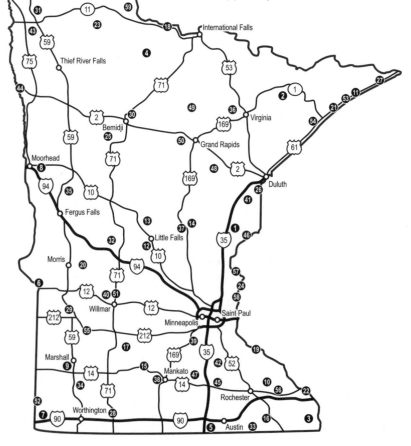

1. Banning State Park, Sandstone, MN 55072. Phone: (320) 245-2668. Located on MN 23 off I-35 exit 195, north of Sandstone. 33 sites, 11 with electric; showers; dump station. 50 foot limit.

2. Bear Head Lake State Park, 9301 Bear Head Lake State Park Rd., Ely, MN 55731. Phone: (218) 365-7229. Located on County Hwy 128 off US 169 east of Tower. 73 sites, 23 with electric; showers; dump station. 60 foot limit.

3. Beaver Creek Valley State Park, 15954 County Road 1, Caledonia, MN 55921. Phone: (507) 724-2107. Located west of Caledonia on County Hwy 1, 24 miles south of I-90 exit 257 (MN 76). 42 sites, 16 with electric; showers; dump station. 55 foot limit.

4. Big Bog Recreation Area, 55716 Hwy 72 NE, Waskish, MN 56685. Phone: (218) 647-8592. Located on MN 72 just north of Waskish. 30 sites; 1 pull-thru; 26 with electric; showers. 60 foot limit.

5. Big Island State Park, 19499 780th Ave., Albert Lea, MN 56007. Phone: (507) 379-3403. Located 3 miles south of Albert Lea on County Hwy 38, near intersection of I-90 & I-35. 97 sites; 32 with electric; showers; dump station. 60 foot limit.

6. Big Stone Lake State Park, 35889 Meadowbrook State Park Rd., Ortonville, MN 56278. Located 8 miles north of Ortonville via MN 7. 37 sites, 10 with electric; showers; dump station. 48 foot limit.

7. Blue Mounds State Park, Luverne, MN 56156. Phone: (507) 283-1307. Located 3 miles north of Luverne (I-90, exit 12) off US 75. 73 sites, 40 with electric; showers; dump station. 50 foot limit.

8. Buffalo River State Park, 155 South St., US Hwy 10, Glyndon, MN 56547. Phone: (218) 498-2124. Located 14 miles east of Moorhead off US 10. From I-94 exit 22, follow MN 9 about 20 miles north to park. 44 sites, 35 with electric; showers; dump station. 50 foot limit.

9. Camden State Park, 1897 County Road 68, Lynd, MN 56157. Phone: (507) 865-4530. Located 10 miles SW of Marshall off MN 23. 80 sites, 7 pull-thru; 29 with electric; showers; dump station. 50 foot limit (60 foot for pull-thru).

10. Carley State Park, c/o Whitewater State Park, Altura, MN 55910. Phone:

(507) 932-3007. Located 20 miles NE of Rochester on Wabasha County Hwy 4. 20 sites (primitive) 30 foot limit.

11. Cascade River State Park, 3481 Hwy 61, Lutsen, MN 55612. Phone: (218) 387-3053. Located on Lake Superior between Lutsen and Grand Marais on MN 61. 40 sites, 3 pull-thru; showers; dump station. 35 foot limit.

12. Charles A. Lindbergh State Park, 1615 Lindbergh Dr., South Little Falls, MN 56345. Phone: (320) 616-2525. Located 1 mile SW of Little Falls off US 10. 38 sites, 15 with electric; showers; dump station. 50 foot limit.

13. Crow Wing State Park, 3124 State Park Rd., Brainerd, MN 56401. Phone: (218) 829-8022. Located 9 miles SW of Brainerd on MN 371. 59 sites, 12 with electric; showers; dump station. 45 foot limit.

14. Father Hennepin State Park, Isle, MN 56342. Phone: (320) 676-8763. Located west of Isle, on Mille Lacs, off MN 27. 103 sites, 41 with electric; showers; dump station. 60 foot limit.

15. Flandrau State Park, 1300 Summit Ave., New Ulm, MN 56073. Phone: (507) 233-9800. Located in New Ulm (US 14 & MN 15); follow signs. 90 sites, 2 pull-thru; 35 with electric; showers; dump station. 66 foot limit.

16. Forestville/Mystery Cave State Park, Preston, MN 55965. Phone: (507) 352-5111. Located east of Wykoff, 4 miles south of MN 16, on County Hwy 5 to County Hwy 118. 73 sites; 23 with electric; showers; dump station. 50 foot limit.

17. Fort Ridgely, 72158 County Hwy 30, Fairfax, MN 55332. Phone: (507) 426-7840. Located SE of Redwood Falls off MN 4, 6 miles south of Fairfax (MN 19). 39 sites, 1 pull-thru; 13 with electric; showers, dump station. 60 foot limit.

18. Franz Jevne State Park, c/o Zippel Bay State Park, 3684 54th Ave. NW, Williams, MN 56686. Phone: (218) 783-6252. Located on Rainey River, east of Birchdale on MN 11. 18 sites, 2 with electric. 30 foot limit.

19. Frontenac State Park, 29223 County 28 Blvd., Frontenac, MN 55026. Phone: (651) 345-3401. Located on US 61 SE of Red Wing, on Mississippi River, on County Hwy 2. 58 sites, 19 with electric; showers; dump station. 53 foot limit.

20. Glacial Lakes State Park, 25022 County Hwy 41, Starbuck, MN 56381. Phone: (320) 239-2860. Located off MN 29 on County Hwy 41, south of

Starbuck. 39 sites, 1 pull-thru; 14 with electric; showers; dump station. 45 foot limit.

21. Gooseberry Falls State Park, 3206 Hwy 61, Two Harbors, MN 55616. Phone: (218) 834-3855. Located on Lake Superior, 13 miles NE of Two Harbors on MN 61. 70 sites, 3 pull-thru; showers; dump station. 40 foot limit.

22. Great River Bluffs State Park, Winona, MN 55987. Phone: (507) 643-6849. Located 14 miles southeast of Winona via US 14/61 and CR 3. Can also be reached from I-94 exit 266 by following County Hwy 3 north 1 mile to park entrance. 31 sites; showers. 60 foot limit.

23. Hayes Lake State Park, 48990 County Hwy 4, Roseau, MN 56751. Phone: (218) 425-7504. Entrance to the park is 15 miles south of Roseau on MN 89, then 9 miles east on County Hwy 4. 35 sites, 18 with electric; showers; dump station. 40 foot limit.

24. Interstate State Park, 307 Milltown Rd., Taylors Falls, MN 55084. Phone: (651) 465-5711. Located on Mississippi River, 1 mile south of Taylors Falls, on US 8. 37 sites, 22 with electric; showers; dump station. 45 foot limit.

25. Itasca State Park, 36750 Main Park Dr., Park Rapids, MN 56470. Phone: (218) 266-2100. Located 21 miles north of Park Rapids on US 71. 224 sites, 100 with electric; showers; dump station. 60 foot limit.

26. Jay Cooke State Park, 500 E Hwy 210, Carlton, MN 55718. Phone: (218) 384-4610. Located 3 miles SW of Carlton (near I-35, southwest of Duluth) on MN 210. 80 sites, 1 pull-thru; 21 with electric; showers; dump station. 60 foot limit.

27. Judge C.R. Magney State Park, 4051 E Hwy 61, Grand Marais, MN 55604. Phone: (218) 387- 3039. Located in northeastern tip of Minnesota, 14 miles NE of Grand Marais on MN 61. 27 sites; showers. 45 foot limit.

28. Kilen Woods State Park, 50200 860th St., Lakefeld, MN 56150. Phone: (507) 662-6258. Located off MN 86, north of I-90 exit 64, on County Hwy 24. 33 sites, 3 pull-thru; 11 with electric; showers; dump station. 50 foot limit.

29. Lac Qui Parle State Park, Montevideo, MN 56266. Phone: (320) 752-4736. Located 10 miles NW of Montevideo, off MN 7 on US 59. 42 sites; 21 with electric; showers; dump station. 50 foot limit.

30. Lake Bemidji State Park, 3401 State Park Rd., Bemidji, MN 56601. Phone: (218) 755-3843. On Lake Bemidji northeast of town via US 71 and County

Hwy 20. 96 sites, 4 pull-thru; 43 with electric; showers; dump station. 50 foot limit.

31. Lake Bronson State Park, Lake Bronson, MN 56734. Phone: (218) 754-2200. Located 2 miles east of Lake Bronson on MN 28 in northwestern Minnesota. 194 sites, 35 with electric; showers; dump station. 50 foot limit.

32. Lake Carlos State Park, 2601 County Hwy 38 NE, Carlos, MN 56319. Phone: (320) 852-7200. Located on County Hwy 38 off MN 29, north of Alexandria (I-94 exit 103). 123 sites, 81 with electric; showers; dump station. 45 foot limit.

33. Lake Louise State Park, 12385 766th Ave., LeRoy, MN 55951. Phone: (507) 324-5249. Located north of LeRoy in southeastern Minnesota near Iowa state line off MN 56. 22 sites, 11 with electric; showers; dump station. 60 foot limit.

34. Lake Shetek State Park, 163 State Park Rd., Currie, MN 56123. Phone: (507) 763-3256. Remote location in southwestern Minnesota, north of Currie on County Hwy 37 on Lake Shetek. 98 sites, 1 pull-thru; 67 with electric; showers; dump station. 60 foot limit.

35. Maplewood State Park, 39721 Park Entrance Rd., Pelican Rapids, MN 56572. Phone: (218) 863-8383. Located 7 miles east of Pelican Rapids off MN 108. 71 sites, 32 with electric; showers; dump station. 50 foot limit.

36. McCarthy Beach State Park, 7622 McCarthy Beach Rd., Side Lake, MN 55781. Phone: (218) 254-7979. Located in northern Minnesota off MN 5, north of Chisholm. 86 sites, 18 with electric; showers; dump station. 50 foot limit.

37. Mille Lacs Kathio State Park, 15066 Kathio State Park Rd., Onamia, MN 56359. Phone: (320) 532- 3523. Located off MN 27, 1/2 mile west of US 169 near Onamia. 70 sites, 3 pull-thru; 22 with electric; showers; dump station. 60 foot limit.

38. Minneopa State Park, 54497 Gadwall Rd., Mankato, MN 56001. Phone: (507) 389-5464. Located 3 miles west of Mankato on MN 68 and US 169. 62 sites, 6 with electric; showers. 60 foot limit.

39. Minnesota Valley Recreation Area, 19825 Park Blvd., Jordan, MN 55352. Phone: (952) 492-6400. Located 40 miles SW of Minneapolis off US 169; follow signs. 25 sites. 60 foot limit.

40. Monson Lake State Park, 1690 15th St. NE, Sunburg, MN 56289. Phone: (320) 366-3797. Located on County Hwy 95, off MN 9, between Sunburg and Benson. 20 sites; showers. 60 foot limit.

41. Moose Lake State Park, 4252 County Hwy 137, Moose Lake, MN 55767. Phone: (218) 485-5420. Located 1/4 mile east of I-35 between exits 114 & 120. 33 sites, 20 with electric; showers. 60 foot limit.

42. Nerstrand-Big Woods State Park, 9700 170th St. E, Nerstrand, MN 55053. Phone: (507) 334-8848. Located east of I-35 between exits 56 & 66, on County Hwy 40. 51 sites, 1 pull-thru; 27 with electric; showers; dump station. 60 foot limit.

43. Old Mill State Park, 33489 240th Ave. NW, Argyle, MN 56713. Phone: (218) 437-8174. In northwestern Minnesota, 15 miles east of Argyle via County Hwy 4. 26 sites, 10 with electric; showers. 67 foot limit.

44. Red River Recreation Area, East Grand Forks, MN 56721. Phone: (218) 773-4950. Located near ND/MN state line on the Red River in East Grand Forks, off US 2. 72 sites, 48 full hook-ups; showers (late 2004); dump station (2005). 40 foot limit.

45. Rice Lake State Park, 8485 Rose St., Owatonna, MN 55060. Phone: (507) 455-5871. Located 7 miles east of Owatonna (I-35 exit 42) on Rose Street. 42 sites, 16 with electric; showers; dump station nearby. 50 foot limit.

46. St. Croix State Park, Hinckley, MN 55037. Phone: (320) 384-6591. Located 15 miles east of Hinckley (I-35 exit 183) on MN 48. 211 sites, 42 with electric; showers; dump station. 60 foot limit.

47. Sakatah Lake State Park, 50499 Sakatah Lake State Park Rd., Waterville, MN 56096. Phone: (507) 362-4438. Located off MN 60, NE of Mankato, near intersection of MN 60 & 13 at Waterville. 62 sites, 14 with electric; showers; dump station. 55 foot limit.

48. Savanna Portage State Park, 55626 Lake Place, McGregor, MN 55760. Phone: (218) 426-3271. Remote location at end of County Hwy 14, north of McGregor (MN 65). 60 sites, 4 pull-thru; 18 with electric; showers; dump station. 55 foot limit.

49. Scenic State Park, 56956 Scenic Hig Hwy 7, Bigfork, MN 56628. Phone: (218) 7743-3362. Remote location 7 miles east of Bigfork (MN 38) on County Hwy 7. 95 sites, 20 pull-thru; 20 with electric; showers; dump station. 50 foot limit.

50. Schoolcraft State Park, 9042 Schoolcraft Lane NE, Deer River, MN 56636. Phone: (218) 247-7215. Located about17 miles west of Grand Rapids off MN 6 via US 2. 28 sites. 40 foot limit.

51. Sibley State Park, 800 Sibley Park Rd. NE, New London, MN 56273. Phone: (320) 354-2055. Located 16 miles north of Wilmar on US 71. 134 sites; 53 with electric; showers; dump station. 60 foot limit.

52. Split Rock Creek State Park, 336 50th Ave., Jasper, MN 56144. Phone: (507) 348-7908. Located in western Minnesota near SD state line, on MN 23, SW of Pipestone (US 75). 28 sites, 19 with electric; showers; dump station. 52 foot limit.

53. Temperance River State Park, 7620 W Hwy 61, Schroeder, MN 55613. Phone: (218) 663-7476. Remote location in northeastern Minnesota on MN 61, just north of Schroeder. 54 sites, 2 pull-thru; 18 with electric; showers. 50 foot limit.

54. Tettegouche State Park, 5702 Hwy 61, Silver Bay, MN 55614. Phone: (218) 226-6365. Located on MN 61 near Silver Bay on Lake Superior. 28 sites; showers. 60 foot limit.

55. Upper Sioux Agency State Park, Granite Falls, MN 56241. Phone: (320) 564-4777. Located on MN 67, 8 miles SE of Granite Falls (US 212 & MN 23). 34 sites, 14 with electric; showers; dump station nearby. 45 foot limit.

56. Whitewater State Park, Altura, MN 55910. Phone: (507) 932-3007. Located 3 miles south of Elba on MN 74, east of Rochester. 106 sites, 5 pull-thru; 47 with electric; showers; dump station. 50 foot limit.

57. Wild River State Park, 39797 Park Trail, Center City, MN 55012. Phone: (651) 583-2125. Located on County Hwy 12 east of I-35 exit 147 (MN 95) on St. Croix River. 96 sites, 2 pull-thru; showers; dump station. 60 foot limit.

58. William O'Brien State Park, 16821 O'Brien Trail N, Marine on St. Croix, MN 55047. Phone: (651) 433-0500. Located on St. Croix River along MN 95 about 16 miles east of I-35 exit 129. 124 sites, 60 with electric; showers; dump station. 60 foot limit.

59. Zippel Bay State Park, 3684 54th Ave. NW, Williams, MN 56686. Phone: (218) 783-6252. Located on County Hwy 8, NW of Baudette and east of Roosevelt, in northern Minnesota on Lake of the Woods. 57 sites; showers; dump station. 60 foot limit.

Mississippi

Of the 28 state parks and recreation areas in Mississippi, 22 locations have RV facilities ranging from "primitive" sites (no hookups) to "improved" or "developed" sites with concrete pads, water, and electric connections. All listed parks also have showers and at least one dump station. Reservations are accepted year round at most locations for a limited number of sites. All other sites are available on a first-come, first-served basis. We recommend calling the particular park to check availability. Offices in all parks are open from 8 AM to 5 PM, 7 days a week. Seniors 62 years and older are eligible for a discount, but you must ask and show proof of age. Visa and MasterCard are accepted. Rate group: A and B depending on site facilities; entrance fee is additional.

Mississippi Dept. of Wildlife, Fisheries and Parks
1505 Eastover Dr.
Jackson, MS 39211
Information (800) 467-2757 / Reservations: Call respective park.
Internet: www.mdwfp.com

Mississippi Park Locator

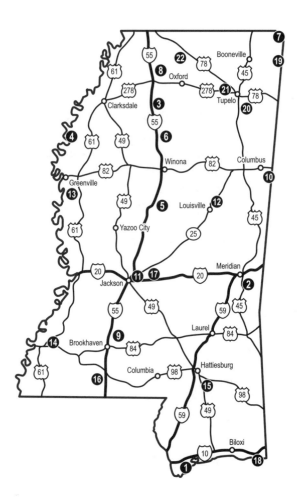

1. Buccaneer State Park, 1150 South Beach Blvd., Waveland, MS 39576.
    Phone: (228) 467-3822. Located 2 miles off US 90 on Beach Blvd in
    Waveland. 149 developed sites, 80 with sewer; laundry.

2. Clarko State Park, 386 Clarko Rd., Quitman, MS 39355. Phone: (601)
    776-6651. Located 20 miles south of Meridian, off US 45. 43 full hook-up
    sites; 15 primitive sites; laundry.

3. George P. Cossar State Park, 165 County Road 170, Oakland, MS 38948.
    Phone: (622) 623-7356. Located 5 miles east of I-55 (Oakland exit) on
    MS 32. 84 developed sites; laundry.

4. Great River Road State Park, Rosedale, MS 38769. Phone: (662) 759-6762. Located in Rosedale, off MS 1 & 8 (35 miles north of Greenville). 61 developed sites; laundry.

5. Holmes County State Park, 5369 State Park Rd., Durant, MS 39063. Phone: (662) 601-3351. Located on MS 424 just east of I-55 exit 150. 28 developed sites; laundry.

6. Hugh White State Park, Grenada, MS 38902. Phone: (662) 226-4934. Located 5 miles east of Grenada (I-55 & MS 8) off MS 8. 173 developed sites; laundry.

7. J. P. Coleman State Park, 613 CR 321, Iuka, MS 38852. Phone: (662) 423-6515. Located 13 miles north of Iuka off MS 25. 75 developed sites; laundry.

8. John W. Kyle State Park, 4235 State Park Rd., Sardis, MS 38666. Phone: (662) 487-1345. Located 9 miles east of Sardis (I-55 exit 252) off MS 315. 200 developed site; laundry.

9. Lake Lincoln State Park, 2573 Sunset Rd. NE, Wesson, MS 39191. Phone: (601) 643-9044. Located off US 51, 4.5 miles east of Wesson (I-55 Wesson exit). 61 improved sites; showers, laundry.

10. Lake Lowndes State Park, 3319 Lake Lowndes Rd., Columbus, MS 39702. Phone: (662) 328-2110. Located 8 miles SE of Columbus (US 82 & 45) off MS 69. 50 sites; showers, laundry.

11. LeFleur's Bluff State Park, 2140 Riverside Dr., Jackson, MS 39202. Office: (601) 987-3923, Campground: (601) 987-3985. Northeast of downtown Jackson at I-55 exit 98. 30 sites with water, electric; showers, dump station.

12. Legion State Park, 635 Legion State Park Rd., Louisville, MS 39339. Phone: (662) 773-8323. Located 2 miles north of Louisville on North Columbus Avenue. 24 sites with full hook-ups.

13. Leroy Percy State Park, Hollandale, MS 38748. Phone: (662) 827-5436. Located 5 miles west of Hollandale (US 61 & MS 12) off MS 12. 16 improved sites; laundry.

14. Natchez State Park, 230-B Wickliff Rd., Natchez, MS 39120. Phone: (601) 442-2658. Located 10 miles NE of Natchez off US 61 at Stanton. 50 sites, showers.

15. Paul B. Johnson State Park, 319 Geiger Lake Rd., Hattiesburg, MS 39401. Phone: (601) 582-7721. Located 10 miles south of Hattiesburg off US 49. 50 sites, showers, laundry.

16. Percy Quin State Park, 1156 Camp Beaver Dr., McComb, MS 39648. Phone: (601) 684-3938. Located 6 miles south of McComb off I-55 exit 13. 107 sites, showers.

17. Roosevelt State Park, 2149 Hwy 13 South, Morton, MS 39117. Phone: (601) 732-6316. Located just north of I-20 exit 77 (MS 13). 109 sites; showers; laundry.

18. Shepard State Park, 1034 Graveline Rd., Gautier, MS 39553. Phone: (228) 497-2244. Located 3 miles west of Pascagoula on Gulf of Mexico, off US 90 at Gautier. 28 sites; showers.

19. Tishomingo State Park, Tishomingo, MS 38873. Phone: (662) 438-6914. Located off the Natchez Trace at mile marker 304. 62 sites, showers, laundry.

20. Tombigbee State Park, 254 Cabin Dr., Tupelo, MS 38804. Phone: (662) 842-7669. Located 6 miles SE of Tupelo off MS 6. 20 sites; showers, laundry.

21. Trace State Park, 2139 Faulkner Rd., Belden, MS 38826. Phone: (662) 489-2958. Located midway between Pontotoc and Tupelo off MS 6. 52 sites with water & electric; showers.

22. Wall Doxey State Park, 3946 Hwy 7 South, Holly Springs, MS 38635. Phone: (662) 252-4231. Located 7 miles south of Holly Springs (US 78 & MS 7) off MS 7. 64 sites; showers; laundry.

Missouri

Thirty-nine State Parks in Missouri have RV camping facilities, ranging from basic (dry-camp) sites to sites with full hook-ups. Water is available in all parks but not necessarily at each site. State Parks are open year round but water service and showers (in parks so equipped) are available normally from April 1 through October 31. Pets are permitted but must be leashed. Seniors (age 65 and older) and persons with disabilities are entitled to a reduced camping fee, with proof of age and/or disability. Missouri has recently installed a centralized reservation system that currently encompasses 23 parks, with more being added this year and next. Reservations require a 48-hour lead time and reservations can be made at the individual park. MasterCard, Visa and Discover credit cards are accepted in Missouri parks. Rate groups: A and B

Missouri Dept. Of Natural Resources
Box 176
Jefferson City, MO 65102
Information: (800) 334-6946 / Reservations: (877) 422-6766
Internet: www.mostatenarks.com

Missouri Park Locator

Missouri Park Locator (*cont.*)

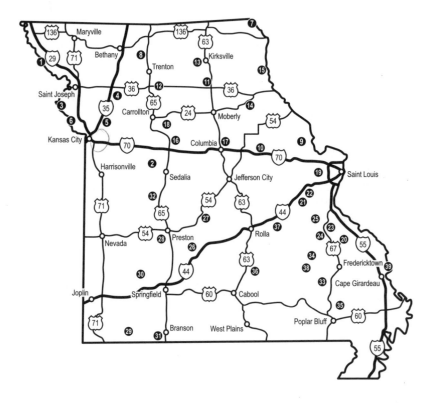

1. Big Lake State Park, 204 Lake Shore Dr., Craig, MO 64437. Phone: (660) 442-3770. Located southwest of Mound City near Kansas state line on MO 111. 75 sites, 60 with electric; showers; laundry; dump station.

2. Knob Noster State Park, 801 SE 10, Knob Noster, MO 65336. Phone: (660) 563-2463. Located on MO 23, outside Knob Noster, off US 50. 77 sites, 40 with electric; showers; laundry; dump station.

3. Lewis and Clark State Park, 801 Lake Crest Blvd., Rushville, MO 64484. Phone: (816) 579-5564. Located on MO 138, on the Missouri River, 20 miles SW of St. Joseph. 70 sites, 44 with electric; showers; laundry; dump station.

4. Wallace State Park, 10621 NE Hwy 121, Cameron, MO 64429. Phone: (816) 632-3745. Located 6 miles south of Cameron, off I-35 exit 42. 87 sites, 42 with electric; showers; dump station.

5. Watkins Woolen Mill State Park, 26600 Park Road North, Lawson, MO 64062. Phone: (816) 580-3387. Located off I-35 exit 26, east of Kearney off MO 92, on Hwy RA. 98 sites, 56 with electric; showers; laundry; dump station. Reservable.

6. Weston Bend State Park, 16600 Hwy 45 N, Weston, MO 64098. Phone: (816) 640-5443. Located 1 mile south of Weston on Missouri River, on MO 45. 36 sites; 21 with electric; showers; laundry; dump station.

7. Battle of Athens State Historic Site, Revere, MO 63465. Phone: (660) 877-3871. Located on Hwy CC, off MO 81, near Iowa state line, on Des Moines River. 29 sites, 15 with electric; water available.

8. Crowder State Park, 76 Hwy 128, Trenton, MO 64683. Phone: (660) 359-6473. Located off US 65, on MO 146, 4 miles west of Trenton. 42 sites, 32 with electric; showers; dump station.

9. Cuivre River State Park, 678 State Route 47, Troy, MO 63379. Phone: (636) 528-7247. Located 3 miles NE of Troy (US 61 & MO 47) on MO 47. 80 sites, 28 with electric; showers; dump station.

10. Graham Cave State Park, 217 Hwy TT, Danville, MO 63361. Phone: (573) 564-3476. Located 2 miles west of Danville (I-70 exit 170) on Hwy TT. 52 sites, 18 with electric; showers; dump station.

11. Long Branch State Park, 28615 Visitor Center Rd., Macon, MO 63552. Phone: (660) 773-5229. Located 2 miles west of the US 63/US36 junction, outside Macon. 83 sites, 40 with electric; showers; dump station.

12. Pershing State Park, 29277 Hwy 130, Laclede, MO 64651. Phone: (660) 963-2299. Located 7 miles west of Brookfield or 18 miles east of Chillicothe, off US 36 on MO 130. 39 sites, 27 with electric; showers; laundry; dump station.

13. Thousand Hills State Park, Kirksville, MO 63501. Phone: (660) 665-6995. Located 2.5 miles SW of Kirksville (US 63) via MO 6 and MO 157. 69 sites, 42 with electric; showers; dump station.

14. Mark Twain State Park, 20057 State Park Office Rd., Stoutsville, MO 65283. Phone: (573) 565-3440. Located on MO 107, NE of Moberly, north of MO 154. 101 sites, 62 with electric; showers; laundry; dump station. Reservable.

15. Wakonda State Park, LaGrange, MO 63448. Phone: (573) 655-2280. Located on Mississippi River, 3 miles south of LaGrange on US 61/24. 79 sites, 30 with electric; showers; laundry; dump station.

16. Arrow Rock State Historic Site, Arrow Rock, MO 65320. Phone: (660) 837-3330. Located 13 miles north of 1-70 exit 98 on MO 41. 45 sites, 23 with electric; showers; dump station.

17. Finger Lakes State Park, 1505 E Peabody Rd., Columbia, MO 65202. Phone: (573) 443-5315. Located 10 miles north of Columbia (1-70 exit 123) off US 63. 36 sites, 17 with electric; showers; dump station. Reservable.

18. Van Meter State Park, Miami, MO 65344. Phone: (660) 886-7537. Located 12 miles NW of Marshall via MO 41 and MO 122. 21 sites, 12 with electric; showers.

19. Dr. Edmund A. Babler Memorial State Park, 800 Guy Park Dr., Wildwood, MO 63005. Phone: (636) 458-3813. Located 20 miles west of St. Louis on Hwy BA, between US 40 and MO 100. 77 sites, 24 with electric; showers; dump station; laundry.

20. Hawn State Park, 12096 Park Dr., Sainte Genevieve, MO 63670. Phone: (573) 883-3603. Located 14 miles SW of I-55 exit 150 via MO 32 and MO 144. 50 sites, 26 with electric; showers; laundry; dump station. Reservable.

21. Meramac State Park, 2800 S Hwy 185, Sullivan, MO 63080. Phone: (573) 468-6072. Located 3 miles NE of Sullivan (1-44 exit 225) on MO 185. 190 sites, 58 with electric; showers; some sewer sites; laundry; dump station. Reservable.

22. Robertsville State Park, Robertsville, MO 63072. Phone: (636) 257-3788. Located 5 miles east of 1-44 exit 247 on Hwy O at Hwy N. 27 sites, 15 with electric; showers; laundry; dump site.

23. St. Francois State Park, 8920 US Hwy 67 N, Bonne Terre, MO 63628. Phone: (573) 358-2173. Located on US 67 about 10 miles north of Park Hills (west of I-55 in southeast MO). 110 sites, 63 with electric; showers; laundry; dump station. Reservable.

24. St. Joe State Park, 2800 Pimville Rd., Park Hills, MO 63601. Phone: (573) 431-1069. Located SW of Park Hills on MO 32, off US 67. 80 sites, 28 with electric; showers; laundry; dump station. Reservable.

25. Washington State Park, DeSoto, MO 63020. Phone: (636) 586-2995. Located 9 miles SW of DeSoto on MO 21. 51 sites, 25 with electric; showers; laundry; dump station. Reservable.

26. Bennett Spring State Park, 26250 Hwy 64A, Lebanon, MO 65536. Phone: (417) 532-4338. Located on MO 64, 12 miles NW of Lebanon (1-44 exit 129). 140 sites, 129 with electric; some sites with sewers; showers; laundry; dump station. NOTE: water available April through October only. Reservable.

27. Lake of the Ozarks State Park, Kaiser, MO 65047. Phone: (573) 348-2694. Located on Lake of the Ozarks south of Osage Beach (US 54) via MO 42 and MO 134. 182 sites, 90 with electric; showers; laundry; dump station. Reservable.

28. Pomme de Terre State Park, Pittsburg, MO 65724. Phone: (417) 852-429 or (417) 745-6909. Located south of Hermitage via MO 254 and MO 64. There are two separate areas to the state park. 257 total sites, 126 with electric; showers; laundry; dump station. Reservable.

29. Roaring River State Park, Cassville, MO 65625. Phone: (417) 847-2539. Located 7 miles south of Cassville on MO 112, near Arkansas state line. 185 sites, 137 with electric; showers; laundry; dump station. Reservable.

30. Stockton State Park, Dadeville, MO 65635. Phone: (417) 276-4259. Located on Stockton Lake about 9 miles south of Stockton via MO 39 and MO 215. 75 sites, 46 with electric; showers; laundry; dump station. Reservable.

31. Table Rock State Park, 5272 Hwy 165, Branson, MO 65616. Phone: (417) 334-4704. Located on MO 165, 5.4 miles west of US 65, SW of Branson. 143 sites, 53 with electric; some sites with sewers; showers; dump station.

32. Harry S. Truman State Park, Warsaw, MO 65355. Phone: (660) 438-7711. Located off MO 7 on Hwy UU, on Lake of the Ozarks, west of US 65 at Warsaw. 201 sites, 102 with electric; showers; laundry; dump station. Reservable.

33. Sam A. Baker State Park, Patterson, MO 63956. Phone: (573) 856-4411. Located 4 miles north of Patterson on MO 143, west of US 67. 214 sites, 109 with electric; showers; laundry; dump station. Reservable.

34. Johnson's Shut-Ins State Park, Middlebrook, MO 63656. Phone: (573) 546-2450. Located in remote section of MO near Mark Twain National Forest, on Hwy N, SW of Park Hills and US 67. 49 sites, 23 with electric; showers; laundry; dump station. Reservable.

35. Lake Wappapello State Park, Williamsville, MO 63967. Phone: (573) 297-3232. Located 16 miles north of Popular Bluff off US 67. 80 sites, 43 with electric; showers; laundry; dump station. Reservable.

36. Montauk State Park, Salem, MO 65560. Phone: (573) 548-2201. Located 21 miles SW of Salem on MO 119, off US 63, south of I-44 exit 186. 154 sites, 67 with electric; showers; laundry; dump station. Reservable.

37. Onondaga Cave State Park, 7556 Hwy H, Leasburg, MO 65535. Phone: (573) 245-6576. Located 7 miles SE of I-44 exit 214 (Leasburg) on Hwy H. 71 sites, 32 with electric; showers; laundry; dump station.

38. Taum Sauk Mountain State Park, c/o Johnson's Shut-Ins State Park, Middlebrook, MO 63656. Phone: (573) 546-2450. Located 9 miles SW of Ironton on Hwy CC, off MO 21/72, near Mark Twain National Forest. 12 rustic sites; water available.

39. Trail of Tears State Park, 429 Moccasin Springs, Jackson, MO 63755. Phone: (573) 334-1711. Located 10 miles east of Fruitland (I-55 exit 105) via US 61 and MO 177. 53 sites, 18 with electric, some with sewers; showers; laundry; dump station. Reservable.

Montana

The Big Sky State offers the RV traveler 23 state parks with facilities. However, all the parks are "dry camp" locations, with water and dump stations available at most. The majority of these parks are in the western and central parts of Montana. Some parks are listed as "primitive" and the campsites are free. Since there are no reservations at the state parks, it is advisable to call your destination park for availability, etc. Pets are permitted in all parks.

NOTE: Several Montana parks have mailing addresses different from their physical locations and some parks share the same telephone number. Follow the location directions listed for each park and indicate the park you are calling about, if you call for information. Also, many of these parks are seasonal and may close earlier than usual, depending on weather conditions. Rate group: B.

Montana Fish, Wildlife & Parks
1420 E. 6th Ave.
Helena, MT 59620
Information: (406) 444-3750
Internet: www.fwp.state.mt.us/parks

Montana Park Locator

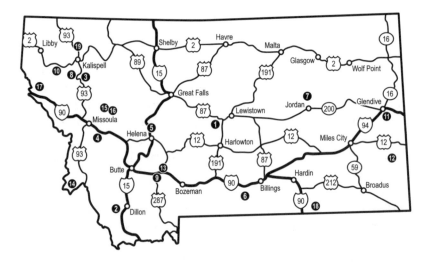

1. Ackley Lake State Park, 4600 Giant Springs Rd., Great Falls, MT 59406.
    Phone: (406) 454-5840. Located SW of Lewistown off US 87 via Secondary
    541 or 400. 23 sites. 24 foot limit.

2. Bannack State Park, 4200 Bannack Rd., Dillon, MT 59725. Phone: (406)
    834-3413. Remote location SW of Dillon off I-15 exit 56, via Secondary
    278, 20 miles west. 28 sites.

3. Flathead Lake area - 5 parks; all have same mailing address: 490 N
    Meridian, Kalispell, MT 59901

    a. Big Arm State Park - Phone: (406) 849-5255. Located on US 93,
        west side of Flathead Lake, 14 miles north of Polson. 40 sites;
        showers. 30 foot limit.
    b. Finley Point State Park - Phone: (406) 887-2715. Located off MT
        35 on SE side of Flathead Lake, 11 miles NE of Polson, on county
        road; follow signs. 16 sites. 40 foot limit.
    c. Wayfarers State Park - Phone: (406) 837-4196. Located on MT 35
        on NE side of Flathead Lake, 1/2 mile south of Bigfork. 30 sites;
        showers; dump station. 50 foot limit.
    d. West Shore State Park - Phone: (406) 844-3066. Located on US
        93 on NW side of Flathead Lake, 20 miles south of Kalispell. 26
        sites. 30 foot limit.
    e. Yellow Bay State Park - Phone: (406) 752-5501. Located on MT
        35 on east side of Flathead Lake, 15 miles north of Polson. 5 sites;
        showers. 30 foot limit.

4. Beavertail Hill State Park, 3201 Spurgin Rd., Missoula, MT 59804. Phone: (406) 542-5500. Located off I-90 exit 130, 26 miles east of Missoula, south of freeway. 28 sites. 28 foot limit.

5. Black Sandy State Park, 930 Custer Ave. W, Helena, MT 59601. Phone: (406) 444-4720. Located about 11 miles north of Helena from I-15 exit 200 via Secondary 453 and county road; follow signs. 33 sites; dump station. 35 foot limit.

6. Cooney Reservoir State Park, Joliet, MT 59041. Phone: (406) 445-2326. Located about 28 miles south of I-90 exit 408 or 434; SW of Billings. 75 sites; showers. 30 foot limit.

7. Hell Creek State Park, Miles City, MT 59301. Phone: (406) 232-0900. Remote location on Fort Peck Lake, 25 miles north of Jordan (MT 200 & 59). 55 sites; showers; dump station. 35 foot limit.

8. Lake Mary Ronan State Park, 490 N Meridian, Kalispell, MT 59901. Phone: (406) 849-5082. Located near Flathead Lake, NW of Polson off US 93; follow signs from 93. 26 sites. 35 foot limit.

9. Lewis & Clark Caverns State Park, Three Forks, MT 59752. Phone: (406) 287-3541. Located on MT 2, 19 miles west of Three Forks. 40 sites; showers; dump station. No size limit.

10. Logan State Park, 490 N Meridian, Kalispel, MT 59901. Phone: (406) 293-7190. Located 45 miles SW of Kalispell on US 2. 41 sites; showers; dump station. 30 foot limit.

11. Makoshika State Park, Glendive, MT 59330. Phone: (406) 377-6256. Located in eastern MT in Glendive (I-94 exit 215); follow signs. 22 sites. 40 foot limit.

12. Medicine Rocks State Park, Miles City, MT 59301. Phone: (406) 232-0900. Remote location in eastern MT, 25 miles south of Baker (US 12 & MT 7) on MT 7. 12 sites. No size limit.

13. Missouri Headwaters State Park, 1400 S 19th St., Bozeman, MT 59715. Phone: (406) 994-4042. Located on MT 286 off MT 205, north of I-90 exit 278. 23 sites. 25 foot limit.

14. Painted Rocks State Park, 3201 Spurgin Rd., Missoula, MT 59804. Phone:

(406) 542-5500. Remote location in southwestern Montana on MT 473, 23 miles off US 93, 17 miles south of Hamilton. 25 sites; no fee. 25 foot limit.

15. Placid Lake State Park, 3201 Spurgin Rd., Missoula, MT 59804. Phone: (406) 677-6804. Located 47 miles NE of Missoula via MT 200 and MT 83. 40 sites; showers. 25 foot limit.

16. Salmon Lake State Park, 3201 Spurgin Rd., Missoula, MT 59804. Phone: (406) 677-6804. Located 42 miles NE of Missoula via MT 200 and MT 83. 20 sites; showers; dump station. 25 foot limit.

17. Thompson Falls State Park, 490 N Meridian Rd., Kalispell, MT 59901. Phone: (406) 752-5501. Located in northwestern Montana, 1 mile northwest of Thompson Falls on MT 200. 17 sites. 30 foot limit.

18. Tongue River Reservoir State Park, Miles City, MT 59301. Phone: (406) 232-0900. Located north of Sheridan, Wyoming, off MT 314 on county road, 6 miles north of Decker. 106 sites; dump station. No size limit.

19. Whitefish Lake State Park, 490 N Meridian, Kalispell, MT 59901. Phone: (406) 862-3991. Located 1 mile west of Whitefish, off US 93 on county road; follow signs. 25 sites; showers. 35 foot limit.

Nebraska

The Cornhusker State has 41 state owned areas with RV facilities. Some of these areas are State Parks and some are State Recreation Areas. Electrical hook-ups are available in more than half these areas and drinking water is available in all locations. Pets on leashes are permitted in all parks but alcoholic beverages are not allowed on state property. Nebraska has recently installed an online reservation system for a few parks. More parks are scheduled to be added to this system in the future. You will have to check the desired park for this service. Otherwise, parks with reservable sites accept requests directly at the park. All state locations require a daily entrance fee in addition to campground charges. Unless indicated, rig size is not a problem in these locations. Rate groups: A and B depending on services provided.

Nebraska Game and Parks Commission
Box 30370
Lincoln, NE 68503
Information: (800) 826-7275 (recorded message)
Internet: www.ngpc.state.ne.us
Internet Reservations (select parks): www.outdoornebraska.org

Nebraska Park Locator

Nebraska Park Locator (*cont.*)

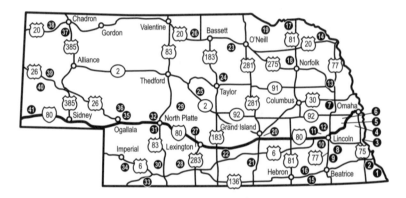

1. Indian Cave State Park, Shubert, NE 68437. Phone: (402) 883-2575. Located in southeastern NE near Missouri River, SE of Auburn off NE 67 on NE 64E. 134 sites with electric; showers; laundry; dump station.

2. Brownville State Recreation Area, c/o Indian Cave State Park, Shubert, NE 68437. Phone: (402) 883-2575. Located in southeastern NE on Missouri River, 19 miles east of Auburn on US 136. 14 sites.

3. Riverview Marina State Recreation Area, c/o Arbor Lodge State Historic Park, Nebraska City, NE 68410. Phone: (402) 873-7222. Located in Nebraska City on the Missouri River. 16 sites with electric (also open camping); showers.

4. Louisville State Recreation Area, Louisville, NE 68037. Phone: (402) 234-6855. Located in southeastern NE outside Louisville (30 miles NE of Lincoln), on NE 50. 241 sites, 205 with electric; showers; dump station.

5. Eugene T. Mahoney State Park, Ashland, NE 68003. Phone: (402) 944-2523. Located in southeastern NE, I-80 exit 426 near Ashland. 149 sites with electric (some 20 -amp); showers; laundry; dump station.

6. Two Rivers State Recreation Area, Waterloo, NE 68069. Phone: (402) 359-5165. Located in eastern NE, 28 miles SW of Omaha on the Platte River near Venice. Five areas: 402 sites, 72 with electric (some with water); showers; dump station.

7. Fremont Lakes State Recreation Area, Ames, NE 68621. Phone: (402) 727-3290. Located in eastern NE, 3 miles west of Fremont on US 30. 200 sites with electric (30/50-amp); numerous primitive sites; showers; dump station.

Note: The next five campgrounds are part of the Salt Valley Lakes State Recreation Area.

8. Wagon Train State Recreation Area (Hickman, NE), c/o Branched Oak State Recreation Area, Raymond, NE 68428. Phone: (402) 783-3400. Located in southeastern NE, 16 miles SE of Lincoln near Hickman on NE 33. 28 sites with electric (30/50-amp); dump station.

9. Stagecoach State Recreation Area (Hickman, NE), c/o Brancherd Oak State Recreation Area, Raymond, NE 68428. Phone: (402) 783-3400. Located in southeastern NE, 21 miles SE of Lincoln, 1 mile west of Hickman. 30 sites with electric (30/50-amp), some open camping; dump station.

10. Conestoga State Recreation Area, Lincoln, NE 68524. Phone: (402) 796-2362. Located in southeastern NE, 10 miles SW of Lincoln, 2 miles north of Denton via NE S-55A, off US 6. 25 sites with electric; dump station.

11. Pawnee State Recreation Area, Lincoln, NE 68524. Phone: (402) 796-2362. Located in southeastern NE, 15 miles west of Lincoln, 1.5 miles west of Emerald off US 34. 78 sites, 68 with electric (30/50-amp); showers; dump station.

12. Branched Oak State Recreation Area, Raymond, NE 68428. Phone: (402) 783-3400. Located in southeastern NE, 16 miles NW of Lincoln, 2.5 miles north of Malcom. 338 sites, 12 full hook up, 253 with electric (some 40 & 50-amp); showers; dump stations.

13. Dead Timber State Recreation Area, Scribner, NE 68057. Phone: (402) 664-3597. Located in eastern NE, 11 miles south of West Point on US 275. 17 sites with electric; some primitive sites.

14. Ponca State Park, Ponca, NE 68770. Phone: (402) 755-2284. Located in northeastern NE near SD state line at junction of NE 12 & 9. 159 sites, 72 with electric (30/50-amp); showers; dump station.

15. Rock Creek Station State Historical Park, Fairbury, NE 68352. Phone: (402) 729-5777. Located in southeastern NE, 6 miles east of Fairbury; follow signs from Fairbury. 25 sites with electric; showers; dump station.

16. Alexandria State Recreation Area, c/o Rock Creek Station RHP, Fairbury, NE 68352. Phone: (402) 729-5777. Located in southeastern NE, 4 miles east of Alexandra, off US 136 and NE 53. 25 sites with electric; dump station.

17. Lewis and Clark State Recreation Area, Crofton, NE 68730. Phone: (402) 388-4169. Located on Missouri River in northeastern NE on SD state line, 9 miles north of Crofton on NE 121, off US 81. Two areas: 354 sites, 174 with electric (30/50-amp); showers; dump stations.

18. Willow Creek State Recreation Area, Pierce, NE 68767. Phone: (402) 329-4053. Located in northeastern NE, 12 miles NW of Norfolk on NE 13. 83 sites, 64 with electric; showers.

19. Niobrara State Park, Niobrara, NE 68760. Phone: (402) 857-3373. Located in northeastern NE near SD state line, 1 mile west of Niobrara on NE 12. 69 sites with electric; showers; dump station.

20. Mormon Island State Recreation Area, Doniphan, NE 68832. Phone: (308) 385-6211. Located in southeastern NE at I-80 exit 212 (Grand Island exit). 34 sites with electric (30/50-amp); showers; dump station.

21. Crystal Lake State Recreation Area, Doniphan, NE 68832. Phone: (308) 385-6210. Located in southern NE, 1.5 miles outside Ayr on NE 74. 70 sites, 20 with electric.

22. Fort Kearney State Recreation Area, Kearney, NE 68847. Phone: (308) 865-5305. Located in south-central NE, off I-80 exit 279, on NE 10 near Kearney on Platte River. 110 sites, 75 with electric (30/50-amp); showers; dump station.

23. Atkinson Lake State Recreation Area, Bassett, NE 68714. Phone: (402) 684-2921. Located in north-central NE outside Atkinson at junction of US 20 & NE 11. 28 sites, 8 with electric.

24. Calamus State Recreation Area, Burwell, NE 68823. Phone: (308) 346-5666. Located on Calamus Reservoir in central NE, 4 miles NW of Burwell on NE 96. 177 sites, 122 with electric, (30/50-amp); showers; dump station.

25. Victoria Springs State Recreation Area, Anselmo, NE 68813. Phone: (308) 749-2235. Located in central NE, 17 miles NW of Broken Bow, off NE 2 on NE S-21A. 100 sites, 20 with electric (30/50-amp); showers.

26. Keller Park State Recreation Area, Bassett, NE 68714. Phone: (402) 684-2921. Located in north-central NE, 9 miles NE of Ainsworth, on US 183 off US 20. 28 sites, 8 with electric; dump station.

27. Johnson Lake State Recreation Area, Elwood, NE 68937. Phone: (308) 785-2685. Located in south-central NE, south of Lexington on US 283, off I-80 exit 237. 267 sites, 113 with electric; showers; dump station.

28. Medicine Creek State Recreation Area, Cambridge, NE 69022. Phone: (308) 697-4667. Located in southern NE, 9 miles NW of Cambridge off US 34 on county road; follow signs. 316 sites, 70 with electric; showers; dump station.

29. Arnold State Recreation Area, Anselmo, NE 68813. Phone: (308) 749-2235. Located in central NE, 38 miles NE of North Platte, outside Arnold on NE 40. 80 sites, 20 with electric; dump station.

30. Red Willow Reservoir State Recreation Area, McCook, NE 69001. Phone: (308) 345-6507. Located in southern NE, 11 miles north of McCook on US 83. 160 sites, 45 with electric; showers; dump station.

31. Maloney Reservoir State Recreation Area, North Platte, NE 69101. Phone: (308) 535-8035. Located in south-central NE, 1 mile south of North Platte on US 83, off I-80 exit 177. 162 sites, 52 with electric (20-amp); showers; dump station.

32. Buffalo Bill State Recreation Area, North Platte, NE 69101. Phone: (308) 535-8035. Located in south-central NE, 2 miles west of North Platte on US 30, next to Buffalo Bill Ranch State Historic Park. 43 sites, 23 with electric (30/50-amp).

33. Swanson Reservoir State Recreation Area, McCook, NE 69001. Phone: (308) 345-6507. Located on Swanson Reservoir in southwestern NE, 25 miles west of McCook on US 34. 212 sites, 62 with electric (30/50-amp); showers; dump stations.

34. Enders Reservoir State Recreation Area, McCook, NE 69001. Phone: (308) 345-6507. Located in southwestern NE near CO state line just outside Enders on US 6. 200 sites, 32 with electric; showers; dump station.

35. Lake Ogallala State Recreation Area, Ogallala, NE 69153. Phone: (308) 284-8800. Located in southwestern NE, 9 miles NE of Ogallala on NE 61 off US 26. 82 sites, 62 with electric (20/30-amp); primitive sites; showers.

36. Lake McConaughy State Recreation Area, Ogallala, NE 69153. Phone: (308) 284-8800. Located in southwestern NE, 10 miles NE of Ogallala (next to Lake Ogallala State Recreation Area) on NE 61. 326 sites, 268 with electric (20/30/50-amp); showers; dump station.

37. Chandron State Park, Chandron, NE 69337. Phone: (308) 432-6167. Located in northwestern NE, 9 miles south of Chandron on US 385. 70 sites with electric; showers; dump station.

38. Fort Robinson State Park, Crawford, NE 69339. Phone: (308) 665-2900. Located in northwestern NE, 3 miles west of Crawford on US 20. 201 sites, 101 with electric (30/50-amp); showers; dump station.

39. Lake Minatare State Recreation Area, Minatare, NE 69356. Phone: (308) 783-2911. Located in western NE, 5 miles NW of Scottsbluff, off US 26 on county roads; follow signs. 152 sites, 52 with electric; showers; dump station.

40. Wildcat Hills State Recreation Area, Gering, NE 69341. Phone: (308) 436-3777. Located in western NE, 10 miles south of Gering (south of Scottsbluff) on NE 71. 30 sites.

41. Oliver Reservoir State Recreation Area, Gering, NE 69341. Phone: (308) 436-3777. Located in southwestern NE, 8 miles west of Kimball, near WY state line, off I-80 exit 8. 175 sites.

Nevada

RV-friendly parks in Nevada are located in convenient places throughout the state. There are 14 such parks, all open year round. User fees are required to enter all Nevada parks and an additional fee is required for campground usage. Because of the altitudes of some parks, winter weather can cause closures. Travelers should contact the respective park to check road and park conditions. You can also check with each park to determine space availability at any time, or to request reservations. Rate group: B. Daily user fee extra.

Nevada Commission on Tourism
401 North Carson St.
Carson City, NV 89701
Information: (775) 687-4384
Internet: www.travelnevada.com

Nevada Park Locator

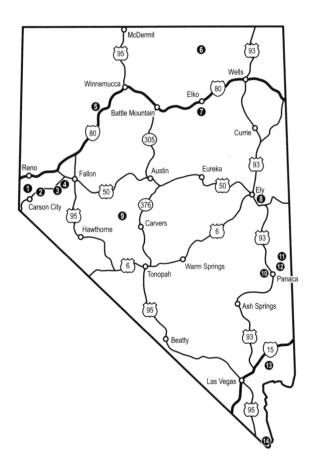

1. Washoe Lake State Park, 4855 East Lake Blvd., Carson City, NV 98704. Phone: (775) 687-4319. Located 10 miles north of Carson City and 15 miles south of Reno. From Carson City take US 395 north to East Lake Blvd exit, then north on East Lake Blvd about 3.1 miles to park entrance. From Reno take US 395 south to the East Lake Blvd intersection, turn left and go south on East Lake Blvd 7.1 miles to park entrance. 49 sites with showers, no hook-ups; dump station. Several sites will accept RVs up to 45 feet.

2. Dayton State Park, US Hwy 50, East Dayton, NV 89403. Phone: (775) 687-5678. Located on US 50, 12 miles east of Carson City, in the town of Dayton. 37 sites, water available, no hook-ups; dump station.

3. Fort Churchill State Historic Park, 1000 Hwy US 95A, Silver Springs, NV 89429. Phone: (775) 577-2345. Located on US 95A 8.5 miles south of Silver Springs (about 40 miles east of Carson City at junction of US 50 & 95A). On the Carson River, 20 sites, water available, no hook-ups; dump station. No Reservations.

4. Lahontan State Recreation Area, 16799 Lahontan Dam, Fallon, NV 89406. Phone: (775) 867-3500. On the Carson River, 18 miles west of Fallon and 45 miles NE of Carson City, via US 50. Access the park from either US 50 east of Silver Springs or US 95 south of Silver Springs. Silver Springs Beach Number Seven offers 26 devloped sites with modern restrooms. Showers and water are available. Primitive on-the-beach camping is available in all areas except for day-use areas and boat ramps. Dump stations are available near both entrances to the park.

5. Rye Patch State Recreation Area, 2505 Rye Patch Reservoir Rd., Lovelock, NV 89419. Phone: (775) 538-7321. Located 22 miles north of Lovelock just off I-80 exit 129. 25 improved sites, showers, water, dump station.

6. Wildhorse State Recreation Areas, HC 31, Elko, NV 89801. Phone: (775) 758-6493. Located on NV 225, 67 miles north of Elko (I-80 exit 301) 23 sites, showers, water, dump station.

7. South Fork State Recreation Area, 353 Lower South Fork Unit 8, Spring Creek, NV 89815. Phone: (775) 744-4346. Remote location on NV 228, 16 miles south of Elko (I-80 exit 301). From Elko, go south 7 miles on NV 227, 5.5 miles south on NV 228 and 3.5 miles SW on Lower South Fork Rd. 25 sites (open early May to November 15th), water, showers, dump station.

8. Cave Lake State Park, Ely NV 89315. Phone: (775) 728-4460. Located 15 miles SE of Ely via US 6/50/93 and Success Summit Road. 23 sites; showers; water; dump station. Winter weather may force closings.

9. Berlin-Ichthyosaur State Park, HC 61, Austin, NV 89310. Phone: (775) 964-2440. Located 23 miles east of Gabbs via NV 844. (Gabbs is located on NV 361, midway between US 50 and US 95 on NV 361) 14 sites; water; dump station. 25 foot limit.

10. Cathedral Gorge State Park, Panaca, NV 89042. Phone: (775) 728-4460. Located 2 miles north of Panaca, just west of US 93. (Panaca is located

in SE Nevada, at junction of US 93 & NV 319) 22 sites; showers; water; dump station.

11. Spring Valley State Park, Star Route, Pioche, NV 89043. Phone: (775) 962-5102. Located 20 miles east of Pioche via NV 322. (Pioche is located in southeastern Nevada at junction of US 93 & NV 322.) Two campgrounds: Horsethief Gulch has 36 sites with water, showers; Ranch Campground has 6 sites with water; dump station. Snow may make winter access difficult.

12. Echo Canyon State Park, HC 74, Pioche NV 89043. Phone: (775) 962-5103. Located 12 miles east of Pioche via NV 322 & 323, and about 12 miles west of Utah/Nevada state line. (Pioche is located in southeastern Nevada at junction of US 93 & NV 322.) 33 sites (first come-first served) water available, dump station.

13. Valley of Fire State Park, Overton, NV 89040. Phone: (702) 397-2088. Located 6 miles from Lake Mead, 55 miles NE of Las Vegas off I-15 at exit 75. 51 sites; showers; water; dump station.

14. Big Bend of the Colorado, Laughlin, NV 89028. Phone: (702) 298-1859. Located 5 miles south of Laughlin, in town limits, 1 mile south of Casino Drive on Needles Hwy. 16 sites; showers; water.

New Hampshire

Ten of New Hampshire's State Parks can accommodate RVs. Most of these parks do not have site facilities and are more tuned to tent camping. In all cases, you should contact the park you seek to determine space availability and *if your rig will fit the space*. Several of the parks are open to RVs with the warning that RVs are welcome ("RVs OK") if the rig will fit the site. Most parks hold some spaces out of the reservation "pool" for drive-in travelers, but you must check with the park. Some parks prohibit pets (see below). Credit cards are accepted. Most parks are open seasonally; some open as late as mid-June. Rate groups: B and C depending on site utilities.

New Hampshire Division of Travel and Tourism Development
Box 1856
Concord, NH 03302
Information: (800) 386-4664 / Reservations: (603) 271-3628
Internet: www.nhparks.state.nh.us (Also for on-line reservations.)

New Hampshire Park Locator

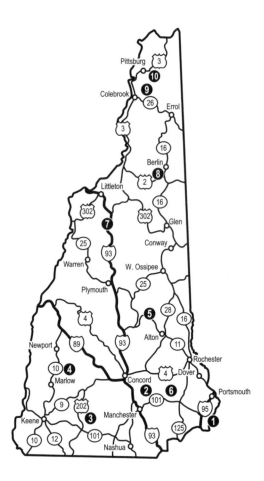

1.   Hampton State Beach, Hampton, NH 03842. Phone: (603) 926-3784.
     Located on Atlantic Ocean in southeastern NH on NH 1A, outside
     Hampton. 28 full hookup sites; showers; store.

2.   Bear Brook State Park, Allenstown, NH 03275. Phone: (603) 485-9874.
     Located SE of Concord off NH 28, 5 miles off US 3. 108 sites (RVs "OK");
     dump station.

3.   Greenfield State Park, Greenfield, NH 03047. Phone: (603) 547-3497.
     Located in southern NH, west of Manchester, on NH 136, near Greenfield.
     257 sites (RVs "OK"); showers; dump station.

4. Pillsbury State Park, Washington, NH 03280. Phone: (603) 863-2860.
    Located 30 miles west of Concord, 7 miles north of Washington on NH
    31. 33 sites.

5. Ellacoya State Beach, Gilford, NH 03246. Phone: (603) 293-7821. Located
    NE of Laconia on Lake Winnipesaukee along NH 11. 38 full hook-up
    sites; showers. No pets.

6. Pawtuckaway State Park, Nottingham, NH 03290. Phone: (603) 895-3031.
    Located NE of Manchester off NH 101, on NH 156. 191 sites; (RVs "OK");
    showers. No pets.

7. Franconia Notch State Park, Franconia, NH 03580. Phone: (603) 823-
    8800. Located in White Mountain National Forest between Plymouth and
    Littleton, off I-93 between exits 34 & 35. 97 sites; showers.

8. Moose Brook State Park, Gorham, NH 03581. Phone: (603) 466-3860.
    Located south of Berlin near Gorham, off US 2. 59 sites (RVs "OK");
    showers.

9. Coleman State Park, Stewartstown, NH 03597. Phone: (603) 538-6965.
    Remote location off NH 26 at Kidderville in northern NH. 24 sites; showers;
    dump station. 35 foot limit.

10. Lake Francis State Park, Pittsburg, NH 03592. Phone: (603) 538-6965.
    Located in far north NH on Lake Francis, 5 miles east of Pittsburg off US
    3. 38 sites; showers; dump station.

New Jersey

New Jersey maintains 16 State Parks or Forests with RV facilities. However, no parks have hook-ups. Water is available in all the parks and most have dump stations. Pets are not allowed in overnight campsites nor are alcoholic beverages permitted in New Jersey parks. Eight of the parks are open year round (see below). While reservations are accepted in all parks, it is possible to obtain space on a drive-in basis. You should call the particular park to verify available space. Rate group: B

New Jersey Dept. of Environmental Protection
Division of Parks and Forestry
State Park Service
Box 404
Trenton, NJ 08625
Information and Reservations: (800) 222-6765
Internet: www.njparksandforests.org

New Jersey Park Locator

1. Allaire State Park, Farmingdale, NJ 07727. Phone: (732) 938-2371. Located on NJ 524, 1.5 miles west of Garden State Pkwy near east end of I-195. 45 sites; showers; dump station.

2. Bass River State Forest, 762 Stage Rd., New Gretna, NJ 08224. Phone: (609) 296-1114. Located on Stage Road west of Garden State Pkwy, 6 miles west of Tuckerton. 178 sites; showers; laundry; dump station.

3. Belleplain State Forest, County Route 550, Woodbine, NJ 08270. Phone: (609) 861-2404. Located in southern NJ on CR 550, 2 miles west of Woodbine. 170 sites; shower; laundry; dump station.

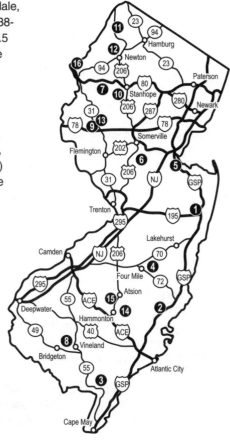

4. Brendan T. Byrne State Forest, New Lisbon, NJ 08064. Phone: (609) 726-1191. Located SE of Browns Mills between NJ 70 & NJ 72. 82 sites; showers; laundry; dump station.

5. Cheesequake State Park, 300 Gordon Rd., Matawan, NJ 07747. Phone: (732) 566-2161. Located off NJ 34 near junction with US 9, 3 miles NW of Matawan. 53 sites; showers; dump station. Seasonal.

6. Delaware and Raritan Canal State Park, Bull Island, 2185 Daniel Bray Hwy (Rte. 29), Stockton, NJ 08559. Phone: (609) 397-2949. Located on the Delaware River northwest of Trenton; on NJ 29, 3 miles NW of Stockton. 69 sites; showers; dump station. Seasonal.

7. Jenny Jump State Forest, Hope, NJ 07844. Phone: (908) 459-4366. Located NW of Great Meadow on State Park Road, 3 miles north of NJ 519. 22 sites; showers. Seasonal.

8. Parvin State Park, 701 Almond Rd., Pittsgrove, NJ 08318. Phone: (856) 358-8616. Located west of Vineland near junction of NJ 540 and 553. 56 sites; showers; laundry; dump station.

9. Spruce Run Recreation Area, 1 Van Sykel's Rd., Clinton, NJ 08809. Phone: (908) 638-8572. Located south of Washington off NJ 31 (I-78 exits 15 or 17). 70 sites; showers; dump station. Seasonal.

10. Stephens State Park, 800 Willow Grove St., Hackettstown, NJ 07840. Phone: (908) 852-3790. Located 2 miles north of Hackettstown off US 46. 40 sites; no facilities. Seasonal.

11. Stokes State Forest, 1 Coursen Rd., Branchville, NJ 07826. Phone: (973) 948-3820. Located in northern NJ off US 206, 3 miles NW of Branchville. 77 sites; showers.

12. Swartswood State Park, Swartswood, NJ 07877. Phone: (973) 383-5230. Located on CR 619, 4 miles NW of Newton (US 206). 67 sites; showers; laundry; dump station. Seasonal.

13. Voorhees State Park, 251 Country Rd., (NJ 513), Glen Gardner, NJ 08826. Phone: (908) 638-6969. Located on NJ 513 near junction with NJ 31, at High Bridge. 50 sites; showers; dump station.

14. Wharton State Forest, 4110 Nesco Rd., Hammonton, NJ 08088. Phone: (609) 561-0024. Located 8 miles east of Hammonton on NJ 542. Godfrey Bridge Campground: 49 sites; no facilities; 21 foot limit.

15. Atsion Recreation Area (Wharton State Forest), 744 Route 206, Shamong, NJ 08088. Phone: (609) 268-0444. Located on US 206, 8 miles north of Hammonton. 50 sites; showers; dump station. Seasonal.

16. Worthington State Forest, Columbia, NJ 07832. Phone: (908) 841-9575. Located on Old Mine Road, 8 miles north of Delaware Water Gap, near I-80 exit 1. 69 sites; showers. Seasonal.

NJ Parks and forests . org

New Mexico

The 27 New Mexico State Parks suitable for RVs rank very high in facilities and locations. Most have full facilities, will accept large rigs and are close to major highways or Interstates. Some parks prohibit alcoholic beverages (check by park) and pets must be on leashes. All the parks have Developed Sites, which means roads are paved or hard gravel, site pads and tables. Other site amenities vary by park. Credit cards are accepted. Rate groups: A, B, and C depending on site facilities.

New Mexico State Parks Division
1220 S. St. Francis Dr.
Box 1147
Santa Fe, NM 87505
Information: (888) 667-2757 / Reservations: (877) 664-7787
Internet: www.nmparks.com

New Mexico Park Locator

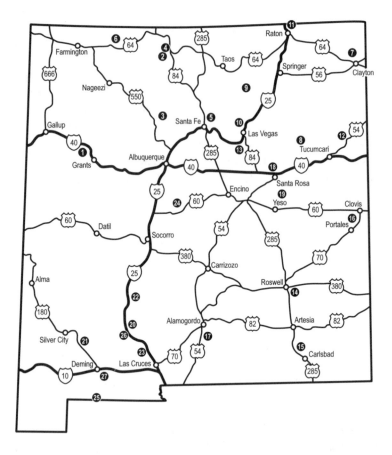

1.   Bluewater Lake State Park, Prewith, NM 87045. Phone: (505) 876-2391.
     Located 28 miles NW of Grants off I-40 between exits 53 & 63. 149 sites,
     14 with electric; showers; dump station. 45 foot limit.

2.   El Vado Lake State Park, Tierra Amarilla, NM 87575. Phone: (505) 588-
     7247. Located 17 miles SW of Tierra Amarilla (US 64 & 84) on MN 112.
     80 sites, 19 with electric; showers; dump station. 35 foot limit.

3.   Fenton Lake State Park, 455 Fenton Lake Rd., Jemez Springs, NM 87025.
     Phone: (505) 829-3630. Located NW of Santa Fe off MN 126, just east of
     US 550. 37 sites, 5 with electric. 40 foot limit.

4.   Heron Lake State Park, Los Ojos, NM 87551. Phone: (505) 588-7470.
     Located 11 miles NW of Tierra Amarilla off US 64/84 via NM 95. 250
     sites, 54 with electric; showers; dump station. 35 foot limit.

5. Hyde Memorial State Park, 740 Hyde Park Rd., Santa Fe, NM 87501. Phone: (505) 983-7175. Located 8 miles NE of Santa Fe off NM 475. 50 sites, 7 with electric; dump station. 53 foot limit.

6. Navajo Lake State Park, 1448 NM 511 #1, Navajo Dam, NM 87419. Phone: (505) 632-2278. Located 25 miles east of Bloomfield off US 64. 246 sites with electric; showers; dump station. 48 foot limit.

7. Clayton Lake State Park, 141 Clayton Lake Rd., Clayton, NM 88415. Phone: (505) 374-8808. Located 12 miles NW of Clayton off NM 370. 37 sites, 7 with electric; showers. 45 foot limit.

8. Conchas Lake State Park, Conchas Dam, NM 88416. Phone: (505) 868-2270. Located 34 miles NW of Tucumcari off NM 104. 195 sites, 40 with electric; showers; dump station. 40 foot limit.

9. Coyote Creek State Park, Guadalupita, NM 87722. Phone: (505) 387-2328. Located 17 miles north of Mora off NM 434, north of Las Vegas in north-central NM. 47 sites, 21 with electric; showers; dump station. 38 foot limit.

10. Storrie Lake State Park, Las Vegas, NM 87701. Phone: (505) 425-7278. Located 4 miles north of Las Vegas off NM 518. 45 sites, 21 with electric; showers; dump station. 40 foot limit.

11. Sugarite Canyon State Park, Raton, NM 87740. Phone: (505) 445-5607. Located near Colorado state line off I-25 exit 452 to NM 72 and NM 526. 40 sites, 12 with electric; showers; dump station. 40 foot limit.

12. Ute Lake State Park, Logan, NM 88426. Phone: (505) 487-2284. Located 3 miles north of Logan off NM 40. 142 sites, 77 with electric; showers; dump station. 40 foot limit.

13. Villanueva State Park, Villanueva, NM 87583. Phone: (505) 421-2957. Located 15 miles south of Las Vegas, off I-25 exits 320 or 323, off NM 3. 31 sites, 12 with electric; showers; dump station. 40 foot limit.

14. Bottomless Lakes State Park, Roswell, NM 88201. Phone: (505) 624-6058. Located on NM 409 east of Roswell via US 380. 26 sites with electric, water; 6 full hook-up; showers; dump station. 50 foot limit.

15. Brantley Lake State Park, Carlsbad, NM 88221. Phone: (505) 457-2384. Located 12 miles north of Carlsbad on Eddy County Road 3, off US 285. 51 sites with electric; showers; dump station. 50 foot limit.

16. Oasis State Park, 1891 Oasis Rd., Portales, NM 88130. Phone: (505) 356-5331. Located in eastern NM, 6.5 miles NW of Portales via NM 467.

23 sites, 12 with electric; showers; dump station. 80 foot limit.

17. Oliver Lee State Park, 409 Dog Canyon, Alamogordo, NM 88310. Phone: (505) 437-8284. Located 12 miles south of Alamogordo, off US 54. 48 sites, 31 with electric; showers; dump station. 38 foot limit.

18. Santa Rosa Lake State Park, Santa Rosa, NM 88433. Phone: (505) 472-3110. Located 7 miles north of Santa Rosa on NM 91; I-40, exit 272. 76 sites, 25 with electric; showers; dump station. 50 foot limit.

19. Sumner Lake State Park, Fort Sumner, NM 88119. Phone: (505) 355-2541. Located on NM 203 via US 84, NW of Fort Sumner. 50 sites, 18 with electric; showers; dump station. 60 foot limit.

20. Caballo Lake State Park, Caballo, NM 87931. Phone: (505) 743-3942. Located 16 miles south of Truth or Consequences off I-25 exits 59 or 63. 135 sites, 63 with electric; showers; dump station. 85 foot limit.

21. City of Rocks State Park, Faywood, NM 88034. Phone: (505) 536-2800. Located north of Deming on NM 61, off US 180. 52 sites, 10 with electric; showers. 65 foot limit.

22. Elephant Butte Lake State Park, Elephant Butte, NM 87935. Phone: (505) 744-5421. Located 5 miles north of Truth or Consequences off I-25 exit 83. 132 sites, 98 with electric; showers; dump station. No length limit.

23. Leasburg Dam State Park, Radium Springs, NM 88054. Phone: (505) 524-4068. Located 15 miles north of Las Cruces on NM 157 at I-25 exit 19. 31 sites, 13 with electric; showers; dump station. 36 foot limit.

24. Manzano Mountains State Park, Mountainair, NM 87036. Phone: (505) 847-2820. Located 16 miles NW of Mountainair (US 60) via NM 55 & 131. 37 sites, 8 with electric; showers; dump station. 40 foot limit.

25. PanchoVilla State Park, Columbus, NM 88029. Phone: (505) 531-2711. Located in Columbus, south of Deming, (near Mexican border) via NM 11. 62 sites with electric & water; showers; dump station. 62 foot limit.

26. Percha Dam State Park, Caballo, NM 87931. Phone: (505) 743-3942. Located near Caballo Lake State Park south of Truth or Consequences at I-25 exit 59. 50 sites, 30 with electric; showers. 85 foot limit.

27. Rockhound State Park, Deming, NM 88030. Phone: (505) 546-6182. Located SE of Deming via NM 11 and NM 141. 29 sites, 15 with electric; showers; dump station. 36 foot limit.

New York

New York *Loves* RVers, with 105 State Parks and Campgrounds equipped for vehicles. These parks stretch from the eastern tip of Long Island to the Empire State's western boundary with Pennsylvania. Many locations are on water, including New York's two Great Lakes, Ontario and Erie, and several are on the picturesque Finger Lakes in western New York. A large number of campgrounds are in the Adirondack Park and on lakes and ponds in that scenic part of the state.

Most of the parks are open May through mid-October, but a few are year round; you will have to check with the particular park if you're enjoying New York in other times of the year. Reservations are available in all parks and are recommended during the "busy" season and weekends. Reservations must be for a minimum of two nights. However, drive-ins are accepted for a single night, space permitting. Pets on leashes are permitted. Credit cards are accepted. Rate group: B and C (special locations; any site utilities extra).

New York State Office of Parks, Recreation and Historic Preservation
The Governor Nelson A. Rockefeller Empire State Plaza
Agency Building 1
Albany, NY 12238
Information : (800) 225-5697 or (518) 474-0456
Reservations: (800) 456-2267
Internet: www.nysparks.com / Reservations: www.ReserveAmerica.com

New York Park Locator

New York Park Locator (*cont.*)

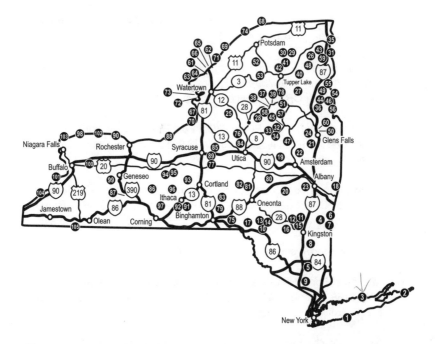

1. Herkscher State Park, Herkscher State Pkwy, East Islip, NY 11730. Phone: (631) 581-2100. Located on south shore of Long Island, south of East Islip, off NY 44. 69 sites; dump station.

2. Hither Hills State Park, 50 S Fairview Ave., Montauk, NY 11954. Phone: (631) 668-2554. Located at eastern end of Long Island just west of Montauk, off NY 27. 168 sites; showers; dump station.

3. Wildwood State Park, Route 25A, Wading River, NY 11792. Phone: (631) 929-4314. Located on NY 25A on Long Island Sound between Wading River and Woodcliff Park. 322 sites with electric; showers; dump station.

4. Lake Taghanic State Park, 1528 Route 82, Ancram, NY 12502. Phone: (518) 851-3631. Located NW of Ancram on NY 82, off Taconic State Parkway (Rte 82 exit). 60 sites; showers.

5. Clarence Fahnestock State Park, Route 301 W, Cold Spring, NY 10516. Phone: (845) 225-7207. Located on NY 301, NE of Cold Spring, off Taconic State Parkway (Rte 301 exit). 80 sites: showers.

6. Taconic State Park (Copake Falls), Route 344, Copake Falls, NY 12517. Phone: (518) 329-3993. Located on state border just north of CT/MA/

NY state lines on NY 344, just outside of Copake Falls. 112 sites; showers; dump station. (See next listing.)

7.   Taconic State Park (Rudd Pond), Rural Route 2 Box 99, Millerton, NY 12546. Phone: (518) 789-3059. Located off NY 2 about 2 miles north of Millerton along CR 62. 40 sites; showers. (See above listing.)

8.   Mills-Norrie State Park, Route 9 (Old Post Road), Staatsburg, NY 12580. Phone: (845) 889-4646. Located on US 9, outside Staatsburg, on Hudson River. 51 sites; showers; dump station.

9.   Beaver Pond State Campground, (Harriman State Park); 800 Route 106, Stony Point, NY 10980. Phone: (845) 947-2792. Located SE of Harriman on NY 106, just east of NYS Thruway. 146 sites; showers; dump station.

Note: The following 7 campgrounds are located in Catskill Park.

10. Mongaup Pond State Campground, Mongaup Pond Road, De Bruce, NY 12758. Phone: (845) 439-4233. Located NE of Livingston Manor off NY 17 exit 96. 163 sites; showers; dump station.

11. North - South Lake State Campground, County Route 18, Haines Falls, NY 12436. Phone: (518) 357-2289. Located NE of Haines Falls off NY 23A. 219 sites; showers; dump station.

12. Devil's Tombstone State Campground, Route 214, Hunter, NY 12442. Phone: (845) 688-7160. Located SE of Hunter on NY 214, near junction of NY 214 & 23A. 24 sites.

13. Little Pond State Campground, Lewbeach, NY 12753. Phone: (845) 439-5480. Located 7 miles NE of Roscoe (NY 17 exit 94) off County Route 54. 75 sites; showers.

14. Beaverkill State Campground, Livingston Manor, NY 12758. Phone: (845) 439-4281. Located north of Livingston Manor (NY 17 exit 96) off CR 54. 95 sites; showers; dump station.

15. Kenneth L. Wilson State Campground, Mount Tremper, NY 12457. Phone: (845) 679-7020. Located SW of Woodstock off NY 212, on Wittenberg Road. 76 sites; showers; dump station.

16. Woodland Valley State Campground, Phoenicia, NY 12464. Phone: (845) 688-7647. Located SW of Mount Tremper off NY 28, on Woodland Valley Road. 72 sites; showers; dump station.

17. Bear Spring Mountain State Campground, Walton, NY 13856. Phone: (607) 865-6989. Located 4 miles SE of Walton off NY 206, on East Trout Brook Road. 41 sites; dump station.

18. Cherry Plain State Park, Berlin, NY 12040. Phone: (518) 733-5400. Located south of Cherry Plain near MA state line, off NY 22 on Miller Road. 20 sites; showers.

19. Caroga Lake State Campground, Route 29A, Caroga Lake, NY 12078. Phone: (518) 835-4241. Located in Adirondack Park, outside Caroga Lake (NY 10 & 29A). 161 sites with showers; dump station.

20. Max V. Shaul State Park, Route 30, Fultonham, NY 12071. Phone: (518) 827-4711. Located SW of Middleburgh on NY 30. 30 sites; showers.

21. Moreau Lake State Park, Gansevoort, NY 12831. Phone: (518) 793-0511. Located NW of Gansevoort, off I-87, exit 17. 148 sites; showers; dump station.

22. Northampton Beach State Campground, Route 30, Mayville, NY 12117. Phone: (518) 863–6000. Located south of Northville in Adirondack Park on NY 30, on Great Scandaga Lake. 224 sites; showers; dump station.

23. Thompson's Lake State Park, Route 157, Voorheesville, NY 12186. Phone: (518) 872-1674. Located west of Voorheesville on NY 157. 140 sites; showers; dump station.

24. Luzerne State Campground, Lake Luzerne, NY 12846. Phone: (518) 696-2031. Located NW of Glens Falls on NY 9N. 174 sites; showers; dump station.

25. Whetstone Gulf State Park, Route 26, Lowville, NY 13367. Phone: (315) 376-6630. Located about 7 miles south of Lowville on NY 26. 62 sites, 12 with electric; showers; dump station.

26. Taylor Pond State Campground, Lyon Mountain, NY 12952. Phone: (518) 647-5250. Remote location west of Clintonville on Taylor Pond. 30 sites.

27. Lake Harris State Campground, Route 28N, Newcomb, NY 12852. Phone: (518) 582-2503. Located on Harris Lake outside Newcomb, on NY 28N. 89 sites; showers; dump station.

28. Nick's Lake State Campground, Old Forge, NY 13420. Phone: (315) 369-3314. Located south of Old Forge off NY 28 on Bisby Road. 112 sites; showers; dump station.

29. Buck Pond State Campground, CR 30, Onchiota, NY 12989. Phone: (518) 891-3449. Located 13 miles north of Saranac Lake via NY 3 and County Road 30. 116 sites; showers; dump station.

30. Meacham Lake State Campground, Route 30, Paul Smiths, NY 12970. Phone: (518) 483-5116. Located 10 miles north of Paul Smiths on NY 30. 224 sites; showers; dump station.

31. Ausable Point State Campground, Route 9, Peru, NY 12972. Phone: (518) 561-7080. Located on Lake Champlain south of Plattsburg along US 9. 123 sites, 43 with electric; showers; dump station.

32. Little Sand Point State Campground, Piseco, NY 12139. Phone: (518) 548-7585. Located south of Piseco on Old Piseco Road, off NY 8. 78 sites; dump station.

33. Point Comfort State Campground, Piseco, NY 12139. Phone: (518) 548-7586. Located south of Piseco off NY 8, next to Little Sand Point State Campground. 76 sites; dump station.

34. Popular Point State Campground, Piseco, NY 12139. Phone: (518) 548-8031. Located south of Piseco on Old Piseco Road, off NY 8. 21 sites; dump station.

35. Cumberland Bay State Park, Route 314E, Plattsburg, NY 12901. Phone: (518) 563-5240. Located on Lake Champlain north of Plattsburg, on NY 314E. 200 sites; showers; dump station.

36. Eagle Point State Campground, Route 9, Pottersville, NY 12860. Phone: (518) 494-2220. Located on Schroon Lake north of Pottersville on US 9. 72 sites; showers; dump station.

37. Brown Tract Pond State Campground, Raquette Lake, NY 13436. Phone: (315) 354-4412. Located SW of Raquette Lake, off NY 28 on Uncas Road. 90 sites; dump station.

38. Eighth Lake State Campground, Route 28, Raquette Lake, NY 13436. Phone: (315) 354-4120. Located on Eighth Lake south of Raquette Lake on NY 28. 126 sites; showers; dump station.

39. Golden Beach State Campground, Route 28, Raquette Lake, NY 13426. Phone: (315) 354-4230. Located east of Raquette Lake on NY 28. 205 sites; showers; dump station.

40. Meadowbrook State Campground, Route 86, Ray Brook, NY 12977.

Phone: (315) 891-4351. Located west of Lake Placid in Ray Brook on NY 86. 62 sites; showers; dump station.

41. Fish Creek Pond State Campground, Route 30, Saranac Lake, NY 12983. Phone: (315) 891-4560. Located NE of Tupper Lake on NY 30. 355 sites; showers; dump station.

42. Rollins Pond State Campground, Route 30 Saranac Lake, NY 12983. Phone: (315) 891-3239. Located on Rollins Pond NE of Tupper Lake off NY 30. 287 sites; showers; dump station.

43. Macomb Reservation State Park, Schuyler Falls, NY 12985. Phone: (518) 643-9952. Located SW of Schuyler Falls on county road, off NY 22B; follow signs. 175 sites; showers; dump station.

44. Paradox Lake State Campground, Route 74, Severance, NY 12872. Phone: (518) 532-7451. Located east of Severance on NY 74, off US 9. 58 sites; showers; dump station.

45. Moffit State Campground, Route 8, Speculator, NY 12164. Phone: (518) 548-7102. Located on Scandaga Lake outside Speculator on NY 8. 261 sites; showers; dump station.

46. Putnam Pond State Campground, Route 74, Ticonderoga, NY 12883. Phone: (518) 585-7280. Located on Putnam Pond SW of Ticonderoga (NY 9N) on NY 74. 72 sites; showers; dump station.

47. Sacandaga State Campground, Route 30, Wells, NY 12190. Phone: (518) 924-4121. Located south of Wells on NY 30. 143 sites; showers; dump station.

48. Wilmington Notch State Campground, Route 86, Wilmington, NY 12997. Phone: (518) 946-7172. Located NE of Lake Placid, south of Wilmington, on NY 86. 54 sites; showers; dump station.

49. Sharp Bridge State Campground, Route 9, North Hudson, NY 12870. Phone: (518) 532-7538. Located north of North Hudson on US 9. 40 sites; showers; dump station.

50. Lake George Battleground State Campground, Route 9, Lake George, NY 12845. Phone: (518) 668-3348. Located north of Glens Falls at I-87 exit 21. 68 sites; showers; dump station.

51. Lake Durant State Campground, Route 28, Blue Mountain Lake, NY 12812. Phone: (518) 352-7797. Located SE of Blue Mountain Lake on NY 28. 61 sites; showers; dump station.

52. Higley Flow State Park, Colton, NY 13625. Phone: (315) 262-2880. Located 14 miles south of Potsdam via NY 57. 135 sites with sewer hookup; 43 with electric; showers; dump station.

53. Cranberry Lake State Campground, Cranberry Lake, NY 12927. Phone: (315) 848-2315. Located on Cranberry Lake along NY 3. 173 sites; showers; dump station.

54. Crown Point State Campground, Crown Point, NY 12928. Phone: (518) 597-3603. Located on Lake Champlain about 7 miles southeast of Port Henry, along NY 903, east of NY 9N. 66 sites; showers; dump station.

55. Lincoln Pond State Campground, County Route 7, Elizabethtown, NY 12932. Phone: (518) 942-5292. Northwest of Witherbee off I-87 exit 30. 35 sites; showers; dump station.

56. Roger's Rock State Campground, Route 9N, Hague, NY 12836. Phone: (518) 585-6746. Located on Lake George between Indian Kettles and Ticonderoga on NY 9N. 332 sites; showers; dump station.

57. Lewey Lake State Campground, Route 30, Indian Lake, NY 12842. Phone: (518) 648-5266. Located 12 miles south of Indian Lake along NY 30. 209 sites; showers; dump station.

58. Limekiln Lake State Campground, Inlet, NY 13360. Phone: (315) 357-4401. Located south of Inlet off NY 28 via CR 14 (Limekiln Rd). 271 sites; showers; dump station.

59. Poke-O-Moonshine State Campground, Route 9, Keeseville, NY 12944. Phone: (518) 834-9045. Located south of Keeseville on US 9 between I-87 exits 32 & 33. 25 sites; dump station.

60. Hearthstone Point State Campground, Route 9N, Lake George, NY 12845. Phone: (518) 668-5193. Located north of Glens Falls at I-87 exit 22, on southwest shore of Lake George. 251 sites; showers; dump station.

61. Grass Point State Park, Alexandria Bay, NY 13607. Phone: (315) 686-4472. Located 27 miles north of Watertown at I-81 exit 50, on St. Lawrence River. 76 sites, 17 with electric; showers; dump station.

62. Keewaydin State Park, Route 12, Alexandria Bay, NY 13607. Phone: (315) 482-3331. Located on St. Lawrence River near Alexandria Bay on NY 12. 41 sites; showers.

63. Burnham Point State Park, Route 12E, Cape Vincent, NY 13618. Phone:

(315) 654-2324. Located about 27 miles northwest of Watertown via NY 12E. 50 sites, 18 with electric; showers; dump station.

64. Cedar Point State Park, Cedar Point State Park Drive, Clayton, NY 13624. Phone: (315) 654-2522. Located east of Burnham Point State Park (see above) on NY 12E. 173 sites, 55 with electric, 33 with sewer; showers; dump station.

65. DeWolfe Point State Park, County Route 191, Fineview, NY 13640. Phone: (315) 482-2012. Located northwest of Alexandria Bay off I-81 exit 51 on Wellesley Island. 14 sites; showers; dump station.

66. Wellesley Island State Park, Cross Island Road, Fineview, NY 13640. Phone: (315) 482-2722. Located on Wellesley Island, I-81 exit 51 on St. Lawrence River. 429 sites, 131 with electric, 57 with sewer; showers; dump station.

67. Southwick Beach State Park, Henderson, NY 13650. Phone: (315) 846-5338. Located outside Woodville on NY 3; on east edge of Lake Ontario. 112 sites, 44 with electric; showers; dump station.

68. Robert Moses State Park, Robertson Bay Road, Massena, NY 13662. Phone: (315) 769-8663. Located in far northern part of state off NY 3, next to Eisenhower Locks on St. Lawrence River. 168 sites, 38 with electric; showers; dump station.

69. Jacques Cartier State Park, Route 12, Morristown, NY 13664. Phone: (315) 375-6371. Located on St. Lawrence River SW of Morristown along NY 12. 98 sites, 22 with electric; showers; dump station.

70. Selkirk Shores State Park, Route 3, Pulaski, NY 13142. Phone: (315) 298-5737. Located 5 miles west of Pulaski on NY 3; on east shore of Lake Ontario. 87 sites; showers; dump station.

71. Kring Point State Park, Alexandria Bay, NY 13679. Phone: (315) 482-2444. On St. Lawrence River NE of Alexandria Bay, off NY 12 on Kring Point Road. 99 sites, 28 with electric; showers; dump station.

72. Wescott Beach State Park, Route 3, Sackets Harbor, NY 13685. Phone: (315)646-2239. Located south of Sackets Harbor on NY 3 in Henderson Bay (Lake Ontario.) 169 sites, 85 with electric; showers; dump station.

73. Long Point State Park, State Park Road, Three Mile Bay, NY 13693. Phone: (315) 649-5258. Located south of Three Mile Bay on Port

Peninsula, off NY 12E via CR 57. 87 sites, 19 with electric; showers; dump station.

74. Coles Creek State Park, Route 37, Waddington, NY 13694. Phone: (315) 388-5636. Located north of Waddington on NY 37 in far northern NY, on St. Lawrence River. 238 sites, 147 with electric; showers; dump station.

75. Oquaga Creek State Park, CR 20, Bainbridge, NY 13733. Phone: (607) 467-4160. Located south of Bennettsville off I-88 exit 8, on CR 20. 95 sites; showers; dump station.

76. Pixley Falls State Park, Route 46, Boonville, NY 13309. Phone: (315) 942-4713. Located about 18 miles north of Rome on NY 46. 22 sites.

77. Chittenango Falls State Park, Route 13, Cazenovia, NY 13035. Phone: (315) 655-9620. Located on Cazenovia Lake SE of Syracuse along NY 13. 22 sites; showers.

78. Lake Eaton State Campground, Route 30, Long Lake, NY 12847. Phone: (518) 624-6646. Located NW of Long Lake on NY 30. 135 sites; showers; dump station.

79. Chenango Valley State Park, Chenango, NY 13746. Phone: (607) 648-5251. Located NE of Johnson City off NY 369. 216 sites, 51 with electric; showers; dump station; golf course.

80. Glimmerglass State Park, CR 31, Cooperstown, NY 13326. Phone: (607) 547-8662. Located on Otsego Lake south of US 20 at East Springfield, on CR 31. 39 sites; showers; dump station.

81. Gilbert Lake State Park, Laurens, NY 13796. Phone: (607) 432-2114. Located north of Oneonta via NY 205 and CR 12. 221 sites, 17 with electric; showers; dump station.

82. Hunt's Pond State Park, New Berlin, NY 13411. Phone: (607) 859-2249. Remote location south of New Berlin (NY 80 & 8), off CR 28. 18 sites.

83. Bowman Lake State Park, Oxford, NY 13830. Phone: (607) 334-2718. North of NY 220, 8 miles west of Oxford. 198 sites; showers; dump station.

84. Delta Lake State Park, Route 46, Rome, NY 13440. Phone: (315) 337-4670. Located on Delta Lake north of Rome on NY 46. 101 sites; showers; dump station.

85. Verona Beach State Park, Route 13, Verona Beach, NY 13162. Phone: (315) 762-4463. Located north of Oneida (I-90 exit 34) on NY 13; on Erie Canal & Oneida Lake. 45 sites; showers; dump station.

86. Keuka Lake State Park, Bluff Point (Branchport), NY 14478. Phone: (315) 536-3666. Located SE of Branchport off NY 54A, on north end of West Branch Keuka Lake. 150 sites, 53 with electric; showers; dump station.

87. Stony Brook State Park, Route 36, Dansville, NY 14437. Phone: (585) 335-8111. Located south of Dansville (I-390 exit 4), on NY 36. 125 sites; showers; dump station.

88. Fair Haven Beach State Park, Route 104A, Fair Haven, NY 13064. Phone: (315) 947-5205. Located on Lake Ontario, 15 miles southwest of Oswego via NY 104A, outside Fair Haven. 185 sites, 44 with electric; showers; dump station.

89. Green Lakes State Park, Fayetteville, NY 13066. Phone: (315) 637-6111. Located 6 miles east of Syracuse off NY 5 on Green Lakes Road. 137 sites, 42 with electric; showers; dump station.

90. Hamlin Beach State Park, Hamlin, NY 14464. Phone: (716) 964-2462. Located about 28 miles NW of Rochester off Lake Ontario State Parkway. 232 sites; showers; dump station.

91. Buttermilk Falls State Park, Route 13S, Ithaca, NY 14850. Phone: (607) 273-5761. Located just south of Ithaca on NY 13. 46 sites; showers; dump station.

92. Robert H. Treman State Park, Route 327, Ithaca, NY 14850. Phone: (607)273-3440. Located SW of Ithaca on NY 327, near junction with NY 13. 72 sites, 11 with electric; showers; dump station.

93. Fillmore Glen State Park, Route 38, Moravia, NY 13118. Phone: (800) 456-2267. Located on NY 38 outside of Moravia, on south end of Owasco Lake. 60 sites, 10 with electric; showers; dump station.

94. Sampson State Park, Route 96A, Romulus, NY 14541. Phone: (315) 585-6392. Located south of Geneva (I-90 exit 42) above east side of Seneca Lake. 309 sites, 245 with electric; showers; dump station.

95. Cayuga Lake State Park, Seneca Falls, NY 13148. Phone: (315) 568-5163. Located 4 miles south of Seneca Falls on NY 89. 286 sites, 36 with electric; showers; dump station.

96. Taughannock Falls State Park, Route 89, Trumansburg, NY 14886. Phone: (607) 387-6739. Located 8 miles north of Ithaca on NY 89; on west side of Cayuga Lake. 76 sites, 16 with electric; showers; dump station.

97. Watkins Glen State Park, Route 14 & 414, Watkins Glen, NY 14891. Phone: (607) 535-4511. Located just outside Watkins Glen on NY 14 & 414, south end of Seneca Lake. 305 sites, 54 with electric; showers; dump station.

98. Golden Hill State Park, Barker, NY 14012. Phone: (716) 795-3885. Located on Lake Ontario, north of Barker on NY 18. 50 sites, 22 with electric; showers; dump station.

99. Letchworth State Park, Castile, NY 14427. Phone: (585) 493-3600. Located south of Mount Morris on NY 408, spanning Genesee River gorge. 270 sites with electric; showers; dump station.

100. Darien Lakes State Park, Darien Center, NY 14040. Phone: (585) 547-9242. Located east of Buffalo off US 20, 3 miles west of NY 77. 141 sites, 45 with electric, 50 with sewer; showers; dump station.

101. Evangola State Park, Route 5, Farnham, NY 14061. Phone: (716) 549-8062. Located SW of Buffalo on NY 5, outside Farnham, on Lake Erie. 82 sites, 37 with electric; showers; dump station.

102. Lakeside Beach State Park, Route 18, Waterport, NY 14571. Phone: (585) 682-4888. Located on Lake Ontario, north of Waterport on NY 18. 274 sites with electric; showers; dump station.

103. Four Mile Creek State Park, Route 18, Youngstown, NY 14174. Phone: (716) 745-3802. Located east of Youngstown along NY 18 on Lake Ontario. 266 sites, 121 with electric; showers; dump station.

104. Lake Erie State Park, Route 5, Brocton, NY 14716. Phone: (716) 792-9214. Located on Lake Erie SW of Dunkirk, north of Brocton, on NY 5. 90 sites; showers; dump station.

105. Allegany State Park, Route 17 (I-86), Salamanca, NY 14779. Phone: (716) 354-9121. Located in southern NY, bordering PA state line, off NY 17/I-86 exit 20, outside Salamanca. (Three campgrounds) 318 sites, 128 with electric; showers; dump station(s). *Contact park office for campsite assignment and location.*

North Carolina

North Carolina has 15 State Parks or Recreation Areas with RV facilities. Most (9) of these parks have dump stations and all have shower facilities in the camping area. Most North Carolina parks are available on a first-come, first-serve basis; reservations, if desired, must be made at the particular park. The state has no centralized reservation system. Pets are permitted on leashes. Seniors age 62 or older are eligible for a discount, depending upon the published fee for the particular campsite. Proof of age is required. Rate groups: A, B, and C, depending upon site amenities.

North Carolina Division of Parks & Recreation
Box 27687
Raleigh, NC 27611
Information: (919) 733-4181
Internet: www.ncsparks.net

North Carolina Park Locator

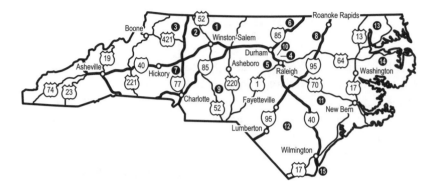

1. Hanging Rock State Park, Danbury, NC 27016. Phone: (336) 593-8480. Located about 25 miles north of Winston-Salem on NC 89. 72 sites.

2. Pilot Mountain State Park, 1792 Pilot Knob Park Rd., Pinnacle, NC 27043. Phone: (336) 325-2355. Located about 20 miles NW of Winston-Salem, off US 52 at Pinnacle exit. 48 sites.

3. Stone Mountain State Park, 3042 Frank Pkwy., Roaring Gap, NC 28668. Phone: (336) 957-8185. Located NW of Winston-Salem and west of I-77 exits 83 or 93, off US 21. 39 sites; dump station.

4. Falls Lake State Recreation Area, 13304 Creedmoor Rd., Wake Forest, NC 27587. Phone: (919) 676-1027. Located about 8 miles north of Raleigh off US 1. 176 sites with electric; dump station.

5. Jordan Lake State Recreation Area, 280 State Park Rd., Apex, NC 27523. Phone: (919) 362-0586. Located about 18 miles west of Raleigh along US 64. 690 sites with electric; dump station.

6. Kerr Lake State Recreation Area, 6254 Satterwhite Point Rd., Henderson, NC 27537. Phone: (252) 438-7791 Located north of Henderson near VA state line, off NC 39. 698 sites; 342 with electric; dump station.

7. Lake Norman State Park, 159 Inland Sea Lane, Troutman, NC 28166. Phone: (704) 528-6350. Located about 7 miles west of I-77 exit 49 via US 21, NC 1301, and NC 1321. 30 sites; dump station.

8. Medoc Mountain State Park, 1541 Medoc State Park Rd., Hollister, NC

27844. Phone: (252) 586-6588. Located west of I-95 between exits 150 & 160 on NC 48. 34 sites with electric; dump station.

9. Morrow Mountain State Park, 49104 Morrow Mountain Rd., Albemarle, NC 28001. Phone: (704) 982-4402. Located east of Albemarle (US 52) on NC 740. 104 sites; dump station.

10. William B. Unstead State Park, 8801 Glenwood Ave., Raleigh, NC 27612. Phone: (919) 571-4170. Located between Raleigh and Durham, off US 70. 29 sites.

11. Cliffs of the Neuse State Park, 345-A Park Entrance Rd., Seven Springs, NC 28578. Phone: (919) 778-6234. Located SE of Goldsboro on NC 111. 33 sites; dump station.

12. Jones Lake State Park, 113 Jones Lake Dr., Elizabethtown, NC 28337. Phone: (910) 588-4550. Located SE of Fayetteville on NC 242. 20 sites.

13. Merchants Millpond State Park, 71 US 158 E, Gatesville, NC 27938. Phone: (252) 357-1191. Located in northeastern NC, outside Sunbury on NC 32. 20 sites.

14. Pettigrew State Park, 2252 Lake Shore Rd., Creswell, NC 27928. Phone: (252) 797-4475. Located in eastern NC, south of Creswell, off US 64; follow signs from Creswell and Cherry. 13 sites.

15. Carolina Beach State Park, Carolina Beach, NC 28428. Phone: (910) 458-8206. Located in southeastern NC, on US 421, south of Wilmington. 80 sites; dump station.

North Dakota

North Dakota has 15 state parks with RV camping spaces and facilities. These parks have more than 1300 sites, most of which are available on a first-come, first-served basis. Some sites are reservable through the toll-free state reservation number or online. All parks require a valid entrance permit (daily or annual) plus daily camping fees. Some sites offer 50-amp electrical service; most are 30-amp. Off-season fees (September 30 through late May) are less than in-season. All locations have drinking water. Rate groups: A and B plus entrance fee.

North Dakota Parks & Recreation
1600 East Century Ave., Ste. 3
Bismarck, ND 58503
Information: (701) 328-5357 / Reservations: (800) 807-4723
Internet: www.ndparks.com

North Dakota Park Locator

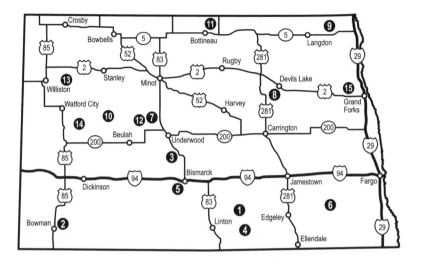

1. Beaver Lake State Park, 3850 70th St. SE, Wishek, ND 58495. Phone:
    (701) 452-2752. Located off ND 3, 17 miles SE of Napoleon (ND 3 & 34).
    25 sites with electric; showers; dump station. Reservations OK.

2. Butte View State Campground, Bowman, ND 58623. Phone: (701) 523-
    3896. Located I mile east of Bowman on US 12. 50 sites with electric;
    showers; dump station. No reservations.

3. Cross Ranch State Park, 1403 River Rd., Center, ND 58530. Phone:
    (701) 794-3731. Located 12 miles SE of Hensler, off ND 200A (exit US
    83 at Washburn). 70 sites with electric; showers; dump station.
    Reservations OK.

4. Doyle Memorial State Recreation Area, Wishek, ND 58495. Phone: (701)
    452-2250. Located on Green Lake, 7 miles SE of Wishek, off ND 3 & 13.
    6 sites with electric; showers; dump station. No reservations.

5. Fort Abraham Lincoln State Park, 4480 Ft. Lincoln Rd., Mandan, ND
    58003. Phone: 701-667-6340. Located 7 miles south of Mandan on ND
    1806 (I-94 exit 147). 96 sites with electric; showers; dump station.
    Reservations OK.

6. Fort Ransom State Park, 5981 Walt Hjelle Pkwy, Ft. Ransom, ND 58033.
    Phone: (701) 973-4331. Located 2 miles north of Fort Ransom, off ND

32, about 25 miles south of I-94 exit 302. 30 sites with electric; showers; dump station. Reservations OK.

7. Fort Stevenson State Park, 1252A 41st Ave. NW, Garrison, ND 58540. Phone: (701) 743-4122. Located 3 miles south of Garrison. Exit US 83 at ND 37 to Garrison. 145 sites with electric; showers; dump station. Reservations OK.

8. Grahams Island State Parks, 152 S Duncan Dr., Devils Lake, ND 58301. Phone: (701) 766-4015. There are 3 areas on Devils Lake. Located SW of Devils Lake off ND 57 and US 2. 70 sites with electric; showers; dump station. Reservations OK.

9. Icelandic State Park, 13571 Hwy 5, Cavalier, ND 58220. Phone: (701) 265-4561. Located 5 miles west of Cavalier on Hwy 5 (about 19 miles west of I-29 exit 203). 165 sites with electric; showers; dump station. Reservations OK.

10. Indian Hills State Recreation Area, Garrison, ND 58540. Phone: (701) 743-4122. Located 31 miles west of Garrison via ND 37 and ND 1804; on Lake Sakakawea. 63 sites with electric; showers; dump station. Contact park for reservations.

11. Lake Metigoshe State Park, #2 Lake Metigoshe State Park, Bottineau, ND 58318. Phone: (701) 263-4651. Located 16 miles NE of Bottineau on ND 43, off ND 14. 130 sites with electric; showers; dump station. Reservations OK.

12. Lake Sakakawea State Park, Riverdale, ND 58565. Phone: (701) 487-3315. Located north of Pick City off ND 200 about 16 miles west of US 83. 300 sites with electric; showers; dump station. Reservations OK.

13. Lewis & Clark State Park, 4904 119th Rd. NW, Epping, ND 58843. Phone: (701) 859-3071. Located 19 miles east of Williston (US 2 & 85) on ND 1804. 87 sites with electric; showers; dump station. Reservations OK.

14. Little Missouri State Park, Killdeer, ND 58640 (satellite of Cross Ranch State Park). Phone: (701) 764-5256. Located 19 miles north of Killdeer (ND 22 & 200) off ND 22. 30 sites with electric. Contact park for reservations.

15. Turtle River State Park, 3084 Park Ave., Arvilla, ND 58214. Phone: (701) 594-4445. Located 22 miles west of Grand Forks and I-29 on US 2. 125 sites with electric; showers; dump station. Reservations OK.

Ohio

Ohio boasts 57 State Parks for RVers, many of which are on lakes or waterways. Most of these parks have electric hook-ups (some 50-amps) and dump stations. Eight parks have sewer and water at the sites. Most of the parks are open year round but some of the facilities are curtailed in cold months. Dump stations are free to campers but charge $10 per use for non-campers. Campsites are available on a first-come basis but one can call ahead for same day rentals. Major credit cards are accepted. Pets are permitted in campgrounds. Six parks (Deer Creek, Hueston Woods, Maumee Bay, Punderson, Salt Fork and Shawnee) have golf courses. Rate groups: B and C depending upon site facilities.

Ohio Department of Natural Resources
Division of Parks and Recreation
1952 Belcher Drive, C-3
Columbus, OH 43224
Information: (800) 282-5393; (800) BUCKEYE
Reservations: (866) 644-6727 or call particular park.
Internet: www.ohiostateparks.org (Also for reservations)

Ohio Park Locator

Ohio Park Locator (cont.)

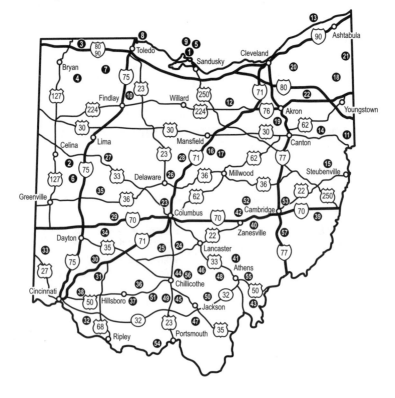

1. East Harbor State Park, Lakeside/Marblehead, OH 43440. Phone: (419) 734-5857. Located on Lake Erie east of Port Clinton on OH 269, off US 2. 570 sites, 365 with electric (50-amp); showers; laundry; dump station. 35+ foot limit.

2. Grand Lake St. Mary's State Park, 834 Edgewater Dr., St. Mary's, OH 45885. Phone: (419) 394-2774. Located west of St. Mary's (I-75 exit 110) on OH 703. 210 sites, 129 with electric; showers; laundry; dump station. 35 foot limit.

3. Harrison Lake State Park, 26246 Harrison Lake Rd., Fayette, OH 43521. Phone: (419) 237-2593. Located 5 miles southwest of Fayette via US 20 and County Hwy 26. 196 sites, 144 with electric (50-amp); showers; laundry; dump station. 35 foot limit.

4. Independence Dam State Park, 27722 State Route 424, Defiance, OH 43512. Phone: (419) 784-3263. Located just east of Defiance on OH 424. 40 sites. 30 foot limit.

5. Kelleys State Park, 4049 E Moores Dock Rd., Port Clinton, OH 43452. Phone: (419) 746- 2546. Located on Lake Erie, on Kelleys Island NE of Port Clinton. 127 sites, 82 with electric (50-amp); showers; dump station. 35 foot limit (See South Bass Island State Park).

6. Lake Loramie State Park, 4401 Ft. Loramie Swanders Rd., Minster, OH 45865. Phone: (937) 295- 2011. Located on Lake Loramie, east of Minster off OH 363. 162 sites, 161 with electric; showers; laundry; dump station. 35+ foot limit.

7. Mary Jane Thurston State Park, 1466 State Route 65, McClure, OH 43534. Phone: (419) 832-7662. Located on OH 65 between US 6 & 24, east of Napoleon. 35 sites. 35 foot limit.

8. Maumee Bay State Park, 1400 State Park Rd., Oregon, OH 43618. Phone: (419) 836-8828. Located on Lake Erie, 7 miles northeast of Oregon via OH 2 and Norden Rd. 252 sites with electric; showers; laundry; dump station. 60 foot limit.

9. South Bass Island State Park, 4049 E Moores Dock Rd., Port Clinton, OH 43452. Phone: (419) 285-2112. Located on South Bass Island in Lake Erie, north of Port Clinton; only accessible by ferry. 135 sites, 10 with electric (50-amp); showers; dump station. 35 foot limit.

10. Van Buren State Park, 12259 Township Road 218, Van Buren, OH 45889. Phone: (419) 832-7662. Located north of Findlay at I-75 exit 164 and OH 613. 78 sites; dump station. 35 foot limit.

11. Beaver Creek State Park, 12021 Echo Dell Rd., East Liverpool, OH 43920.
    Phone: (330) 385-3091. Located north of East Liverpool, off OH 7, about
    6 miles north of OH 11. 53 sites; dump station. 35 foot limit.

12. Findley State Park, 25381 State Route 58, Wellington, OH 44090. Phone:
    (440) 647-4490. Located 3 miles south of Wellington on OH 58. 272 sites;
    showers; laundry; dump station. 40 foot limit.

13. Geneva State Park, 4499 Padanarum Rd., Geneva, OH 44041. Phone:
    (440) 466-8400. On Lake Erie, north of Geneva and I-90 exit 218 via OH
    534. 91 sites with electric; showers; laundry; dump station. 40 foot limit.

14. Guilford Lake State Park, 6835 E Lake Rd., Lisbon, OH 44432. Phone:
    (330) 222-1712. Located off OH 172 between Canton and OH 11. 41
    sites with electric (50-amp); showers; dump station. 35 foot limit.

15. Jefferson Lake State Park, 501 Township Road 261-A, Richmond, OH
    43944. Phone: (330) 222-1712. Located 5 miles northwest of Richmond
    via OH 43 and County Hwy 54. 97 sites; dump station. 35 foot limit.

16. Malabar Farm State Park, 4050 Bromfield Rd., Lucas, OH 44843. Phone:
    (419) 892-2784. Located SE of Mansfield and I-71 exits 165 or 169; follow
    signs. 15 sites.

17. Mohican State Park, 3116 State Route 3, Loudonville, OH 44842. Phone:
    (419) 994-5125. Located SE of Mansfield on OH 3, near Loudonville. 186
    sites, 153 with electric (50-amp); showers; laundry; dump station. 40 foot
    limit.

18. Mosquito Lake State Park, 1439 State Route 305, Cortland, OH 44410.
    Phone: (330) 637-2856. Located on Mosquito Lake, north of Warren on
    OH 305. 234 sites, 217 with electric (50-amp); showers; laundry; dump
    station. 35 foot limit.

19. Portage Lakes State Park, 5031 Manchester Rd., Akron, OH 44319.
    Phone: (330) 644-2220. Located SE of Barberton off OH 93 near OH
    619. 74 sites; dump station. 35 foot limit.

20. Punderson State Park, 11755 Kinsman Rd., Newbury, OH 44065. Phone:
    (440) 564-1195. Located 15 miles east of Beachwood and I-271 exit 29
    via OH 87. 191 sites with electric; showers; laundry; dump station. 35 foot
    limit.

21. Pymatuning State Park, 6260 Pymatuning Park Rd., Andover, OH 44003. Phone: (440) 293-6684. Located on Pymatuning Reservoir north of Andover, off OH 85. 370 sites, 349 with electric; showers; laundry; dump station. 35 foot limit.

22. West Branch State Park, 5708 Esworthy Rd., Ravenna, OH 44266. Phone: (330) 296-3239. Located on Kerwin Reservoir, east of Akron, off OH 5. 103 sites, 50 with electric (50-amp); showers; laundry; dump station. 35 foot limit.

23. Alum Creek State Park, 3615 S Old State Rd., Delaware, OH 43015. Phone: (740) 548-4631. Located between US 23 & I-71, 15 miles north of Columbus. 287 sites with electric (50-amp); showers; laundry; dump station. 35 foot limit.

24. A.W. Marion State Park, 7317 Warner-Huffer Rd., Circleville, OH (mail: c/o Deer Creek State Park, below). Phone: (740) 869-3124. Located 6 miles northeast of Circleville via US 22 and Ringold Southern Rd. 58 sites, 29 with electric, (50-amp); dump station. 35 foot limit.

25. Deer Creek State Park, 20635 Waterloo Rd., Mt. Sterling, OH 43143. Phone: (740) 869-3508. Located south of Mt. Sterling, off OH 207. 227 sites with electric; showers; laundry; dump station. 40 foot limit.

26. Delaware State Park, 5202 US 23 N, Delaware, OH 43015. Phone: (740) 363-4561. Located on Delaware Lake about 8 miles north of Delaware on US 23. 211 sites, 161 with electric (20-amp); showers; laundry; dump station. 35 foot limit.

27. Indian Lake State Park, 12774 State Route 235 N, Lakeview, OH 43331. Phone: (937) 843-3553. Located about 12 miles northwest of Bellefontaine via US 33. 461 sites, 418 with electric (some 50-amp); showers; laundry; dump station. 35 foot limit.

28. Mount Gilead State Park, 4119 State Route 95, Mt. Gilead, OH 43338. Phone: (419) 946-1961. Located outside Mt. Gilead on OH 95, off US 42. 65 sites, 59 with electric (50-amp); dump station. 40+ foot limit.

29. Buck Creek State Park, State Park, 1901 Buck Creek Lane, Springfield, OH 45502. Phone: (937) 322-5284. Located east of Springfield on Brown Reservoir, off OH 4. 101 sites, 89 with electric; showers; laundry; dump station. 35 foot limit.

30. Caesar Creek State Park, 8570 E State Route 73, Waynesville, OH 45068. Phone: (573) 897-3055. Located on Caesar Creek Lake along OH 73, west of I-71 exit 45. 284 sites with electric; showers; laundry; dump station. 40 foot limit.

31. Cowan Lake State Park, 1750 Osborn Rd., Wilmington, OH 45177. Phone: (937) 382-1096. Located SW of Wilmington, off US 68 and OH 350. 254 sites, 237 with electric (50-amp); showers; laundry; dump station. 35 foot limit.

32. East Fork State Park, Bethel, OH 45106. Phone: (513) 734-4323. Located on East Fork Lake, southeast of Cincinnati on OH 133, between OH 32 & 125. 399 sites with electric; showers; laundry; dump station. 30 foot limit.

33. Hueston Woods State Park, 6301 Park Office Rd., College Corner, OH 45003. Phone: (513) 523-1060. Located near Indiana state line, NW of Oxford, off US 27. 488 sites, 252 with electric; showers; laundry; dump station. 35 foot limit.

34. John Bryan State Park, 3790 State Route 370, Yellow Springs, OH 45387. Phone: (937) 767-1274. Located on OH 370, northeast of Dayton, off OH 343, near Clifton. 100 sites, 10 with electric (50-amp); dump station. 40 foot limit.

35. Kiser Lake State Park, 4889 N State Route 235, St. Paris, OH 43072. Phone: (937) 362-3822. Located on OH 235 between Urbana and Sidney, north of US 36. 114 sites; dump station. 40 foot limit.

36. Paint Creek State Park, 14265 US Route 50, Bainbridge, OH 45612. Phone: (937) 981-7061. Located on Paint Creek Lake, NW of Bainbridge, off US 50. 195 sites with electric (20-amp); showers; laundry; dump station. 50 foot limit.

37. Rocky Fork State Park, 9800 North Shore Dr., Hillsboro, OH 45133. Phone: (937) 393-4284. Located on Rocky Fork Lake, east of Hillsboro, off US 50. 230 sites, 130 with electric (50-amp); showers; laundry; dump station. 35+ foot limit.

38. Stonelick State Park, 2895 Lake Dr., Pleasant Plain, OH 45162. Phone: (513) 625-7544. Located on Stonelick Lake, east of Cincinnati, off OH 727. 113 sites, 107 with electric (50-amp); showers; laundry; dump station. 35+ foot limit.

39. Barkcamp State Park, 65330 Barkcamp Rd., Belmont, OH 43718. Phone: (740) 484-4064. Located near Belmont off I-70 exit 208, between Wheeling, WV and Cambridge, OH. 150 sites with electric (50-amp); showers; dump station. 35 foot limit.

40. Blue Rock State Park, 7924 Cutler Lake Rd., Blue Rock, OH 43720. Phone: (740) 674-4794. Located SE of Zanesville off OH 60. 94 sites; showers; dump station. 40 foot limit.

41. Burr Oak State Park, 10220 Burr Oak Lodge Rd., Glouster, OH 45732. Phone: (740) 767-3570. Located on Burr Oak Reservoir between Athens and New Lexington, off OH 13. 100 sites; showers; laundry; dump station. 30 foot limit.

42. Dillon State Park, 5265 Dillon Hills Dr., Nashport, OH 43830. Phone: (740) 452-1083. Located on Dillon Lake between Newark and Zanesville, off OH 146. 193 sites, 181 with electric (50-amp); showers; laundry; dump station. 40 foot limit.

43. Forked Run State Park, 63300 State Route 124, Reedsville, OH 45772. Phone: (740) 378-6206. Located on the Ohio River, SE of Athens, south of Reedsville, on OH 124. 192 sites; showers; laundry; dump station. 30 foot limit.

44. Great Seal State Park, 635 Rocky Rd., Chillicothe, OH 45601. Phone: (740) 663-2125. Located outside Chillicothe, off US 23 (follow signs). 15 sites. Small rigs. (See Scioto Trail State Park)

45. Scioto Trail State Park, 144 Lake Rd., Chillicothe, OH 45601. Phone: (740) 663-2125. Located about 7 miles south of Chillicothe, off US 23. 73 sites, 40 with electric (50-amp); dump station. 35 foot limit.

46. Hocking Hills State Park, 19852 State Route 664 S, Logan, OH. Phone: (740) 385-6842. Located SW of Logan on OH 664 in Hocking State Forest. 172 sites, 159 with electric (some 20-amp, some 50-amp); showers; laundry; dump station. 50 foot limit.

47. Jackson Lake State Park, 35 Tommy Been Rd., Oak Hill, OH 45656. Phone: (740) 682-6197. South of Jackson via OH 93 and OH 279. 34 sites with electric (50-amp); dump station. 35 foot limit.

48. Lake Hope State Park, 27331 State Route 278, McArthur, OH 45651.

Phone: (740) 596-9938 or 596-5253. Located NE of McArthur, off US 50 on OH 278. 219 sites, 46 with electric (50-amp); showers; laundry; dump station. 35 foot limit.

49. Lake White State Park, 2767 State Route 551, Waverly, OH 45690. Phone: (740) 947-4059. Located on Lake White, SW of Waverly via US 23 and OH 104. 10 sites. 35 foot limit.

50. Lake Alma State Park, Wellston, OH 45692. Phone: (740) 384-4474. Located north of Wellston, off OH 32/124; follow signs. 83 sites, 72 with electric (some 50-amp); dump station. 40 foot limit.

51. Pike Lake State Park, 1847 Pike Lake Rd., Bainbridge, OH 45612. Phone: (740) 493-2212. Located 7 miles south of Bainbridge via county roads. 78 sites with electric (50-amp); dump station. 35 foot limit.

52. Muskingum River State Park, 7924 Cutler Lake Rd., Blue Rock, OH 43720. Phone: (740) 674-4794. Located on Muskingum River, north of Zanesville, off OH 60. 20 sites. Small rigs.

53. Salt Fork State Park, 14755 Cadiz Rd., Lore City, OH 43755. Phone: (740) 432-1508. Located northeast of Cambridge and I-77 exit 47 via US 22. 212 sites with electric (50-amp); showers; laundry; dump station. 35 foot limit.

54. Shawnee State Park, 4401 State Route 125, Portsmouth, OH 45663. Phone: (740) 858-4561. West of Portsmouth on Roosevelt Lake along OH 125. 106 sites, 103 with electric (some 20-amp; some 50-amp); showers; laundry; dump station. 35 foot limit.

55. Strouds Run State Park, 11661 State Park Rd., Athens, OH 45701. Phone: (740) 592-2302. Located off US 50, just east of Athens. 75 sites; dump station. 35 foot limit.

56. Tar Hollow State Park, 16396 Tar Hollow Rd., Laurelville, OH 43135. Phone: (740) 887-4818. Located east of Chillicothe via US 50 and OH 327. 113 sites, 28 with electric (50-amp); showers; laundry; dump station. 35 foot limit.

57. Wolf Run State Park, 16170 Wolf Run Road, Caldwell, OH 43724. Phone: (740) 732-5035. East of Belle Valley and I-77 exit 28 via OH 821 and OH 215. 138 sites, 71 with electric (50-amp); showers; laundry; dump station. 35 foot limit.

Oklahoma

When it comes to state parks with RV facilities, The Sooner State takes a back seat to no one! Oklahoma offers the RVer 46 state parks and/or resorts, all of which have some campground sites equipped with an electric hook-up. Many parks have numerous full hook-up sites and all have drinking water in the respective park, if not at the site. Rig size is not a problem in any of the listed parks. All are open year round and they accept major credit cards. Reservations are accepted at some parks, so the traveler should check with the particular park. Senior discounts are available for residents of participating states, so you must inquire at check-in and request this discount. Proof of age is required. Pets on leashes are OK. Rate groups: B and C, no additional entrance fee.

Oklahoma Tourism & Recreation Dept.
Travel & Tourism Division
Box 52002
Oklahoma City, OK 73152
Information: (800) 652-6552 / Reservations: (800) 654-8240
Internet: www.oklahomaparks.com

Oklahoma Park Locator

Oklahoma Park Locator (*cont.*)

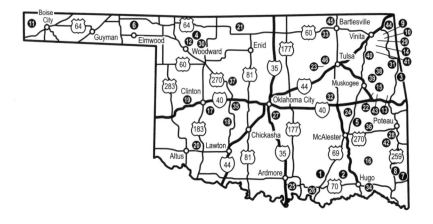

1. Boggy Depot State Park, Atoka, OK 74525. Phone: (580) 889-5625.
    Located off OK 7, 11 miles west of Atoka, on Park Lane Road. 106 sites;
    6 full hook-ups; 20 with electric, water; 80 primitive; showers; dump station.

2. McGee Creek State Park, Atoka, OK 74525. Phone: (580) 889-5822.
    Located on McGee Creek Dam Road, SE of Atoka via OK 3, north of
    Farris. 86 sites; 41 with electric, water; 45 primitive; showers; dump station.

3. Adair State Park, Stilwell, OK 74960. Phone: (918) 696-7143. Located in
    eastern OK, outside Adair on OK 51. 26 sites; 6 with electric, water; 20
    primitive sites; showers.

4. Alabaster Caverns State Park, Freedom, OK 73842. Phone: (580) 621-
    3381. Located in northern OK between US 64 & 412, on OK 50. 23 sites;
    11 with electric, water; 12 primitive; showers; dump station.

5. Arrowhead State Park, Canadian, OK 74425. Phone: (918) 339-2204.
    Located in eastern OK, 15 miles north of McAlester on US 69. 150 sites;

20 full hook-ups; 61 with electric, water; 69 primitive; showers; dump station. Golf course. (Also see Lake Eufaula State Park.)

14

6. Beaver Dunes State Park, Beaver, OK 73932. Phone: (580) 625-3373. Located in "Panhandle" on US 270 between US 64 & 412. 17 sites; 7 with electric (50-amp), water; 10 primitive; showers; dump station.

7. Beavers Bend State Resort Park, Broken Bow, OK 74728. Phone: (580) 494-6300. Located on Broken Bow Lake in southeastern OK, 11 miles north of Broken Bow on US 259A. 380 sites; 15 full hook-ups; 15 with electric, water; 350 primitive; showers; dump station. (Also see Hochatown State Park.)

8. Hochatown State Park, Broken Bow, OK 74728. Phone: (580) 494-6300. Located on Broken Bow Lake, on US 259, 13 miles north of Broken Bow. 202 sites, 24 full hook-ups; 27 with electric, water; 151 primitive; showers; dump station. Golf course.

9. Bernice State Park, Grove, OK 74344. Phone: (918) 786-9447. Located 8 miles off I-44 exit 302 in northeastern OK, off OK 89A. 34 sites with electric, water; showers; dump station. (See Honey Creek State Park.)

10. Honey Creek State Park, Grove, OK 74344. Phone: (918) 786-9447. Located in northeastern OK, south of Grove off US 59. 106 sites; 53 with electric, water; 53 primitive.

11. Black Mesa State Park, Kenton, OK 73946. Phone: (580) 426-2222. Located in west tip of the "Panhandle," 27 miles NW of Boise City on CR 325. 63 sites; 33 with electric, water; 30 primitive; showers; dump station.

12. Boiling Springs State Park, Woodward, OK 73802. Phone: (580) 256-7664. Located in northern OK, 8 miles NE of Woodward on OK 34C. 88 sites; 10 full hook-up; 66 with electric, water; 12 primitive; showers; dump station.

13. Brushy Lake State Park, Sallisaw, OK 74955. Phone: (918) 775-6507. Located in eastern OK, 8 miles north of Sallisaw, on US 59. 58 sites; 23 with electric, water; 35 primitive; showers; dump station.

14. Cherokee State Park, Disney, OK 74340. Phone: (918) 435-8066. Located in northeastern OK, outside Langley on OK 82. 124 sites; 34 with electric, water; 90 primitive; showers; dump station.

15. Cherokee Landing State Park, Park Hill, OK 74451. Phone: (918) 457-5716. Located in eastern OK, 14 miles south of Tahlequah on OK 82. 164 sites; 116 with electric, water; 48 primitive; showers; dump station.

16. Clayton Lake State Park, Clayton, OK 74536. Phone: (918) 569-7981. Located in southeastern OK, 5 miles south of Clayton on US 271. 58 sites; 25 with electric, water; 33 primitive; showers; dump station.

17. Crowder Lake State Park, Weatherford, OK 73096. Phone: (405) 343-2443. Located in western OK, 10 miles south of Weatherford (I-40 exit 80) off OK 54, follow signs. 8 sites; 5 full hook-ups; 3 primitive; showers; dump station.

18. Fort Cobb State Park, Fort Cobb, OK 73038. Phone: (405) 643-2249. Located on Fort Cobb Lake in west-central OK, 25 miles south of I-40, 6 miles north of Fort Cobb. 360 sites; 308 with electric, water; 52 primitive. Golf course.

19. Foss State Park, Foss, OK 73647. Phone: (580) 592-4433. Located on Foss Lake in western OK, 7 miles north of I-40 exit 53, off OK 44, follow signs. 6 campgrounds with 142 sites; 100 with electric, water; 42 primitive; showers; dump stations.

20. Great Plains State Park, Mountain Park, OK 73559. Phone: (580) 560-2032. Located in southwestern OK, 6 miles north of Snyder via US 183. 95 sites; 14 full hook-ups; 44 with electric, water; 37 primitive; showers; dump station.

21. Great Salt Plains State Park, Jet, OK 73749. Phone: (580) 626-4731. Located on Great Salt Plains Lake, 8 miles north of Jet (US 64) on OK 38. 170 sites; 64 with electric, water; 106 primitive; showers; dump station.

22. Greenleaf State Park, Braggs, OK 74423. Phone: (918) 487-5196. Located on Greenleaf Lake in eastern OK, 17 miles southeast of Muskogee via US 62 and OK 10. 98 sites; 22 full hook-up; 76 with electric, water; showers; dump station.

23. Lake Keystone State Park, Mannford, OK 74044. Phone: (918) 865-4991. Located 16 miles west of Tulsa via US 64/412 (Keystone Expressway) and OK 151. 148 sites; 40 full hook-up; 36 with electric, water; 72 primitive; showers; dump station.

24. Lake Eufaula State Park, Checotah, OK 74426. Phone: (918) 689-5311. Located 14 miles southwest of Checotah off I-40 exit 259 and OK 150. 198 sites; 34 full hook-ups; 59 with electric, water; 105 primitive; showers; dump station. (Also see Arrowhead State Park.)

25. Lake Murray State Resort Park, Ardmore, OK 73401. Phone: (580) 223-9339. Located south of Ardmore in southern OK, east of I-35 exits 24 or 29. 261 sites; 56 full hook-up; 295 with electric, water; showers; dump station. Golf course.

26. Lake Texoma State Resort Park, Kingston, OK 73439. Phone: (580) 564-2566. Located in southern OK near TX state line, 4 miles east of Kingston on US 70. 400 sites; 153 full hook-up; 42 with electric, water; 205 primitive; showers; dump station. Golf course.

27. Lake Thunderbird State Park, Norman, OK 73026. Phone: (405) 350-3572. Located in central OK, 13 miles east of I-35 exit 108A via OK 9. 549 sites; 30 full hookup; 228 with electric (50-amp), water; 291 primitive; showers; dump station.

28. Lake Wister State Park, Wister, OK 74966. Phone: (918) 655-7756. Located 2 miles south of Wister in eastern OK, on US 270. 197 sites; 16 full hook-up; 86 with electric, water; 95 primitive; showers; dump station.

29. Disney/Little Blue State Park, Disney, OK 74340. Phone: (918) 435-8066. Located outside Disney in northeastern OK, on OK 28. 80 primitive sites.

30. Little Sahara State Park, Waynoka, OK 73860. Phone: (580) 824-1471. Located in northwestern OK, 4 miles south of Waynoka, between US 412 & 64 on US 281. 180 sites; 90 with electric (30 & 50-amp), water; 90 primitive; showers.

31. Natural Falls State Park, West Siloam Springs, OK 74338. Phone: (918) 422-5802. Located in eastern OK near AR state line, 3 miles west of West Siloam Springs on US 412. 74 sites; 44 with electric, water; 30 primitive; showers; dump station.

32. Okmulgee & Dripping Springs State Parks, Okmulgee, OK 74447. Phone: (918) 756-5971. Two parks, 3 miles apart. Located south of Tulsa in eastern OK, 6 miles west of Okmulgee on OK 56. 244 sites (total); 122 with electric, water; 122 primitive; showers; dump stations.

33. Osage Hills State Park, Pawhuska, OK 74056. Phone: (918) 336-4141. Located in northeastern OK on US 60, 12 miles west of Bartlesville. 55 sites; 20 with electric, water; 35 primitive; showers; dump station.

34. Raymond Gary State Park, Fort Towson, OK 74735. Phone: (580) 873-2307. Located in southeastern OK, near TX state line; 15 miles east of Hugo on US 70; on lake Raymond Gary. 119 sites; 10 full hook-up; 9 with electric, water; 100 primitive; showers; dump station.

35. Red Rock Canyon State Park, Hinton, OK 73047. Phone: (405) 542-6344. Located west of Oklahoma City, 5 miles south of I-40 exit 101 via US 281. 81 sites; 5 full hook-up; 46 with electric, water; 30 primitive; showers; dump station.

36. Robbers Cave State Park, Wilburton, OK 74578. Phone: (918) 465-2562.

Located in southeastern OK, 4 miles north of Wilburton on OK 2, north off US 270. 115 sites; 19 full hook-up; 62 with electric, water; 34 primitive; showers; dump station.

37. Roman Nose State Resort Park, Watonga, OK. Phone: (580) 623-4215. Located NW of Oklahoma City, 7 miles north of Watonga, off US 270/281 on OK 8A. 96 sites; 32 full hook-up; 64 primitive; showers; dump station. Golf course.

38. Western Hills Guest Ranch/Sequoyah Resort Park, Wagoner, OK 74477. Phone: (918) 772-2046. Located on Fort Gibson Lake in eastern OK, 8 miles east of Wagoner, off US 69 on OK 51. 367 sites; 28 full hook-up; 149 with electric, water; 190 primitive; showers; dump station. Golf course.

39. Sequoyah Bay State Park, Wagoner, OK 74477. Phone: (918) 683-0878. Located in eastern OK, 4 miles south of Wagoner on OK 16, follow signs. 84 sites with electric, water; showers; dump station.

40. Snowdale State Park, Salina, OK 74340. Phone: (918) 435-8066. Located in northeastern OK, 8 miles east of Pryor via OK 20. 84 sites; 18 with electric, water; 66 primitive; showers; dump station.

41. Spavinaw State Park, (Spavinaw) Disney, OK 74340. Phone: (918) 435-8066. Located on Lake Hudson in northeastern OK, 14 miles east of Pryor on OK 20. 86 sites; 26 with electric, water; 60 primitive; dump station.

42. Talimena State Park, Talihina, OK 74571. Phone: (918) 567-2052. Located in southeastern OK, 7 miles north of Talihina on US 271. 45 sites; 10 with electric, water; 35 primitive; showers; dump station.

43. Lake Tenkiller State Park, Vian, OK 74962. Phone: (918) 489-5643. Located on Lake Tenkiller in eastern OK, off I-40 exit 297 (Vian), 10 miles north on OK 82, follow signs. 239 sites; 37 full hook-up; 50 with electric, water; 152 primitive; showers; dump station.

44. Twin Bridges State Park, Fairland, OK 74343. Phone: (918) 540-2545. Located in far northeastern OK, 6 miles NE of Fairland at OK 137/US 60. 172 sites; 62 with electric, water; 110 primitive; showers; dump station.

45. Wah-Sha-She State Park, Copan, OK 74022. Phone: (918) 532-4627. Located on Hulah Lake in northeastern OK near KS state line, 10 miles west of Copan via OK 10. 106 sites; 46 with electric, water; 60 primitive; showers; dump station.

46. Walnut Creek State Park, New Prue, OK 74060. Phone: (918) 242-3362. On Keystone Lake northwest of Tulsa off US 412 (Cimarron Turnpike), 13 miles north on 209th West Avenue, follow signs. 79 sites; 8 full hook-up; 71 with electric, water; showers; dump station.

Oregon

There are 45 State Parks or Recreation Areas in Oregon with RV facilities. About half of these locations accept reservations, however, space permitting, all will accept campers on a "first-come" basis. Travelers on the Oregon Coast should be aware that this area is very popular in late Spring through early Autumn and sites are often hard to procure. The reservation system requires two days notice. RVers should always call these Reservable locations before stopping. Most Oregon parks have campsites with electric and a good number feature full hook-up sites. Parks with primitive sites do have water in the park. Unless otherwise noted, all parks are open year round. Discovery Season, October 1 through April 30, offers lower camping fees and smaller crowds. Rate groups: B and C depending on site facilities.

Oregon Parks and Recreation Dept.
1115 Commercial St. NE, Ste. 1
Salem, OR 97301
Information: (800) 551-6949 or (503) 378-6305
Reservations: (800) 452-5687
Internet: www.oregonstateparks.org

Oregon Park Locator

Oregon Park Locator (*cont.*)

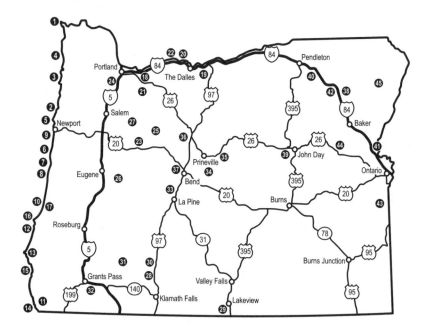

1. Fort Stevens State Park, Hammond, OR 97121. Phone: (503) 861-1671. Located in northwestern OR off US 101, west of Astoria at the mouth of the Columbia River. 477 sites, 174 full hook-ups, 303 sites with electric; showers; dump station. 50 foot limit.

2. Devil's Lake State Recreation Area, Lincoln City, OR 97367. Phone: (541) 994-2002. Located in northwestern OR on the coast off US 101, outside Lincoln City. 32 sites, 28 full hook-ups, 4 with electric; showers. 45 foot limit.

3. Cape Lookout State Park, Tillamook, OR 97141. Phone: (503) 842-4981. Located in northwestern OR off US 101 on Three Capes Scenic Loop, 12 miles SW of Tillamook; follow signs from 101. 39 sites, 38 full hook-ups, 1 with electric; showers; dump station. 60 foot limit.

4. Nehalem Bay State Park, Nehalem Bay, OR 97131. Phone: (503) 368-5141. Located in northwestern OR, 3 miles south of Manzanita junction, off US 101. 270 sites with electric; showers; dump station. 60 foot limit.

5. Beverly Beach State Park, Newport, OR 97365. Phone: (541) 265-9278. Located on central OR coast, 7 miles north of Newport on US 101. 129 sites, 54 full hook-ups, 75 with electric; showers; dump station. 65 foot limit.

6. Beachside State Recreation Site, Waldport, OR 97394. Phone: (541) 563-3220. Located on central OR coast, 3 miles south of Waldport on US 101. 33 sites with electric; showers. 30 foot limit. Seasonal.

7. Carl G. Washburne Memorial State Park, Florence, OR 97439. Phone: (541) 997-3641. Located on central OR coast, 14 miles north of Florence on US 101, near Heceta Head Lighthouse. 58 full hook-up sites; showers; dump station. 45 foot limit. No reservations. Seasonal.

8. Jessie M. Honeyman Memorial State Park, Florence, OR 97439. Phone: (541) 997-3641. Located on central OR coast, 3 miles south of Florence on US 101, next to Oregon Dunes National Recreation Area. 166 sites, 47 full hook-ups, 119 with electric; showers; dump station. 60 foot limit.

9. South Beach State Park, Newport, OR 97366. Phone: (541) 867-4715. Located on central OR coast, 2 miles south of Newport on US 101. 233 sites, 227 with electric, 6 primitive; showers; dump station. 60 foot limit.

10. Umpqua Lighthouse State Park, Reedsport, OR 97467. Phone: (541) 271-4118. Located on south-central OR coast, 6 miles south of Reedsport on US 101, near mouth of Winchester Bay. 20 full hook-up sites; showers. 45 foot limit.

11. Alfred A Loeb State Park, Brookings, OR 97415. Phone: (541) 469-2021. Located in southwestern OR, 10 miles NE of Brookings off US 101, on Chetco River (follow signs from 101.) 48 sites with electric; showers. 50 foot limit. No reservations.

12. Bullards Beach State Park, Bandon, OR 97411. Phone: (541) 347-2209. Located on southern OR coast, 2 miles north of Bandon on US 101, at mouth of Coquille River. 185 sites, 102 full hook-ups, 83 with electric; showers; dump station. 55 foot limit.

13. Cape Blanco State Park, Sixes, OR 97476. Phone: (541) 332-6774. Located on southern OR coast outside Sixes, 9 miles north of Port Orford off US 101. 53 sites with electric; showers; dump station. 65 foot limit. No reservations.

14. Harris Beach State Park, Brookings, OR 97415. Phone: (541) 469-2021. Located on southern OR coast, north side of Brookings, on US 101. 86

sites, 36 full hook-ups, 50 with electric; showers; dump station. 50 foot limit.

15. Humbug Mountain State Park, Port Orford, OR 97465. Phone: (541) 332-6774. Located on southern OR coast, 6 miles south of Port Orford on US 101. 3 sites with electric; showers; dump station. 55 foot limit. No reservations.

16. Sunset Bay State Park, Coos Bay, OR 97420. Phone: (541) 888-4902. Located on southern OR coast, 12 miles SW of Coos Bay off US 101; follow signs. 65 sites, 29 full hook-ups, 36 with electric; showers. 47 foot limit.

17. William M. Tugman State Park, Lakeside, OR 97449. Phone: (541) 888-4902. Located on southern OR coast, 8 miles south of Reedsport, off US 101 on Eel Lake. 100 sites with electric; showers. 50 foot limit.

18. Ainsworth State Park, Hood River, OR 97031. Phone: (503) 695-2301. Located in northwestern OR, 35 miles east of Portland on Historic Columbia River Hwy, off I-84 exit 35. 45 full hook-up sites, some pull-thru; showers; dump station. 60 foot limit. No reservations. Seasonal.

19. Deschutes River State Recreation Area, Wasco, OR 97065. Phone: (541) 739-2322. Located in northwestern OR, 15 miles east of The Dalles, off I-84 exit 97, on Deschutes & Columbia Rivers. 58 sites, 33 with electric, 25 primitive.

20. Memaloose State Park, Hood River, OR 97031. Phone: (541) 478-3008. Located in northwestern OR, 11 miles west of The Dalles on I-84 (westbound access only, at rest area). Eastbound I-84 travelers should use exit 76 and return westbound 3 miles on Interstate. 44 full hook-up sites; showers; dump station. 60 foot limit. Seasonal.

21. Milo McIver State Park, Estacada, OR 97023. Phone: (503) 630-7150. Located in northwestern OR, 25 miles SW of Portland off OR 211, via OR 224 off I-205; follow signs from 224. 44 sites with electric; showers; dump station. 50 foot limit. Seasonal.

22. Viento State Park, Hood River, OR 97031. Phone: (541) 374-8811. Located in northern OR, 8 miles west of Hood River at I-84 exit 56. 57 sites with electric; showers. 30 foot limit. No reservations. Seasonal.

23. Cascadia State Park, Detroit, OR 37342. Phone: (503) 854-3406. Located in central OR, 14 miles east of Sweet Home (I-5 exits 216 or 233) on US 20. 25 primitive sites. 35 foot limit. No reservations. Seasonal.

24. Champoeg State Heritage Area, St. Paul, OR 97137. Phone: (503) 678-1251. Located in western OR about 15 miles south of Portland and 5 miles west of I-5 exit 278. 85 sites, 12 full hook-ups, 67 with electric, 6 with electric, some pull-thrus; showers; dump station. 60 foot limit.

25. Detroit Lake State Recreation Area, Detroit, OR 97342. Phone: (503) 854-3346. Located in west-central OR, 50 miles east of Salem on OR 22. 178 sites, 106 full hook-ups, 72 with electric; showers. 60 foot limit. Seasonal.

26. Fall Creek State Recreation Area, Lowell, OR 97452. Phone: (541) 973-1173. Located in western OR, 27 miles SE of Eugene-Springfield (I-5 exit 186), north of Lowell off OR 58. 42 primitive sites. 45 foot limit. No reservations. Seasonal.

27. Silver Falls State Park, Sublimity, OR 97385. Phone: (503) 873-8681. Located in western OR, 26 miles east of Salem on OR 214, off OR 22 from I-5 exit 253. 47 sites with electric; showers; dump station. 60 foot limit.

28. Collier Memorial State Park, Chiloquin, OR 97624. Phone: (541) 783-2471. Located in southern OR, 30 miles north of Klamath Falls on US 97. 50 full hook-up sites; showers; dump station. 100 foot limit. No reservations. Seasonal.

29. Goose Lake State Recreation Area, LaPine, OR 97739. Phone: (541) 947-3111. Located in southern OR at CA/OR state line on US 395, 1 mile west of New Pine Creek. 47 sites with electric; showers; dump station. 50 foot limit. No reservations. Seasonal.

30. Jackson F. Kimball State Recreation Area, Chiloquin, OR 97624. Phone: (541) 783-2471. Located in southern OR near Crater Lake National Park, 3 miles north of Fort Klamath on OR 232, off US 97. 10 primitive sites; no water. 45 foot limit. No reservations. Seasonal.

31. Joseph H. Stewart State Recreation Area, Trail, OR 97541. Phone: (541) 560-3334. Located in southern OR, 35 miles NE of Medford on OR 62. 151 sites with electric; showers; dump station. 80 foot limit. No reservations. Seasonal.

32. Valley of the Rogue State Park, Gold Hill, OR 97525. Phone: (541) 582-1118. Located in southwestern OR, 12 miles east of Grants Pass at I-5 exit 45B. 146 sites, 98 full hook-ups, 48 with electric; showers; dump station. 75 foot limit.

33. LaPine State Park, LaPine, OR 97739. Phone: (541) 536-2428. Located in central OR, 27 miles SW of Bend, off US 97. 137 sites, 87 full hook-ups, 50 with electric, some pull-thrus; showers; dump station. 85 foot limit.

34. Prineville Reservoir State Park, Prineville, OR 97754. Phone: (541) 447-4363. Located in central OR, 16 miles SE of Prineville off US 26. 45 sites, 22 full hook-ups, 23 with electric; showers. 50 foot limit.

35. Jasper Point (Prineville Reservoir), Prineville, OR 97754. Phone: (541) 447-3875. Located in central OR, 18 miles SE of Prineville off US 26. 30

sites, with electric. 35 foot limit. No reservations. Seasonal.

36. The Cove Palisades State Park, Culver, OR 97734. Phone: (541) 546-3412. Located in central OR, 15 miles SW of Madras off US 97 on Lake Billy Chinook. 87 full hook-up sites; showers; dump station. 60 foot limit.

37. Tumalo State Park, Bend, OR 97701. Phone: (541) 382-3586. Located in central OR, 5 miles NW of Bend off US 20 on Deschutes River. 23 full hook-up sites; showers. 44 foot limit.

38. Catherine Creek State Park, Union, OR 97883. No telephone. Located in northeastern OR, 8 miles SE of Union on OR 203. 20 primitive sites. 50 foot limit.

39. Clyde Holliday State Recreation Site, Mount Vernon, OR 97865. Phone: (541) 932-4453. Located in central OR, 6 miles west of John Day on US 26, near US 395. 31 sites with electric; showers; dump station. 60 foot limit. No reservations. Seasonal.

40. Emigrant Springs State Heritage Area, Meacham, OR 97859. Phone: (541) 983-2277. Located in northeastern OR, 26 miles SE of Pendelton off I-84 exits 228 or 238. 18 full hook-up sites; showers. 60 foot limit. No reservations.

41. Farewell Bend State Recreation Area, Huntington, OR 97907. Phone: (541) 869-2365. Located in eastern OR 1 mile north of I-84 exit 353 on the Snake River. 136 sites, 91 with electric, 45 primitive; showers; dump station. 60 foot limit.

42. Hilgard Junction State Recreation Area, Meacham, OR 97859. Phone: No telephone. Located in northeastern OR, 8 miles west of LaGrande off I-84 exit 252, on Grande Ronde River. 18 primitive sites; dump station. 30 foot limit. No reservations. Seasonal.

43. Lake Owyhee State Park, Adrian, OR 97901. Phone: (541) 339-2331. Located in eastern OR, 33 miles SW of Nyssa (I-84 exit 374), off OR 201; follow signs. 31 sites with electric; showers; dump station. 55 foot limit. No reservations. Seasonal.

44. Unity Lake State Recreation Area, Meacham, OR 97859. Phone: (541) 932-4453. Located in eastern OR, 50 miles east of John Day off US 26 on OR 245. 35 sites with electric; showers; dump station. 60 foot limit. No reservations.

45. Wallowa Lake State Park, Joseph, OR 97846. Phone: (541) 432-4185. Located in northeastern OR, 6 miles south of Joseph off OR 82, at the foot of the Wallowa Mountains. 121 full hook up sites; some pull-thru; showers; dump station. 90 foot limit.

Pennsylvania

The Commonwealth of Pennsylvania is one of the richest states in number of RV sites with nearly 7,000 spread among 50 State Parks. While none of the parks offer sewer or water hook-ups, most have electric connections (not at all sites in every park) and drinking water is available in all the parks. (Not all parks are equipped to provide holding tank water because of hand pump delivery.) As a rule, Pennsylvania parks do not allow pets in camping areas, however there are some exceptions, call to verify. Also, alcoholic beverages are not allowed in these parks. While most of the parks are open from Spring through late Autumn, parks open year round are often closed because of snow during winter months. Reservations require a 48-hour advance notice. Several parks do not accept reservations- call to verify. Seniors (62 & older) are eligible for a discount on all park rates. Major credit cards are accepted. Rate groups: A, B and C depending upon site type and day of the week.

Pennsylvania Dept. of Conservation and Natural Resources
Bureau of State Parks
Box 8551
Harrisburg, PA 17105
Information and Reservations: (888) 727-2757
Internet: www.dcnr.state.pa.us

Pennsylvania Park Locator

Pennsylvania Park Locator (*cont.*)

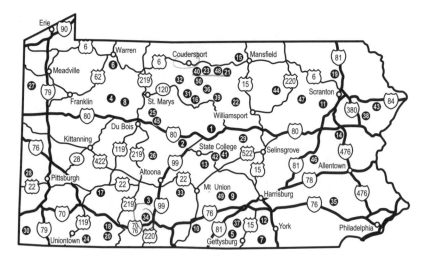

1. Bald Eagle State Park, 149 Main Park Rd., Howard, PA 16841. Phone: (814) 625-2775. Located on PA 150, 10 miles north of Milesburg and I-80 exit 158. 99 sites, 84 with electric; some 50-amp; 35 primitive sites; showers; dump station. Seasonal.

2. Black Moshannon State Park, 4216 Beaver Rd., Philipsburg, PA 16866. Phone: (814) 342-5960. Located on PA 504, 9 miles east of Philipsburg. 80 sites with electric; showers; dump station. Seasonal.

3. Blue Knob State Park, 124 Park Rd., Imler, PA 16655. Phone: (814) 276-3576. Located 9 miles west of I-99 exit 7 near Imler, via PA 869. 43 sites, 25 with electric; showers; dump station. Seasonal.

4. Cook Forest State Park, Cooksburg, PA 16217. Phone: (814) 744-8407. Located near Cooksburg; I-80 exit 73 (PA 949) or I-80 exit 78 (PA 36), north about 15 miles. 226 sites, some with electric; showers; dump station; laundry.

5. Caledonia State Park, 40 Rocky Mountain Rd., Fayetteville, PA 17222. Phone: (717) 352-2161. Located on US 30 midway between Gettysburg (US 15) and Chambersburg (I-81). Two campgrounds; 184 sites, some with electric; showers; dump station.

6. Chapman State Park, Clarendon, PA 16313. Phone: (814) 723-0250. Located off US 6 near Clarendon. 83 sites, some with electric; water available; dump station.

7. Codorus State Park, 1066 Blooming Grove Rd., Hanover, PA 17331. Phone: (717) 637-2816. Located on PA 216, SE of Hanover. 185 sites, many with electric; 50 foot limit; showers; dump station. Seasonal.

8. Clear Creek State Park, Sigel, PA 15860. Phone: (814) 752-2368. Located on PA 949; I-80 exit 73 (PA 949) or I-80 exit 78 (PA 36), north about 12 miles. 53 sites, some with electric; dump station. Seasonal.

9. Colonel Denning State Park, 1599 Doubling Gap Rd., Newville, PA 17241. Phone: (717) 776-5272. Located on PA 233, 8 miles north of Newville; 9 miles south of Landisburg. 52 sites, some with electric; dump station. Seasonal.

10. Cowans Gap State Park, 6235 Aughwick Rd., Fort Loudon, PA 17224. Phone: (717) 484-3948. Located off PA 75 between Chambersburg and McConnellsburg; north of US 30 at Fort Loudon. 224 sites, some with electric; showers; dump station. Seasonal.

11. Frances Slocum State Park, 565 Mount Oilivet Rd., Wyoming, PA 18644. Phone: (570) 696-3525. Located 10 miles NW of Wilkes-Barre; 5 miles east of Dallas; off US 11 to PA 309. 85 sites, some with electric; showers; dump station.

12. Gifford Pinchot State Park, 2200 Rosstown Rd., Lewisberry PA 17339.

Phone: (717) 432-5011. Located on PA 177 between Rossville and Lewisberry, south of Harrisburg; I-83 exit 35. 339 sites, some with electric; showers; dump station. Seasonal.

13. Greenwood Furnace State Park, Huntingdon, PA 16652. Phone: (814) 667-1800. Located on PA 305, northwest of Belleville; southeast of State College. 51 sites, 46 with electric (30 & 50 amps); showers; dump station. Seasonal.

14. Hickory Run State Park, White Haven, PA 18661. Phone: (570) 443-0400. Located on PA 534, south of I-80/I-476 junction (via PA 940). 381 sites, some with electric; showers; dump station. Seasonal.

15. Hills Creek State Park, 111 Spillway Rd., Wellsboro, PA 16901. Phone: (570) 724-4246. Located between Wellsboro and Mansfield, off US 6 via PA 287 at Tioga. 102 sites, some with electric; showers; dump station. Seasonal.

16. Kettle Creek State Park, 97 Kettle Creek Park Ln., Renovo, PA 17764. Phone: (570) 923-6004. Located on PA 4001, 7 miles NW of Westport (PA 120). 71 sites, 50 with electric; water available; dump station. Seasonal.

17. Keystone State Park, 1150 Pittsburgh St., Derry, PA 15627. Phone: (724) 668-2939. Located about 45 miles east of Pittsburgh, off US 22 at New Alexandria. 100 sites, some with electric; showers; dump station. Seasonal.

18. Kooser State Park, 943 Glades Pike, Somerset, PA 15501. Phone: (814) 445-8673. Located on PA 31 between Donegal and Somerset (I-76/70 exits 91 & 110). 47 sites, 14 with electric; dump station. Seasonal.

19. Lackawanna State Park, Dalton, PA 18414. Phone: (570) 945-3239. Located on PA 407 west of I-81 exit 199; US 6/11 use PA 438 to PA 407. 96 sites, 61 with electric; showers; dump station. Seasonal.

20. Laurel Hill State Park, 1454 Laurel Hill Park Rd., Somerset, PA 15501. Phone: (814) 445-7725. Located south of PA 31 between Donegal and Somerset (I-76/70 exits 91 & 110), follow signs to Trent Road. 264 sites, 149 with electric; showers; dump station. Seasonal.

21. Leonard Harrison State Park, 4797 Route 660, Wellsboro, PA 16901. Phone: (570) 724-3601. Located on PA 660, 10 miles southwest of Wellsboro. 30 sites, some with electric; dump station. Seasonal.

22. Little Pine State Park, 4205 Little Pine Creek Rd., Waterville, PA 17776. Phone: (570) 753-6000. Located about 25 miles NW of Williamsport (US 15 & 220) via PA 287 to English Center, follow signs. 98 sites, most with electric; showers; dump station. 30 foot maximum length. Seasonal.

23. Lyman Run State Park, 454 Lyman Run Rd., Galeton, PA 16922. Phone: (814) 435-5010. Located off US 6, 15 miles east of Coudersport; 7 miles west of Galeton. 29 sites with electric; dump station. Seasonal.

24. Ohiopyle State Park, Ohiopyle, PA 15470. Phone: (724) 329-8591. Located SE of Uniontown, off PA 381. RVs recommended using US 40; PA 2019 is very steep. 199 sites, some with electric; showers; dump station. Seasonal.

25. Parker Dam State Park, 28 Fairview Rd., Penfield, PA 15849. Phone: (814) 765-0630. Located off PA 153, 8 miles north of I-80 exit 111; follow signs. 110 sites, 80 with electric; showers; dump station. Seasonal.

26. Prince Gallitzin State Park, 966 Marina Rd., Patton, PA 16668. Phone: (814) 674-1000. Located NW of Altoona via PA 36 and PA 53. Remote campground. 437 sites, some with electric; showers; laundry; store; dump station. Seasonal.

27. Pymatuning State Park, 2660 Williams Field Rd., Jamestown, PA 16134. Phone: (724) 932-3141. Located on Pymatuning Reservoir, off US 322, 1.5 miles north of Jamestown. 657 sites, about half with electric; showers; dump station. Seasonal.

28. Raccoon Creek State Park, 3000 State Route 18, Hookstown, PA 15050. Phone: (724) 899-2200. Located west of Pittsburgh on PA 18, off US 22 or 30. 172 sites, some with electric; showers; dump station. Seasonal.

29. Raymond B. Winter State Park, 17215 Buffalo Rd., Mifflinburg, PA 17844. Phone: (570) 966-1455. Located on PA 192, 18 miles west of Lewisburg. 59 sites, some with electric; showers; dump station. Seasonal.

30. Ryerson Station State Park, 361 Bristoria Rd., Wind Ridge, PA 15380. Phone: (724) 428-4254. Located off PA 21, 3 miles west of Wind Ridge (southwestern PA, near WV state line). 50 sites, 16 with electric; showers; dump station. Seasonal.

31. Sinnemahoning State Park, 8288 First Fork Rd., Austin, PA 16720. Phone:

(814) 647-8401. Located on PA 872, 8 miles north of PA 120; 35 miles south of Coudersport (US 6). 35 sites, some with electric; showers; dump station. Seasonal.

32. Sizerville State Park, 199 E Crowley Run Rd., Emporium, PA 15834. Phone: (814) 486-5605. Located on PA 155, 6 miles north of Emporium (PA 120). 18 sites with electric; shower; dump station. Seasonal.

33. Trough Creek State Park, James Creek, PA 16657. Phone: (814) 658-3847. Located on PA 994, SE of Entriken (off PA 26). 32 sites with electric; dump station. Seasonal.

34. Shawnee State Park, 132 State Park Rd., Schellsburg, PA 15559. Phone: (814) 733-4218. Located SE of Johnstown at junction of US 30 and PA 96. 293 sites, 65 with electric; showers; dump station. Seasonal.

35. French Creek State Park, 843 Park Rd., Elverson, PA 19520. Phone: (610) 582-9680. Located off PA 345 SW of Pottstown and NE of I-76 exit 298. 201 sites, 57 with electric; showers; dump station.

36. Ole Bull State Park, Cross Fork, PA 17729. Phone: (814) 435-5000. Located on PA 144, 18 miles south of Galeton (US 6). 81 sites, 45 with electric; dump station.

37. Pine Grove Furnace State Park, 1100 Pine Grove Rd., Gardners, PA 17324. Phone: (717) 486-7174. Located SW of Harrisburg on PA 233, 8 miles south of I-81 exit 37. 74 sites, some with electric; dump station; store. Seasonal.

38. Tobyhanna State Park, Tobyhanna, PA 18466. Phone: (570) 894-8336. Located SE of Scranton, 2 miles north of Tobyhanna on PA 423. (I-380 is 2.5 miles south of park.) 140 sites; hand pump water; dump station.

39. Hyner Run State Park, Hyner, PA 17738. Phone: (570) 923-6000. Located in north-central PA on PA 120, 6 miles east of Renovo; 3 miles north of Hyner. 30 sites (rustic); dump station. Seasonal.

40. Patterson State Park, c/o Lyman Run, Galeton, PA 16922. Phone: (814) 435-5010. Located on PA 44, 6.5 miles south of Sweden Valley (US 6). 10 sites (rustic); no facilities. Seasonal.

41. Poe Paddy State Park, c/o Reeds Gap, Milroy, PA 17063. Phone: (717)

667-3622. Located east of State College off US 322. (Follow gravel road from Poe Valley State Park.) 39 sites (rustic); no facilities.

42. Poe Valley State Park, c/o Reeds Gap, Milroy, PA 17063. Phone: (814) 349-2460. Located east of State College, 12 miles east of Potters Mills (US 322) via state forest roads; follow signs. 76 sites (rustic); dump station. Seasonal.

43. Promised Land State Park, Greentown, PA 18426. Phone: (570) 676-3428. Located on PA 390, south of I-84 exits 20 or 26. 232 sites (four areas), some with electric; showers; dump station. Seasonal.

44. Worlds End State Park, Forksville, PA 18616. Phone: (570) 924-3287. Located NE of Williamsport on PA 154 about 7 miles NW of US 220. 70 sites, 35 with electric; showers; dump station.

45. S.B. Elliott State Park, c/o Parker Dam, Penfield, PA 15849. Phone: (814) 765-0630. Located on PA 153 just off I-80 exit 111, NW of Clearfield. 25 sites (rustic); dump station. Seasonal.

46. Locust Lake State Park, c/o Tuscarora, Barnesville, PA 18214. Phone: (570) 467-2404. Located SW of Mahonoy City, 2 miles from PA 54 and I-81 interchange. 140 sites, some with electric; showers; dump station.

47. Ricketts Glen State Park, 695 State Route 487, Benton, PA 17814. Phone: (570) 477-5675. Located on PA 487, 30 miles north of Bloomsburg between Williamsport and Wilkes-Barre. 120 sites (rustic); showers; dump station. Recommended RV access via Dushore (US 220 to PA 487) because of very steep road from Red Rock (south).

48. Colton Point State Park, Wellsboro, PA 16901. Phone: (570) 724-3061. Located 5 miles south of US 6 at Ansonia, SW of Wellsboro. 25 sites (rustic); dump station. Seasonal.

49. Fowlers Hollow State Park, c/o Colonel Denning, Newville, PA 17241. Phone: (717) 776-5272. Located west of Harrisburg, off PA 274. (Remote location; no easy access.) 18 sites (rustic); dump station.

50. Cherry Springs State Park, c/o Lyman Run, Galeton, PA 16922. Phone: (814) 435-5010. Located in Cherry Springs on PA 44, south of US 6. 30 sites (rustic); dump station.

Rhode Island

Rhode Island has only four State Parks with RV facilities and all these parks are located along the south shore, on or near the Atlantic Ocean. Pets on leases are permitted at some parks and not at others. You should contact the respective park for site availability and rules regarding pets (and alcohol use) at that park. All State Parks operate on a seasonal basis. Rate groups: B (RI residents): C (non-residents).

Rhode Island Division of Parks & Recreation
2321 Hartford Ave.
Johnston, RI 02919
Information: (401) 222-2632
Internet: www.riparks.com

Rhode Island Park Locator

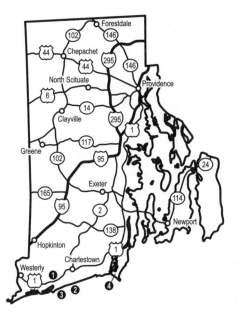

1. Burlingame State Park, US 1, Charlestown, RI 02813. Phone: (401) 322-
    7337. Located near Watchaug Pond, just north of US 1, west of
    Charlestown. 755 sites; showers; 2 dump stations

2. Charlestown Breachway State Park, US 1, Charlestown, RI 02813. Phone:
    (401) 322-8910. Located south of Charlestown, off US 1 on Block Island
    Sound. 75 sites; showers.

3. East Beach State Park, c/o Burlingame State Park, Charlestown, RI 02813.
    Phone: (401) 322-0450. Located on Block Island Sound, SW of
    Charlestown. 25 sites; showers.

4. Fishermen's Memorial State Park, State Route 108, 1011 Point Judith
    Rd., Narragansett, RI 02882. Phone: (401) 789-8374. Located near the
    end of RI 108, south of US 1 and Narragansett. 40 full hook-up sites; 107
    sites with water, electric; showers. Note: In season minimum stays may
    be required, check with park.

South Carolina

South Carolina has 32 State Parks with RV facilities. Unless otherwise noted, these facilities include water and electric at each site, showers nearby and at least one dump station in the park. Most parks have a limited number of pull-thru sites (check with the particular park to ascertain availability). All parks but Edisto Beach accept reservations. Reservations should be made with the particular park; no central reservation number. Unless otherwise noted, there are no rig size limitations. Rate groups: B and C depending on site facilities.

South Carolina Dept. of Parks, Recreation & Tourism
Box 71
Columbia, SC 29202
Information: (888) 887-2757
Internet: www.SouthCarolinaParks.com

South Carolina Park Locator

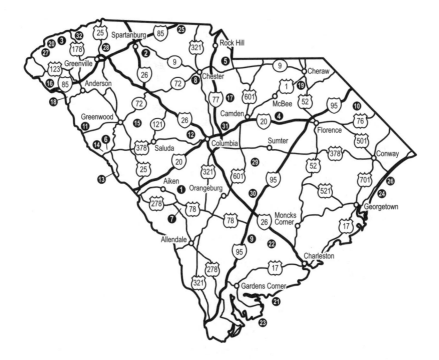

1. Aiken State Natural Area, 1145 State Park Rd., Windsor, SC 29856. Phone: (803) 649-2857. Located 16 miles east of Aiken (US 1 & 78) off SC 302 & 4. 25 sites.

2. Croft State Natural Area, 450 Croft State Park Rd., Spartanburg, SC 29302. Phone: (864) 585-1283. Located 17 miles SE of Spartanburg (I-26 & I-85) off US 176. 50 sites.

3. Keowee-Toxaway State Natural Area, 108 Residence Dr., Sunset, SC 29685. Phone: (864) 868-2605. Located off SC 288 about 18 miles NW of Greenville. 10 sites.

4. Lee State Natural Area, 487 Loop Rd., Bishopville, SC 29010. Phone: (803) 428-5307. Located off I-20, NE of Wisacky exit. 25 sites.

5. Andrew Jackson State Park, 196 Andrew Jackson Park Rd., Lancaster, SC 29720. Phone: (803) 285-3344. Located SE of Rock Hill, off US 521 at SC/NC state line. 360 sites.

6. Baker Creek State Park, Route 3, McCormick, SC 29835. Phone: (864) 443-2457. Located SW of McCormick, off US 378 & SC 28. 50 sites.

7. Barnwell State Park, 223 State Park Rd., Blackville, SC 29817. Phone: (803) 2874-2212. Located off SC 3, SW of Blackville (US 78 & SC 3). 25 sites.

8. Chester State Park, 759 State Park Dr., Chester, SC 29706. Phone: (803) 385-2680. Located 3 miles southwest of Chester via SC 72. 25 sites.

9. Colleton State Park, Canadys, SC 29433. Phone: (843) 538-8206. Located near Colleton, off I-95 exit 68. 25 sites.

10. Little Pee Dee State Park, 1298 State Park Rd., Dillon, SC 29536. Phone: (843) 774-8872. Located off SC 57 about 8 miles SE of Dillon (I-95 exit 193). 32 sites.

11. Calhoun Falls State Recreation Area, 46 Maintenance Rd., Calhoun Falls, SC 29628. Phone: (864) 447- 8267. Located in Calhoun Falls on SC 72, about 3 miles from GA state line. 86 sites.

12. Dreher Island State Recreation Area, 3677 State Park Rd., Prosperity, SC 29127. Phone: (803) 364-4152. Located off US 76 about 30 miles west of Columbia. From I-26 exit 91, follow signs. From US 378, take SC 391 north and follow signs. 97 sites.

13. Hamilton Branch State Recreation Area, Route 1, Plum Branch, SC 28845. Phone: (864) 333-2233. Located on SC 28 midway between McCormick, SC and Augusta, GA. 190 sites.

14. Hickory Knob State Resort Park, Route 4, McCormick, SC 29835. Phone: (864) 391-2450. Located off US 378 about 6 miles SW of McCormick, at GA state line. 44 sites.

15. Lake Greenwood State Recreation Area, 302 State Park Rd., Ninety-Six, SC 29666. Phone: (864) 543-3535 Located 16 miles east of Greenwood, off SC 34 & 702. 125 sites.

16. Lake Hartwell State Recreation Area, 19138-A South Hwy 11, Fair Play, SC 29643. Phone: (864) 972-3352. Located on Tugaloo River, north of I-85 exit 1 via SC 11. 117 sites.

17. Lake Wateree State Recreation Area, 881 State Park Rd., Winnsboro, SC 29180. Phone: (803) 482-6401. Located off US 21 midway between Columbia and Rock Hill. Follow signs from US 21. 72 sites.

18. Sadlers Creek State Recreation Area, 940 Sadlers Creek Park Rd., Anderson, SC 29626. Phone: (864) 226-8950. Located off US 29 about 13 miles southwest of Anderson. 37 sites.

19. Cheraw State Park, 100 State Park Rd., Cheraw, SC 29520. Phone: (843)

537-9656. Located near junction of US 1 & 52, about 5 miles south of Cheraw. 17 sites.

20. Devils Fork State Park, 161 Holcombe Circle, Salem, SC 29676. Phone: (864) 944-2639. Located off SC 107 near SC-GA-NC state lines. 59 sites.

21. Edisto Beach State Park, 8377 State Cabin Rd., Edisto Island, SC 29438. Phone: (843) 869-4430 Located at end of SC 174, off US 17, on the Atlantic Ocean. 89 sites.

22. Givhans Ferry State Park, 746 Givhans Ferry Rd., Ridgeville, SC 29472. Phone: (843) 873-0692. Located off SC 61 near Givhans (I-26 exit 187). 25 sites.

23. Hunting Island State Park, 2555 Sea Island Pkwy, Hunting Island, SC 29920. Phone: (843) 838-2011. Located at end of US 21, SE of Beaufort, on the Atlantic Ocean. 183 sites.

24. Huntington Beach State Park, 16148 Ocean Hwy, Murrells Inlet, SC 29576. Phone: (843) 237-4440. Located about 18 miles SW of Myrtle Beach, off US 17, on the Atlantic Ocean. 127 sites.

25. Kings Mountain State Park, 1277 Park Rd., Blacksburg, SC 29702. Phone: (803) 222-3209. Located about 8 miles west of Clover via SC 55 and SC 161; adjacent to Kings Mountain National Military Park. 116 sites.

26. Myrtle Beach State Park, 4401 South Kings Hwy., Myrtle Beach, SC 29575. Phone: (843) 238-5325. Located on US 17 about 7 miles SW of Myrtle Beach, on the Atlantic Ocean. 347 sites.

27. Oconee State Park, 624 State Park Rd., Mountain Rest, SC 29664. Phone: (864) 638- 5353. Located off SC 107, NW of Clemson. 140 sites.

28. Paris Mountain State Park, 2401 State Park Rd., Greenville, SC 29609. Phone: (864) 244-5565. Located off US 25 about 14 miles north of Greenville. 40 sites.

29. Poinsett State Park, 6660 Poinsett Park Rd., Wedgefield, SC 29168. Phone: (803) 494-8177. Located off SC 261 about 20 miles SW of Sumter. 50 sites.

30. Santee State Park, 251 State Park Rd., Santee, SC 29142. Phone: (803) 854-2408. Located on Lake Marion near Santee, on SC 6 at I-95 exit 98. 163 sites.

31. Sesquicentennial State Park, 9564 Two Notch Rd., Columbia, SC 29223. Phone: (803) 788-2706. Located off US 1, 4 miles northeast of Columbia. 87 sites.

32. Table Rock State Park, 158 E Ellison, Pickens, SC 29671. Phone: (864) 878-9813. Located 12 miles north of Pickens via US 178 and SC 11. 100 sites.

South Dakota

South Dakota has 11 State Parks and 27 Recreation Areas that will accommodate RVs. Most of these parks and areas are part of the state-wide reservation system. All these areas require a daily (or annual) license fee in addition to the fees charged for campsite usage. These sites are divided into three categories: *Preferred* Campgrounds (most popular) have restrooms and showers; some with electric hook-ups. *Modern* Campgrounds also have restrooms and showers; some electric and *Basic* Campgrounds have vault toilets, no showers and some (few) electric facilities. Some facilities are limited in winter months when water systems are shut down. Credit cards are accepted. Rate group: A, admission fee extra.

South Dakota Dept. of Game, Fish and Parks
Foss Building
523 East Capitol
Pierre, SD 57501
Information: (605) 773-3391 / Reservations: (800) 710-2267
Internet: www.sdgfp.info/Parks or www.CampSD.com (reservations)

South Dakota Park Locator

South Dakota Park Locator (*cont.*)

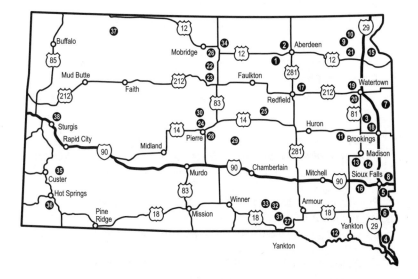

1. Mina Lake State Recreation Area, 37908 Youth Camp Rd, Aberdeen, SD 57401. Phone: (605) 225-5325. Located 11 miles west of Aberdeen off US 12. 37 sites, 36 with electric; showers; dump station. Reservations accepted.

2. Richmond Lake State Recreation Area, 37908 Youth Camp Rd, Aberdeen, SD 57401. Phone: (605) 225-5325. Located 10 miles NW of Aberdeen off US 281. 25 sites, 23 with electric; showers.

3. Lake Poinsett State Recreation Area, c/o Oakwood Lakes State Park, 46109 202nd St, Bruce, SD 57220. Phone: (605) 627-5411. Located 12 miles north of Arlington, off US 81. 108 sites with electric; showers; dump station.

4. Union Grove State Park, c/o Newton Hills State Park, 28771 482nd Ave, Canton, SD 57013. Phone: (605) 987-2263. Located 11 miles south of Beresford off I-29 exit 38. 24 sites, 11 with electric; showers. No reservations.

5. Big Sioux State Recreation Area, 410 Park Ave, Brandon, SD 57005. Phone: (605) 582-7243. Located 4 miles SW of Brandon, off I-90 exit 406 (Sioux Falls area). 50 sites, 43 with electric; showers; dump station. Reservations accepted.

6. Newton Hills State Park, 28771 482nd Ave, Canton, SD 57013. Phone: (605) 987-2263. Located 6 miles south of Canton, off US 18 (I-90 exit 62). 128 sites, 113 with electric; showers, dump station. Reservations accepted.

7. Lake Cochrane State Recreation Area, 400 W Kemp Ave, Watertown, SD 57201. Phone: (605) 882-5200. Located 10 miles east of Clear Lake, off SD 22 (I-29 exit 164). 25 sites with electric; showers. Reservations accepted.

8. Palisades State Park, 25495 485th Ave, Garretson, SD 57030. Phone: (605) 594-3824. Located south of Garretson about 10 miles north of I-90 exit 406. 37 sites, 16 with electric; showers. Reservations accepted.

9. Fort Sisseton State Historic Park, 11907 434th Ave, Lake City, SD 57247. Phone: (605) 448-5474. Located 10 miles south of Lake City off SD 10. 14 sites, 10 with electric; showers. Reservations accepted.

10. Roy Lake State Park, 11545 Northside Dr, Lake City, SD 57247. Phone: (605) 448-5701. Located 3 miles west of Lake City off SD 10; 81 sites, 73 with electric; showers; dump station. Reservations accepted.

11. Lake Thompson State Recreation Area, 21176 Flood Club Rd, Lake Preston, SD 57249. Phone: (605) 847-4893. Located off US 14, 3 miles west then 3 miles south of Lake Preston. 103 sites, 97 with electric; showers; dump station. Reservations accepted.

12. Lewis and Clark, Pierson Ranch & Chief White Crane Recreation Areas, 43349 SD Hwy 52, Yankton, SD 57078. Phone: (605) 668-2985. Located about 6 miles west of Yankton (US 81 at NE/SD state line) on SD 52. 588 sites, 561 with electric; showers; dump station. Reservations accepted.

13. Lake Herman State Park, RR 3 Box 79, Madison, SD 57042. Phone: (605) 256-5003. Located 2 miles west of Madison (US 81 & SD 34) off SD 34. 72 sites, 70 with electric; showers, dump station. Reservations accepted.

14. Walkers Point State Recreation Area, c/o Lake Herman State Park, RR 3 Box 79, Madison, SD 57042. Phone: (605) 256-5003. Six miles southeast

of Madison via SD 34, SD 19, and CR 44. 43 sites, 42 with electric; showers; dump station. Reservations accepted.

15. Hartford Beach State Park, RR 1 Box 50, Corona, SD 57227. Phone: (605) 432-6374. Located 13 miles north of Milbank via SD 15. 43 sites, 36 with electric; showers; dump station. Reservations accepted.

16. Lake Vermillion State Recreation Area, 26140 451st Ave, Canistota, SD 57012. Phone: (605) 296-3643. Located 5 miles south of I-90 at Montrose, exit 370. 66 sites, 62 with electric; showers; dump station. Reservations accepted.

17. Fisher Grove State Park, c/o Lake Louise State Recreation Area, 35250 191st St, Miller, SD 57362. Phone: (605) 472-1212. Located off US 212, 7 miles east of Redfield (junction US 212 & 281). 28 sites, 19 with electric; showers; dump station. No Reservations.

18. Oakwood Lakes State Park, 46109 202nd St, Bruce, SD 57220. Phone: (605) 627-5441. Located off US 14, 7 miles north and 3 miles west of Volga (I-29 exit 140). 68 sites, 65 with electric; showers; dump station. Reservations accepted.

19. Sandy Shore State Recreation Area, 400 W Kemp Ave, Watertown, SD 57201. Phone: (605) 882-5200. Located off US 212, 5 miles west of Watertown (I-29 exit 177). 20 sites, 12 with electric; showers. Reservations accepted.

20. Pelican Lake State Recreation Area, 400 W Kemp Ave, Watertown, SD 57201. Phone: (605) 882-5200. Located 9 miles south of Watertown in eastern SD, off US 212. 25 sites with electric.

21. Pickerel Lake State Recreation Area, RR 1 Box 113, Grenville, SD 57239. Phone: (605) 486-4753. Located in northeastern SD, 10 miles north of Waubay off US 12. 64 sites, 56 with electric; showers; dump station.

22. Swan Creek State Recreation Area, c/o West Whitlock State Recreation Area, HC 3 Box 73A, Gettysburg, SD 57442. Phone: (605) 765-9410. Located off US 83, 9 miles west of Akaska in north-central SD. 23 sites with electric; showers; dump station. Reservations accepted.

23. West Whitlock State Recreation Area, HC 3 Box 73A, Gettysburg, SD 57442. Phone: (605) 765-9410. Located off US 212, 18 miles west of Gettysburg in north-central SD. 100 sites, 87 with electric; showers; dump station. Reservations accepted.

24. Oahe Downstream State Recreation Area, 20439 Marina Loop Rd, Fort Pierre, SD 57532. Phone: (605) 224-5605. Located off SD 1806, below Oahe Dam, 5 miles north of Fort Pierre. 206 sites with electric; showers, dump station. Reservations accepted.

25. Lake Louise State Recreation Area, 35250 191st St, Miller, SD 57362. Phone: (605) 853-2533. Located off US 14, 14 miles NW of Miller (junction US 14 & SD 45). 39 sites, 29 with electric; showers; dump station. Reservations accepted.

26. Indian Creek State Recreation Area, 12905 288th Ave, Mobridge, SD 57601. Phone: (605) 845-7112. Located off US 12, 2 miles SE of Mobridge in north-central SD. 113 sites with electric; showers; dump station. Reservations accepted.

27. North Point and Randall Creek State Recreation Areas, 38180 297th St, Lake Andes, SD 57356. Phone: (605) 487-7046. Located off US 281 & US 18, SW of Pickstown. 245 sites with electric; showers; dump station. Reservations accepted.

28. Farm Island State Recreation Area, 1301 Farm Island Rd, Pierre, SD 57501. Phone: (605) 224-5605. Located 4 miles east of Pierre via SD 34. 90 sites, 76 with electric; showers; dump station. Reservations accepted.

29. West Bend State Recreation Area, 1301 Farm Island Rd, Pierre, SD 57501. Phone: (605) 875-3220. Located off SD 34, 26 miles east and 9 miles south of Pierre. 126 sites, 110 with electric; showers; dump station. Reservations accepted.

30. Cow Creek and Okobojo Point State Recreation Areas, c/o Ohae Downstream State Recreation Area, 20439 Marina Loop Rd, Fort Pierre, SD 57532. Phone: (605) 224-5605. Located off SD 1804, about 15 to 17 miles NW of Pierre. 46 sites. No Reservations.

31. North Wheeler and Pease Creek State Recreation Areas, c/o North Point State Recreation Area, 38180 297th St, Lake Andes, SD 57356. Phone: (605) 487-7046. Located off SD 1804, 4 miles west of Platte (junction of SD 44 & 45). 46 sites, 39 with electric; Pease Creek has showers. No Reservations.

32. Platte Creek State Recreation Area, c/o Snake Creek State Recreation Area, 35316 SD Hwy 44, Platte, SD 57369. Phone: (605) 337-2587.

Located off SD 54, 8 miles west and 6 miles south of Platte (junction of SD 44 & 45). 54 sites, 36 with electric; showers; dump station. Reservations accepted.

33. Snake Creek and Buryanek State Recreation Areas, 35316 SD Hwy 44, Platte, SD 57369. Phone: (605) 337-2587. Located off SD 44 on Missouri River, about 12 miles west of Platte. 159 sites, 152 with electric; showers; dump station (Snake Creek). Reservations accepted.

34. Lake Hiddenwood State Recreation Area, c/o Indian Creek State Recreation Area, 12905 288th Ave, Mobridge, SD 57601. Phone: (605) 765-9410. Located 5 miles NE of Selby, off US 12 & 83. 14 sites, 7 with electric. No reservations.

35. Custer State Park – Eight campgrounds in Custer State Park complex. Located near Mt. Rushmore, junction US 16 & 385. Reservations recommended; call specific area for space availability. Information: (605) 255-4515; Reservations (800) 710-2267.
    a. Blue Bell State Park campground, 35 sites; showers.
    b. Game Lodge State Park campground, 58 sites (designed for big rigs); showers; dump station.
    c. Legion Lake State Park campground, 25 sites; showers.
    d. Sylvan Lake State Park campground, 39 sites; showers.
    e. Center Lake State Park campground, 71 sites, no hook-ups; showers.
    f. Stockade Lake State Park campground, 69 sites; showers.
    g. Grace Coolidge State Park campground, 26 sites. No reservations.
    h. French Creek State Park Horse Camp- horse campers only; showers.

36. Angostura State Recreational Area, HC 52 Box 131A, Hot Springs, SD 57747. Phone: (605) 745-6996. Located on Angostura Reservoir, 10 miles SE of Hot Springs, off US 18 & 385. 167 sites, 139 with electric; showers; dump station. Reservations accepted.

37. Shadehill State Recreation Area, 19150 Summerville Rd, Shadehill, SD 57653. Phone: (605) 374-5114. Located off SD 73, 14 miles south of Lemmon in northwestern SD on North Fork Grand River. 52 sites with electric; showers; dump station. Reservations accepted.

38. Bear Butte State Park, Box 688, Sturgis, SD 57785. Phone: (605) 347-5240. Located off SD 79, 6 miles NE of Sturgis, I-90 exit 30. 15 sites.

Tennessee

There are 32 Tennessee State Parks with RV sites. Most offer water and electric hook-ups; several with 50-amp service. Many have laundry facilities and most have dump stations. Tennessee has no central reservation system and all the parks with campgrounds operate on a first-come, first-served basis. It is wise to contact the particular park to check for space before proceeding there. All the parks are very busy during the summer months. Many are open year round and you should check for facilities in autumn and winter months. Unless specified in listing, there are no rig size limitations. Only Tennessee residents are eligible for senior citizen discounts. Rate groups: B and C depending on site facilities.

Tennessee State Parks
Dept. of Environment and Conservation
401 Church Street
Nashville, TN 37243
Information: (866) 836-6757
Internet: www.tnstateparks.com

Tennessee Park Locator

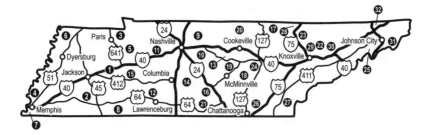

1. Natchez Trace State Park, 24845 Natchez Trace Rd., Wildersville, TN 38388. Phone: (800) 250-8616 or (731) 968-3742. Located 6 miles NE of Lexington off I-40 exit 116, between Nashville and Memphis. 190 full hook-up sites; showers; 50-amp; laundry; store.

2. Chicksaw State Park, 20 Cabin Ln., Henderson, TN 38340. Phone: (731) 989-5141. Located 8 miles west of Henderson (on US 45) on TN 100. 52 sites; water; electric; dump station.

3. Paris Landing State Park, 16055 Hwy 49N, Buchanan, TN 38222. Phone: (731) 641-4465 or (800) 250-8614. Located 18 miles NE of Paris, on US 79. 54 sites; water; electric; showers; dump station.

4. Meeman-Shelby Forest State Park, 910 Riddick Rd., Millington, TN 38053. Phone: (901) 876-5215 or (800) 471-5293. Located 18 miles north of Memphis. I-40 exit on to US 51 to Millington; follow signs. 49 sites; water; electric; showers; dump station.

5. Nathan Bedford Forest State Park, 1825 Pilot Knob Rd., Eva, TN 38333. Phone: (731) 584-6356. Located near Eva on local roads. I-40 exit 126 (US 641) north to Camden (US 70), follow signs. 38 sites; water; electric (50-amp); showers; dump station.

6. Reelfoot Lake State Park, Tipton, TN 38079. Phone: (731) 253-7756 or (866) 836-6757. Located in northwestern TN on Reelfoot Lake. From US 51 follow TN 22 from Union City to park; or TN 183 from Obion to park. 86 sites; water; electric; showers; laundry; dump station.

7. T.O. Fuller State Park, 1500 Mitchell Rd., Memphis, TN 38109. Phone: (901) 543-7581. Located in West Memphis; I-55 exit 9 (Mitchell Road); follow signs. 45 sites; water; electric; showers; dump station. No reservations.

8. Pickwick Landing State Park, Pickwick Dam, TN 38365. Phone: (731) 689-3129 or (800) 250-8615. Located on TN 57, south of Savannah (US 64); follow TN 128 to TN 57. 48 sites; water; electric (some 50-amp; 31 sites 20-amp); showers; dump station.

9. Bledsoe Creek State Park, 400 Zieglers Fort Rd., Gallatin, TN 37066. Phone: (615) 452-3706. Located 7 miles east of Gallatin on TN 25 (NE Nashville, via US 31E). 26 sites; water; electric; showers; dump station. No reservations.

10. Cedars of Lebanon State Park, 328 Cedars Forest Rd., Lebanon, TN 37090. Phone: (615) 443-2769. Located 31 miles east of Nashville; 6 miles south of I-40 on US 231. 117 sites; water; electric; showers; dump station; store. No reservations.

11. Montgomery Bell State Park, 1020 Jackson Hill Rd., Burns, TN 37029. Phone: (615) 797-9052 or (800) 250-8613. Located on US 70, 7 miles east of Dickson; I-40 exit 182. 80 sites; water, electric (30 & 50-amp); showers; dump station. No reservations. (Some sites will accept only pop-up campers; call if in doubt.)

12. David Crockett State Park, 1400 West Gaines, Lawrenceburg, TN 38464. Phone: (931) 762-9408. Located off US 64, 1/2 mile west of Lawrenceburg. 107 sites; water; electric; showers; dump station.

13. Edgar Evins State Park, 1630 Edgar Evins State Park Rd., Silver Point, TN 38582. Phone: (931) 858-2246 or (800) 250-8619. Located between Cookeville and Lebanon, 60 miles east of Nashville; I-40 exit 268 (TN 56). 60 sites; water; electric (some 50-amp); showers; dump station; laundry. 30 foot limit.

14. Henry Horton State Park, 4358 Nashville Hwy, Chapel Hill, TN 37034. Phone: (931) 364-2319 or (800) 250-8612. Located on US 31-A, 40 miles south of Nashville; or I-65 exit 46, follow signs. 54 sites; water; electric; showers; dump station. No reservations.

15. Mousetail Landing State Park, Linden, TN 37096. Phone: (731) 847-0841. Located on Tennessee River on TN 438, near junction with US 412. 19 sites; water; electric; showers; laundry, dump station.

16. Old Stone Fort State Park, 732 Stone Fort Dr., Manchester, TN 37855. Phone: (931) 723-5073. Located off US 41 in Manchester; use I-24 exit

111, follow signs. 51 sites; water; electric; showers; dump station (summer only). No reservations.

17. Pickett State Park, 4605 Pickett Pkwy, Jamestown, TN 38556. Phone: (931) 879-5821. Located on TN 154, NE of Jamestown (US 127), in Upper Cumberland Mountains. 20 sites; water; electric; showers; dump station. No reservations.

18. Fall Creek Falls State Park, Pikeville, TN 37367. Phone: (423) 881-5298 or (800) 250-8611. Located 18 miles NW of Pikeville via TN 30 and TN 284. 228 sites; water; electric; showers; dump station.

19. Rock Island State Park, 82 Beach Rd., Rock Island, TN 38581. Phone: (931) 686-2471. Located on TN 287 between McMinnville and Crossville; off US 70S at Campaign. 60 sites; water; electric; showers; laundry; dump station.

20. Standing Stone State Park, 1647 Standing Stone Park Hwy, Hilham, TN 38568. Phone: (931) 823-6347 or (800) 713-5157. Located on TN 52, 9 miles NW of Livingstone (TN 111 & 52). 36 sites; water; electric; showers; dump station. Seasonal.

21. Tims Ford State Park, 570 Tims Ford Dr., Winchester, TN 37398. Phone: (931) 962-1183. Located on Tims Ford Reservoir on TN 82, NW of Winchester. Two campgrounds: Tims Ford has 52 sites with water and electric (30-amp); showers; dump station; laundry. 35 foot maximum. Fairview has 88 sites (30 full hook-up, 38 with water and electric (30-amp), and 20 with water only); showers; dump station.

22. Big Ridge State Park, 1015 Big Ridge Rd., Maynardville, TN 37807. Phone: (865) 992-5523. Located about 35 miles north of Knoxville. From I-75 exit 122, follow TN 61 east about 12 miles to park. 50 sites; water; electric; showers.

23. Cove Lake State Park, 110 Cove Lake Ln., Caryville, TN 37714. Phone: (423) 566-9701. Located 30 miles NW of Knoxville on US 25W at I-75 exit 134 in Caryville. 100 sites; water; electric; showers; dump station. No reservations.

24. Cumberland Mountain State Park, 24 Office Dr., Crossville, TN 38555. Phone: (931) 484-6138. Located on US 127 about 4.5 miles SE of Crossville. 147 sites; water; electric; showers. No reservations.

25. Davy Crockett Birthplace State Park, 1245 Davy Crockett Park Rd., Limestone, TN 37681. Phone: (423) 257-2167; Campground: (423) 257-4500. Located on US 11E & 321, SW of Johnson City. 74 sites (25 with sewer); water; electric; showers; dump station.

26. Harrison Bay State Park, 8411 Harrison Bay Rd., Harrison, TN 37341. Phone: (423) 344-6214. Located northeast of Chattanooga via TN 58. 128 sites; water; electric; showers; dump station. Some sites 65 foot plus.

27. Hiwassee and Ocoee Rivers State Park, Delano, TN 37325. Phone: (423) 263-0050. Located 6 miles north of Benton on TN 30, off US 411. 43 sites (primitive); showers.

28. Indian Mountain State Park, 143 State Park Circle, Jellico, TN 37762. Phone: (423) 784-7958. Located near Jellico at KY state line; I-75 exit 160 to US 25W, follow signs. 49 sites; water; electric; showers; dump station.

29. Norris Dam State Park, 125 Village Green Circle, Lake City, TN 37769. Phone: (865) 426-7461. Located on US 441, 2.5 miles south of I-75 exit 128. 75 sites; water; electric, showers; laundry; dump station. No reservations.

30. Panther Creek State Park, 2010 Panther Creek Park Rd., Morristown, TN 37814. Phone: (423) 587-7046. Located on Cherokee Reservoir, 6 miles west of Morristown, off US 11E. 50 sites; water; electric; dump station. No reservations.

31. Roan Mountain State Park, 1015 Hwy 143, Roan Mountain, TN 37681. Phone: (423) 772-0190 or (800) 250-8620. Located in northeastern Tennessee about 25 miles southeast of Johnson City. 87 sites; water; electric; showers; dump station.

32. Warrior's Path State Park, Hemlock Road, Kingsport, TN 37663. Phone: (423) 239-8531. Located on Patrick Henry Reservoir, off TN 36; I-81 exit 59. 94 sites; water; electric; showers; dump station. No reservations.

Texas

Texas offers the RVer 61 state locations with facilities, ranging from primitive to full hook-ups. Many parks are on lakes and near major highways. Some parks offer "specials" (which usually require multiple nights stay.) And while only Texas residents qualify for fee discounts all the parks accept major credit cards. Many parks have overflow parking areas that offer traveling RVers a dry camp site for one night at a reduced price. It is necessary when calling a particular park to inquire about these areas and if they are available. Several parks with overflow areas also have water nearby. Reservations require 48 hours advance requests; same day reservations- call the park directly. Rate group: A, B, and C depending upon site utilities; entrance fees are $2 to $5 extra.

Texas Parks & Wildlife
4200 Smith School Road
Austin, TX 78744
Information: (800) 792-1112 (Mon thru Fri)
Reservations: (512) 389-8900 (Mon thru Sat)
Internet: www.tpwd.state.tx.us/park

Texas Park Locator

Texas Park Locator (*cont.*)

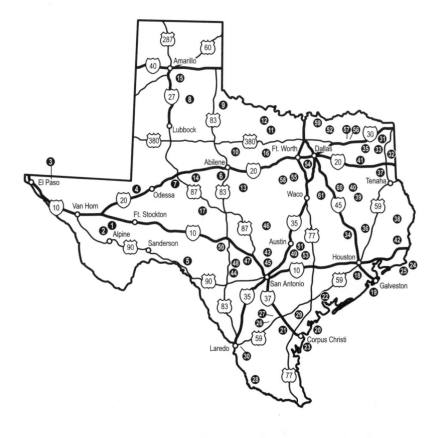

NOTE: Most of the parks listed here are reachable via a road designated as "FM" followed by a number. This abbreviation means Farm to Market Road. Some of these roads are paved, some are gravel. All are marked with the appropriate number.

1. Balmorhea State Park, Toyahvale, TX 79786. Phone: (432) 375-2370. Located SW of Balmorhea on TX 17. I-10 westbound use exit 206; I-10 eastbound, exit 192. Follow signs to Ranch Road 3078. 38 sites; water; electric; showers; dump station.

2. Davis Mountain State Park, Fort Davis, TX 79734. Phone: (432) 426-3337. Located 4 miles west of Fort Davis. Follow TX 17 from Fort Davis north to TX 118, west to park entrance. 33 sites with water; 34 sites with water and electric; 27 full hook-up sites; showers; dump station.

3. Hueco Tanks State Historic Site, 6900 Hueco Tanks Rd. No. 1, El Paso, TX 79938. Phone: (915) 857-1135. Located 32 miles east of El Paso; US 62/180 east to Ranch Road 2775. 3 sites with water; 17 with water and electric; showers; dump station.

4. Monahans Sandhills State Park, Monahans, TX 79756. Phone: (432) 943-2092. Located 31 miles west of Odessa; I-20 exit 86, follow signs to Park Road 41. 26 sites; water; electric; dump station.

5. Seminole Canyon State Park, Comstock, TX 78837. Phone: (432) 292-4464. Located 9 miles west of Comstock (about 30 miles NW of Del Rio) on US 90. 84 sites with water; 23 water and electric; showers; dump station.

6. Abilene State Park, 150 Park Rd. 32, Tuscola, TX 79562. Phone: (325) 572-3204. Located SW of Abilene on Park Road 32, off US 83, near junction with US 84. 76 sites with water and electric; 3 full hook-up; showers; dump station.

7. Big Spring State Park, 1 Scenic Dr., Big Spring, TX 79720. Phone: (432) 263-4931. Located in Big Spring (junction of I-20 & US 87). 2 sites, water and electric.

8. Caprock Canyons State Park, Quitaque, TX 79255. Phone: (806) 455-1492. Located on FM 1065, 3.5 miles north of Quitaque, off TX 86. 44 sites with water and electric; several dry camp sites; showers; dump station.

9. Copper Breaks State Park, 777 Park Rd. 62, Quanah, TX 79252. Phone: (940) 839-4331. Located off TX 6 between US 70 & 287. 25 sites with water and electric; 11 with water; showers; dump station.

10. Fort Griffin State Park, 1701 N US 283, Albany, TX 76430. Phone: (325) 762-3592. Located 15 miles north of Albany (NE of Abilene) on US 283/ 183. 15 sites with water, electric; 2 full hook-up; 25 dry sites; showers; dump station.

11. Fort Richardson State Park, 228 Park Rd. 61, Jacksboro, TX 76458. Phone: (940) 567-3506. Located NW of Fort Worth, off US 281/380, about 2.5 miles south of Jacksboro. 37 sites with water and electric; 5 full hook-up; 7 dry-camp sites; showers; dump station.

12. Lake Arrowhead State Park, 229 Park Rd. 63, Wichita Falls, TX 76310. Phone: (940) 528-2211. Located off FM 1954 SE of Wichita Falls. Access FM 1954 from US 281 or US 287. 48 sites with water, electric; 29 water; 15 dry-camp sites; showers; dump station.

13. Lake Brownwood State Park, Brownwood, TX 76801. Phone: (325) 784-5223. Located 16 miles north of Brownwood (US 67 & 377) off TX 279. 46 sites with water, electric; 20 full hook-up sites; showers; dump station.

14. Lake Colorado City State Park, 4582 FM 2836, Colorado City, TX 79512. Phone: (325) 728-3931. Located on FM 2836, off I-20 exit 213, 11 miles SW of Colorado City. 98 sites with water, electric; 34 water; (9 pull-thru sites); showers; dump station.

15. Palo Duro Canyon State Park, 11450 Park Rd. 5, Canyon, TX 79015. Phone: (806) 488-2227. Located 12 miles east of Canyon (I-27 exit 106) on TX 217. 80 sites with water, electric; showers; dump station.

16. Possum Kingdom State Park, Caddo, TX 76429. Phone: (940) 549-1803. Located NW of Mineral Wells off US 180 at Caddo to FM 33, follow signs. 61 sites with water and electric; 55 water; (over-flow sites available); showers; dump station.

17. San Angelo State Park, 2900-2 Mercedes Rd., San Angelo, TX 76901. Phone: (325) 949-4757. Located just west of San Angelo on FM 2288, off US 67. 63 sites with water, electric; showers; dump station.

18. Brazos Bend State Park, FM 762, Needville, TX 77461. Phone: (979) 553-5101. Located SW of Houston off FM 1462, from TX 288 at Rosharon. 77 sites with water, electric; dump station.

19. Galveston Island State Park, 14901 FM 3005, Galveston, TX 77554. Phone: (409) 737-1222. Located near I-45 exit 1A on Seawall Boulevard on Gulf of Mexico. 150 sites with water, electric; 20 dry-camp sites; showers; dump station.

20. Goose Island State Park, 202 S Palmetto St., Rockport, TX 78382. Phone: (361) 729-2858. Located next to the IC Waterway, 10 miles NE of Rockport, off TX 35. 102 sites with water, electric; some dry-camp sites; showers; dump station.

21. Lake Corpus Christi State Park, Mathis, TX 78368. Phone: (361) 547-2635. Located 35 miles NW of Corpus Christi, 4 miles SW of Mathis off TX 359; I-37 exit 34. 83 sites with water, electric; 25 full hookup sites; showers; dump station.

22. Lake Texana State Park, 46 Park Rd. 1, Edna, TX 77957. Phone: (361) 782-5718. Located 6.5 miles east of Edna (US 59) on TX 111. 141 sites with water, electric; showers; dump station.

23. Mustang Island State Park, Port Aransas, TX 78373. Phone: (361) 749-5246. Located SE of Corpus Christi on TX 358; access via JFK Causeway to TX 361. 48 sites with water, electric (50-amp); 340 primitive sites; showers; dump station.

24. Sabine Pass Battleground State Park, Sabine Pass, TX 77655. Phone: (409) 971-2451. Located on the Gulf of Mexico, 15 miles south of Port Arthur near Sabine Pass on TX 87. 10 sites with water, electric; 10 primitive sites; dump station.

25. Sea Rim State Park, Sabine Pass, TX 77655. Phone: (409) 971-2559. Located on TX 87, on Gulf of Mexico, 20 miles south of Sabine Pass. 20 sites with water, electric; 10 with water; primitive sites on the beach; showers; dump station.

26. Choke Canyon State Park, Calliham Unit, Calliham, TX 78007. Phone: (361) 786-3868. Located 12 miles west of Three Rivers on TX 72. 40 sites with water, electric (50-amp); showers; dump station.

27. Choke Canyon State Park, South Shore Unit, Three Rivers, TX 78071. Phone: (361) 786-3538. Located 3.5 miles west of Three Rivers on TX 72. 20 sites with water, electric; showers; dump station.

28. Falcon State Park, Falcon Heights, TX 78545. Phone: (956) 848-5327. Located north of Roma on Falcon Reservoir (about 90 miles SE of Laredo) on FM 2098, off US 83. 31 full hook-up sites; 31 with water; electric; all 50-amp & pull-thru; showers; dump station.

29. Goliad State Park, 108 Park Rd. 6, Goliad, TX 77963. Phone: (361) 645-3405. Located south of Goliad on US 183 & 77A. 24 sites with water and electric; 14 with water; showers; dump station.

30. Lake Casa Blanca International State Park, Laredo, TX 78044. Phone: (956) 725-3826. Located 3 miles east of Laredo on US 59. 66 sites with water, electric; showers; dump station.

31. Atlanta State Park, 927 Park Rd. 42, Atlanta, TX 75551. Phone: (903) 796-6476. Located 11 miles NW of Atlanta, near Arkansas state line, off US 59. 16 full hook-up sites; 44 with water, electric; showers; dump station.

32. Caddo Lake State Park, 245 Park Rd. 2, Karnack, TX 75661. Phone: (903) 679-3351. Located 15 miles NE of Marshall off TX 43. 8 full hook-up sites; 18 with water and electric; 20 with water; (some 50-amp service); showers; dump station.

33. Daingerfield State Park, 455 Park Rd. 17, Daingerfield, TX 75638. Phone: (903) 645-2921. Located on TX 49 east of Daingerfield. Accessible via I-30 to Mt. Pleasant, south on TX 49; 10 full hook-up sites; 30 with water, electric; showers; dump station.

34. Huntsville State Park, Huntsville, TX 77342. Phone: (936) 285-5644. Located 6 miles SW of Huntsville, off I-45 exit 103. 62 sites with water and electric; 125 with water; showers; dump station.

35. Lake Bob Sandlin State Park, Pittsburg, TX 75686. Phone: (903) 572-5531. Located 12 miles southeast of Mount Vernon and I-30 exit 146 via TX 37 and FM 21. 75 sites with water, electric; showers; dump station.

36. Lake Livingston State Park, 300 State Park Rd. 65, Livingston, TX. Phone: (936) 365-2201. Located 1 mile south of Livingston on US 59. 66 full hook-up sites; 69 with water and electric; 26 with water; showers; dump station.

37. Martin Creek Lake State Park, 9515 CR 2181 D, Tatum, TX 75691. Phone: (903) 836- 4336. Located 20 miles SE of Longview; I-20 exit 589 to US 259 to TX 43. 60 sites with water, electric; showers; dump station.

38. Martin Dies, Jr. State Park, Jasper, TX 75951. Phone: (409) 384-5231. Located on US 190 between Jasper and Livingston. 115 sites with water and electric; 67 with water; showers; dump station.

39. Mission Tejas State Park, Grapeland, TX 75844. Phone: (936) 687-2394. Located 21 miles NE of Crockett on TX 21. 5 full hook-up sites; 10 with water and electric; 4 with water; showers; dump station.

40. Rusk/Palestine State Park, (2 areas) Rusk, TX 75785. Phone: (903) 683-5126. Rusk is located 3 miles west of Rusk, off US 84; Palestine is located 3 miles east of Palestine on US 84. 32 full hook-up sites; 62 with water and electric; 12 with water; showers; dump station. Call for site availability. Parks are located several miles apart.

41. Tyler State Park, 789 Park Rd. 16, Tyler, TX 75706. Phone: (903) 597-5338. Located north of Tyler on FM 14, off I-20 exit 562. 39 full hook-up sites; 48 with water, electric; showers; dump station.

42. Village Creek State Park, Lumberton, TX 77657. Phone: (409) 755-7322. Located 10 miles north of Beaumont off US 96. 25 sites with water, electric; showers; dump station.

43. Blanco State Park, Blanco, TX 78606. Phone: (830) 833-4333. Located on south side of Blanco, 40 miles north of San Antonio on US 281 (SW of Austin - US 290 to 281). 16 full hook-up sites; 12 with water, electric; showers; dump station.

44. Garner State Park, Concan, TX 78838. Phone: (830) 232-6132. Located on the Frio River, 31 miles north of Uvalde, on US 83. 146 sites with water and electric; 206 with water; showers; dump station.

45. Guadalupe River State Park, 3350 Park Rd., Spring Branch, TX 78070. Phone: (830) 438-2656. Located 30 miles north of San Antonio on US 281. 48 sites with water, electric; showers; dump station.

46. Inks Lake State Park, 3630 Park Rd. 4 W, Burnet, TX 78611. Phone: (512) 793-2223. Located 9 miles west of Burnet off TX 29. 137 sites with water and electric; 50 with water; showers; dump station.

47. Kerrville-Schreiner State Park, 2385 Bandera Hwy, Kerrville, TX 78028. Phone: (830) 257-5392 or (830) 257-CAMP. Located 3 miles SW of Kerrville on TX 173. 42 full hook-up sites; 42 with water and electric; 58 with water; 7 primitive; showers; dump station.

48. Lost Maples State Natural Area, 37221 FM 187, Vanderpool, TX 78885. Phone: (830) 966-3413. Located about 70 miles NW of San Antonio on FM 187 (off US 83). 30 sites with water, electric; showers; dump station.

49. McKinney Falls State Park, 5808 McKinney Falls Pkwy, Austin, TX 78744. Phone: (512) 243-1643. Located 13 miles south of Austin, between US 183 and I-35 exit 228. 84 sites with water, electric; showers; dump station.

50. South Llano River State Park, 1927 Park Rd. 73, Junction, TX 76849. Phone: (325) 446-3994. Located 7 miles SW of Junction (I-10 exit 456) on US 377. 58 sites with water, electric; showers; dump station.

51. Bastrop State Park, Bastrop, TX 78602. Phone: (512) 321-2101. Located 30 miles SE of Austin near junction of TX 71 & 21. 24 full hook-up sites; 30 with water and electric; showers; dump station.

52. Bonham State Park, Bonham, TX 75418. Phone: (903) 583-5022. Located NE of Dallas and 1.5 miles SE of Bonham. Use TX 78 to FM 271, follow signs. 14 sites with water and electric; also dry sites; showers; dump station.

53. Buescher State Park, Smithville, TX 78957. Phone: (512) 237-2241. Located 2 miles north of Smithville and about 20 miles east of Austin via TX 71 to FM 155, follow signs. 32 sites with water and electric; 25 with water; showers; dump station.

54. Cedar Hill State Park, 1570 West FM 1382, Cedar Hill, TX 75104. Phone: (972) 291-3900. Located 10 miles SW of Dallas on FM 1382 between I-20 and US 67. 355 sites with water and electric; 2 dry-camp sites; showers; dump station.

55. Cleburne State Park, 5800 Park Rd. 21, Cleburne, TX 76033. Phone: (817) 645-4215. Located about 40 miles SW of Fort Worth and 10 miles SW of Cleburne off US 67. 27 full hook-up sites; 31 with water, electric; showers; dump station.

56. Cooper Lake State Park, Doctors Creek Unit, 1664 FM 1529 S, Cooper, TX 75432. Phone: (903) 395-3100. Located on NE side of Cooper Lake near Cooper about 18 miles north of I-30 exit 122 on TX 19; follow signs. 42 sites with water, electric; showers; dump station.

57. Cooper Lake State Park, South Sulphur Unit, 1690 FM 3505, Sulphur Springs, TX 75482. Phone: (903) 945-5256. Located on south side of Cooper Lake, about 13 miles north of 1-30 exit 122 via TX 19 to TX 71 to FM 3505. 87 sites with water and electric; some dry-camp sites; showers; dump station.

58. Dinosaur Valley State Park, Glen Rose, TX 76043. Phone: (254) 897-4588. Located on FM 205, SW of Glen Rose, off US 67. 46 sites with water and electric; showers; dump station.

59. Eisenhower State Park, 50 Park Rd. 20, Denison, TX 75020. Phone: (903) 465-1956. Located off FM 1310 on Lake Texoma, NW of Denison (US 75, exit 72 to TX 91 to FM 1310). 50 full hook-up sites; 45 with water and electric; showers; dump station.

60. Fairfield Lake State Park, 123 State Park Rd. 64, Fairfield, TX 75840. Phone: (903) 389-4514. Located 6 miles NE of Fairfield (I-45 exit 197), follow signs. 134 sites with water and electric; several dry camp sites; showers; dump station.

61. Fort Parker State Park, Mexia, TX 76667. Phone: (254) 562-5751. Located 7 miles south of Mexia on TX 14. 35 sites with water and electric; several dry camp sites; showers; dump station.

Utah

The Beehive State has 28 State Parks with RV sites or facilities. While all the parks offer drinking water, two locations, Dead Horse Point and Goblin Valley, have limited water supplies and RVers should fill their water tanks ahead of time, just to be sure. All the parks charge a day-use fee in addition to the camping charge. Most of the parks are open year round, however many close the shower facilities in winter. If traveling to any park in winter months, you should call ahead to verify road conditions and status. Most parks, especially those on lakes or reservoirs, are very busy from May through September and require reservations. Summer travelers should call ahead to verify site availability. Rate groups: A, B, and C depending on site facilities.

Utah Division of Parks & Recreation
1594 West North Temple, Ste. 116
Box 146001
Salt Lake City, UT 84114
Information: (801) 538-7220 / Reservations: (800) 322-3770
Internet: www.stateparks.utah.gov

Utah Park Locator

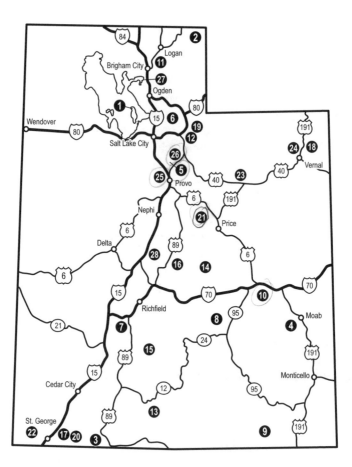

1. Antelope Island State Park, Syracuse, UT 84075. Phone: (801) 773-2941.
    Located in the Great Salt Lake (via Causeway) west of Ogden off I-15,
    on Antelope Island. 26 sites; 65 foot limit; showers; dump station.

2. Bear Lake State Park, Garden City, UT 84028. Phone: (435) 946-3343.
    Two locations on Bear Lake located at UT/ID state line. Some areas
    seasonal. Bear Lake Marina, located on US 89, 2 miles north of Garden
    City and Bear Lake Rendezvous Beach, on the south shore, near
    Laketown on UT 30; 178 sites; most with full hook-ups; showers; dump
    stations.

3. Coral Pink Sand Dunes State Park, Kanab, UT 84741. Phone: (435) 648-

2800. Located NW of Kanab off US 89, follow signs. 22 sites; 45 foot limit; showers; dump station.

4. Dead Horse Point State Park, Moab, UT 84532. Phone: (435) 259-2614. Located west of Moab on UT 313, 18 miles off US 191. 21 sites with electric; 45 foot limit; showers; dump station. Limited water.

5. Deer Creek State Park, Midway, UT 84049. Phone: (435) 654-0171. Located on US 189 between Heber City and Provo, on Deer Creek Reservoir. 58 sites; 35 foot limit; showers; dump station.

6. East Canyon State Park, Morgan, UT 84050. Phone: (801) 829-6866. Located NE of Salt Lake City on UT 65 & 66; off I-80 & I-84. 31 sites; 35 foot limit; showers; dump station.

7. Fremont Indian State Park & Museum, 11550 W Clear Creek Canyon Rd., Sevier, UT 84766. Phone: (435) 527-4631. Located 21 miles SW of Richfield on I-70 exit 17. 31 sites; dump station.

8. Goblin Valley State Park, Green River, UT 84525. Phone: (435) 564-3633. Located between Hanksville and Green River (I-70 exit 158), off UT 24. 21 sites; 30 foot limit; showers; dump station. Limited water.

9. Goosenecks State Park, Mexican Hat, UT 84513. Phone: (435) 678-2238. Located southwest of Blanding near Mexican Hat (US 163), 4 miles off UT 261. 4 primitive sites; no facilities; dump station.

10. Green River State Park, Green River, UT 84525. Phone: (435) 564-3633. Located in Green River City off I-70 exit 158. 42 sites; 45 foot maximum; no hook-ups; showers; dump station.

11. Hyrum State Park, 495 W 300 S, Hyrum, UT 84319. Phone: (435) 245-6866. Located in Hyrum, 8 miles south of Logan. 31 sites; 40 foot maximum; no facilities.

12. Jordanelle State Park, Heber City, UT 84032. Phone: (435) 649-9540. Located on Jordanelle Reservoir near Heber City, SE of Salt Lake City, off US 40. 103 sites with water and electric; showers; 70 foot limit.

13. Kodachrome Basin State Park, Cannonville, UT 84718. Phone: (435) 678-8562. Located 9 miles south of UT 12 and Cannonville, east of Bryce Canyon National Park. 27 sites; 45 foot maximum; showers; dump station.

14. Millsite State Park, Huntington, UT 84528. Phone: (435) 687-2491. Located 4 miles west of UT 10 (I-70 exit 89), NW of Ferron. 20 sites; 35 foot maximum; showers; dump station.

15. Otter Creek State Park, Antimony, UT 84712. Phone: (435) 624-3268. Located 4 miles from Antimony on UT 22; about 12 miles east of US 89 at Kingston. 24 sites; 40 foot maximum; showers; dump station.

16. Palisade State Park, 2200 East Palisade Rd. Sterling, UT 84665. Phone: (435) 835-7275. Located off US 89, SE of Manti. 53 sites; 45 foot maximum; showers; dump station.

17. Quail Creek State Park, St. George, UT 84771. Phone: (435) 897-2378. Located 3 miles east of I-15 exit 16, on UT 9. 23 sites; 35 foot limit; no facilities.

18. Red Fleet State Park, 8750 N Hwy 191, Vernal, UT 84078. Phone: (435) 789-4432. Located in northeast corner of UT, 13 miles north or Vernal, off US 191. 38 sites; 35 foot limit; dump station.

19. Rockport State Park, 9040 N Hwy 302, Peoa, UT 84061. Phone: (435) 336-2241. Located 45 miles east of Salt Lake City near Wanship, on UT 32. 36 sites; 40 foot limit; showers; dump station.

20. Sand Hollow State Park, 4405 W 3600 S, Hurricane, UT 84737. Phone: (435) 879-2378. Located 4 miles east of I-15 exit 16 and 1 mile south of UT 9 on Turf Sod Rd. Primitive sites; no facilities. New park; opened in 2003. Still under construction.

21. Scofield State Park, Price, UT 84501. Phone: (435) 448-9449 or (435) 637-2732. Located west of Helper, off US 6, on UT 96. Two areas: Scofield Mountain View, located 6 miles north of Scofield. 34 sites; 30 foot limit; showers; dump station. Seasonal. Scofield Madsen Bay, located on north end of Reservoir. 40 sites; 35 foot maximum; showers.

22. Snow Canyon State Park, 1002 N Snow Canyon Rd., Ivins, UT 84738. Phone: (435) 628-2255. Located 11 miles NW of St. George, on UT 18. 17 sites with water, electric; 21 sites no hook-ups; showers; 35 foot limit.

23. Starvation State Park, Duchesne, UT 84021. Phone: (435) 738-2326. Located 4 miles NW of Duchesne (US 40 & 191) on US 40. 54 primitive sites; 40 foot limit; no utilities; showers; dump station.

24. Steinaker State Park, 4335 N Hwy 191, Vernal, UT 84078. Phone: (435) 789-4432. Located 7 miles north of Vernal, off US 191. 31 sites; 35 foot maximum; dump station.

25. Utah Lake State Park, 4400 W Center St., Provo, UT 84601. Phone: (801) 375-0731. Located on Utah Lake, 5 miles west of Provo, off I-15. 54 sites; 40 foot maximum; showers; dump station. Seasonal.

26. Wasatch Mountain State Park, Midway, UT 84049. Phone: (435) 654-1791. Located near Heber City, off US 40/189. Four campgrounds. 139 sites, 35 foot maximum; water, electric; 35 full hook-up sites; showers. Dump station.

27. Willard Bay State Park, 900 W 650 N #A, Willard, UT 84340. Phone: (435) 734-9494. Located adjacent to Watkins Reservoir, NW of Ogden. Two locations: Willard Bay North Marina, located 15 miles north of Ogden, off I-15 exit 360. 101 sites; 39 full hook-ups; 38 foot limit; showers; dump station. Willard Bay South Marina, located 8 miles north of Ogden, off I-15 exit 354. 30 sites; 35 foot limit; no facilities.

28. Yuba State Park, Levan UT 84639. Phone: (435) 758-2611. Located 25 miles south of Nephi, off I-15 exits 188 or 202. 68 sites in two different camping areas; 45 foot limit; showers; dump station.

Vermont

Thirty-two of Vermont's 40 state parks have RV facilities. However, none of the parks have hook-ups. All but two parks have dump stations and all have showers. All offer drinkable water. The parks accept Visa and MasterCard. Parks are open in the Spring-Summer season only; many close on Labor Day. It is wise to call ahead to (1) check available space and; (2) if open. No reservations accepted; all sites are first-come first-served. Unless noted in the listing, all sites will accept "big rigs." Rate groups: B and C.

Vermont Dept. of Forests, Parks & Recreation
103 South Main St.
Waterbury, VT 05671
Information: (802) 244-1481
Internet: www.campvermont.com
E-mail: info@campvermont.com

Vermont Park Locator

1. Allis State Park, 284 Allis State Park Rd., Randolph, VT 05060. Phone: (802) 276-3175. Located on VT 65 off I-89, Brookfield exit. 18 sites.

2. Ascutney State Park, 1826 Back Mtn. Rd., Windsor, VT 05089. Phone: (802) 674-2060. Located off VT 44A (US 5; I-91 exit 8) near Windsor. 39 sites.

3. Big Deer State Park, 126 Boulder Beach Rd., Groton, VT 05046. Phone: (802) 584-3822. Located off VT 232 about 19 miles NW of Groton, via US 302. 28 sites; no dump station; no big rigs.

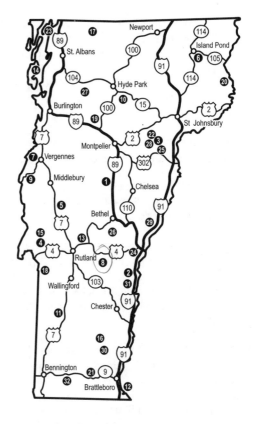

4. Bomoseen State Park, 22 Cedar Mtn. Rd., Fair Haven, VT 05743. Phone: (802) 265-4242. Located 4 miles north of Hydeville, off VT 4A. 56 sites; some pull-thru.

5. Branbury State Park, 3570 Lake Dunmore Rd. Route 53, Salisbury, VT 05733. Phone: (802) 247-5925. Located 9 miles north of Brandon on Route 53, on Lake Dunmore. 39 sites.

6. Brighton State Park, Island Pond, VT 05846. Phone: (802) 723-4360. Located off VT 105, 2 miles east of Island Pond (VT 105 & 111). 63 sites.

7. Button Bay State Park, 5 Button Bay State Park Rd., Vergennes, VT 05491. Phone: (802) 475-2377. Located on Lake Champlain, 6.5 miles west of Vergennes (VT 22A & US 7). 72 sites.

7/1 ᕋ2

NW, VT State Parks. Ca

8. Coolidge State Park, 855 Coolidge State Park Rd., Plymouth, VT 05056. Phone: (802) 672-3612. Located off VT 110A, NE of Plymouth Notch; 6 miles SW of Bridgewater Corners (US 4). 25 sites.

9. D.A.R. State Park, 6750 State Route 17W, Addison, VT 05491. Phone: (802) 759-2354. Located on Lake Champlain, 7 miles west of Addison via VT 17 (off VT 22 A). 47 sites.

10. Elmore State Park, Lake Elmore, VT 05657. Phone: (802) 888-2982. Located on VT 12, 5 miles southeast of Morrisville (VT 100 & 15). 45 sites.

11. Emerald Lake State Park, 374 Emerald Lake Lane, East Dorset, VT 05253. Phone: (802) 362-1655. Located on US 7 about 9 miles north of Manchester. 69 sites.

12. Fort Dummer State Park, 517 Old Guilford Rd., Brattleboro, VT 05301. Phone: (802) 254-2610. Located off I-91 exit 1, south of Brattleboro. 51 sites.

13. Gifford Woods State Park, 34 Gifford Woods, Killington, VT 05751. Phone: (802) 775-5354. Located near Killington at US 4 and VT 100 junction. 27 sites.

14. Grand Isle State Park, 36 East Shore Rd. S, Grand Isle, VT 05458. Phone: (802) 372-4300. Located 20 miles north of Burlington via US 2. 122 sites; some pull-thru.

15. Half Moon Pond State Park, 1621 Black Pond Rd., Hubbardton, VT 05743. Phone: (802) 273-2848 Located about 5 miles south of Hubbardton, off VT 30 on marked roads. 60 sites; no big rigs.

16. Jamaica State Park, Jamaica, VT 05343. Phone: (802) 874-4600. Located on the West River, off VT 30 outside Jamaica. 43 sites.

17. Lake Carmi State Park, 460 Marsh Farm Rd., Enosburg Falls, VT 05450. Phone: (802) 933-8383. Located off VT 236, about 9 miles NW of Enosburg Falls (VT 105 & 108). 141 sites.

18. Lake St. Catherine State Park, 3034 VT 30 S, Poultney, VT 05764. Phone: (802) 287-9158. Located about 3 miles south of Poultney on VT 30. 50 sites.

19. Little River State Park, 3444 Little River Rd., Waterbury, VT 05676. Phone: (802) 244-7103. Located about 6 miles north of Waterbury (I-89 exit 10) off US 2; follow signs. 81 sites.

20. Maidstone State Park, Guildhall, VT 058905. Phone: (802) 676-3930.

Located near NH state line, 5 miles north of Maidstone on VT 102 to marked State Forest Hwy. 45 sites; no big rigs.

21. Molly Stark State Park, 705 Route 9 East, Wilmington, VT 05363. Phone: (802) 464-5460. Located about 4 miles east of Wilmington on VT 9 in southern Vermont. 23 sites.

22. New Discovery State Park, 4239 VT 232, Marshfield, VT 05658. Phone: (802) 426-3042. Located 23 miles northeast of Montpelier via US 2 and VT 232. 46 sites.

23. North Hero State Park, 3803 Lakeview Rd., North Hero, VT 05474. Phone: (802) 372-8389. Located on Lake Champlain about 20 miles west of Swanton via VT 79 and US 2. 99 sites.

24. Quechee Gorge State Park, 764 Dewey Mills Rd., White River, VT 05001. Phone: (802) 295-2990 (summer) or 888-409-7579 (Oct.-May). Located off US 4 in Quechee (I-89 exit 1). 47 sites.

25. Ricker Pond State Park, 526 State Forest Rd., Groton, VT 05046. Phone: (802) 584-3821. Located off VT 232, 5 miles NW of Groton (US 302). 32 sites.

26. Silver Lake State Park, Barnard, VT 05031. Phone: (802) 234-9451. Located on Silver Lake, 1 mile north of Barnard on VT 12. 40 sites.

27. Smugglers Notch State Park, 6443 Mountain Rd., Stowe, VT 05672. Phone: (802) 253-4014. Located about 10 miles NW of Stowe on VT 108. 7 sites; no big rigs.

28. Stillwater State Park, 126 Boulder Beach Rd., Groton, VT 05046. Phone: (802) 584-3822. Located NW of Groton, off US 302 and VT 232. 60 sites.

29. Thetford Hill State Park, Thetford, VT 05074. Phone: (802) 785-2266. From I-91 exit 14, go 1 mile north on VT 113 to Thetford Hill and then south 1 1/2 miles on Academy Rd. 14 sites.

30. Townshend State Park, 2755 State Forest Rd., Townshend, VT 05353. Phone: (802) 365-7500. Located in Townshend, off VT 30 on the West River. 30 sites; no dump station; no big rigs.

31. Wilgus State Park, Ascutney, VT 05030. Phone: (802) 674-5422. Located off VT 5 in Weathersfield Bow. 19 sites.

32. Woodford State Park, 142 State Park Rd., Woodford, VT 05201. Phone: (802) 447-7169. Located on VT 9 about 11 miles east of Bennington. 83 sites.

Virginia

Virginia has 19 State Parks with RV accessibility. All listed parks have dump stations. Most locations have water and electricity at the sites, several with 50-amp service. Individual parks cannot take reservations (except Breaks Interstate Park) but you can check availability by calling a park. The state-wide reservation service requires 48 hours advance notice and is not open on weekends. Rate groups: B and C depending on site facilities; Kiptopeke State Park considered a premium park.

Virginia Dept. of Conservation and Recreation
203 Governor St., Ste. 302
Richmond, VA 23219
Information: (804) 786-1712 / Reservations: (800) 933-7275
Internet: www.dcr.state.va.us

Virginia Park Locator

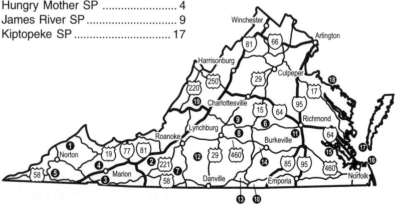

1. Breaks Interstate Park, Breaks, VA 24607. Phone: (800) 982-5122 or
    (540) 865-4413. Located on VA/KY state line, off VA-KY 80. 122 sites
    with electric; showers. No size limit.

2. Claytor Lake State Park, Dublin, VA 24084. Phone: (540) 643-2500.
    Located northeast of Pulaski at I-81 exit 101; east to park. 110 sites with
    water, electric; showers. 35 foot limit.

3. Grayson Highlands State Park, 829 Grayson Highland Ln., Mouth of
    Wilson, VA 24363. Phone: (276) 579-7092. Located 34 miles south of
    Marion and I-81 exit 45 via VA 16, US 58, and VA 362. 32 sites with water,
    electric; showers. 40 foot limit.

4. Hungry Mother State Park, 2854 Park Blvd., Marion, VA 24354. Phone:
    (276) 781-7400; Located on VA 16, 4 miles north of Marion (I-81 exit 47).
    32 sites with water, electric; showers. 36 foot limit.

5. Natural Tunnel State Park, Duffield, VA 24244. Phone: (276) 940-2674.
    Located on VA 871 about 13 miles northwest of Gate City via US 23. 18
    sites with water, electric; showers. 38 foot limit.

6. Bear Creek Lake State Park, 929 Oak Hill Rd., Cumberland, VA 23040.
    Phone: (804) 492-4410. Located off VA 622, via US 60 north from
    Cumberland. 29 sites; (23 sites - 20 foot limit; 6 sites - 35 foot limit) water;
    electric; showers.

7. Fairy Stone State Park, 967 Fairystone Lake Dr., Stuart, VA 24171. Phone:
    (276) 930-2424. Located on VA 57 about 24 miles NW of Martinsville via
    US 58 and VA 57 & 623. 51 sites with water, electric; showers. 30 foot
    limit.

8. Holiday Lake State Park, Appomattox, VA 24522. Phone: (434) 248-6308.
    Located in the Appomattox-Buckingham State Forest east of Appomattox;
    access from VA 24, 636 and 640. 30 sites with water, electric; showers.
    30 foot limit.

9. James River State Park, Gladstone, VA 24533. Phone: (434) 933-4355.
    Located NE of Lynchburg on VA 647 via US 29 & VA 655. 9 sites (primitive);
    showers; dump station. 30 foot limit.

10. Occoneechee State Park, 1192 Occoneechee Park Rd., Clarksvillle, VA
    23927. Phone: (434) 374-2210. Located 1.5 miles east of Clarksville on

US 58, near junction with US 15. 37 sites with water and electric; 51 primitive sites; showers. 30 foot limit.

11. Pocahontas State Park, 10301 State Park Rd., Chesterfield, VA 23838. Phone: (804) 796-4255. Located about 20 miles southwest of Richmond. From I-95, take exit 61 and go west on VA 10 to VA 655. 59 sites with water, electric; showers. 40 foot limit.

12. Smith Mountain Lake State Park, 1235 State Park Rd., Huddleston, VA 24104. Phone: (540) 297-6066. Located on Smith Mountain Lake, SE of Roanoke off VA 626. 29 sites (24 sites - 30 foot limit; 5 sites - 50 foot limit) with water, electric; showers.

13. Staunton River State Park, 1170 Staunton Trail, Scottsburg, VA 24589. Phone: (434) 572-4623. Located 18 miles east of South Boston via US 360 and VA 344. 34 sites (6 sites - 20 foot limit; some to 45 foot limit.) with water, electric; showers.

14. Twin Lakes State Park, 788 Twin Lakes Rd., Green Bay, VA 23942. Phone: (434) 392-3435. Located 5 miles SW of Burkeville via US 360 and VA 621. 27 sites with water, electric; showers. 35 foot limit.

15. Chippokes Plantation State Park, 695 Chippokes Park Rd., Surry, VA 23883. Phone: (757) 294-3525. Located NW of Norfolk on the James River, off VA 10. 32 sites; water, electric; showers. 40 foot limit.

16. First Landing State Park, 2500 Shore Dr., Virginia Beach, VA 23451. Phone: (757) 412-2300. Located on US 60 at Cape Henry in Virginia Beach. 233 sites; water, electric; showers. 50 foot limit.

17. Kiptopeke State Park, 3540 Kiptopeke Dr., Cape Charles, VA 23310. Phone: (757) 331-2267. Located on eastern shore, 3 miles north of Chesapeake Bay Bridge Tunnel on VA 704, via US 13. 94 sites with water, electric; 40 with sewer; 50 foot limit.

18. Westmoreland State Park, 1650 State Park Rd., Montross, VA 22520. Phone: (804) 493-8821. Located 5 miles north of Montross via VA 3 and VA 347. 56 sites; 42 with water, electric; showers; 14 primitive sites. 40 foot limit.

19. Douthat State Park, Millboro, VA 24460. Phone: (540) 862-8100. Located 5 miles north of Clifton Forge and I-64 exit 27 via VA629. 55 sites with water, electric; showers. 45 foot limit.

Parks. wa. gov

Washington

There are 73 RV-friendly State Parks in Washington. Many of these parks offer sites with full hook-ups and only a few are classified as "primitive." Almost every Washington park has some primitive sites in addition to the other listed sites. In the listings, "standard sites" means the campsites have no utilities but water and showers are nearby. The park listing will indicate the number of standard sites, plus the sites that have utilities and their type. Some parks accept reservations but all sites are available on a first-come basis. The reservation system requires 48 hours advance request. *The last two listings are parks in Washington's San Juan Islands. These parks are accessible only via the Washington Ferry System.* Numerous parks in the system are located on the islands in Puget Sound, as indicated. These islands are connected to the mainland by bridges and do not require ferry access. Rate groups: B and C depending on site utilities.

State of Washington
Parks & Recreation Commission
7150 Cleanwater Lane
Box 42650
Olympia, WA 98504
Information: (360) 902-8844 / Reservations: (888) 226-7688
Internet: www.parks.wa.gov

cancel line on 2 ls

Camp out

Washington Park Locator

Washington Park Locator (*cont.*)

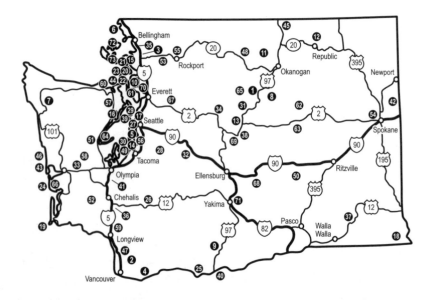

1. Alta Lake State Park, Paternos, WA 98846. Phone: (509) 923-2473. Located 4 miles SW of Paternos on WA 153 near junction of US 97. 157 standard sites; 32 with electric, water; dump station. 40 foot limit.

2. Battle Ground Lake State Park, Battle Ground, WA 98604. Phone: (360) 687-4621. Located 21 miles NE of Vancouver on WA 503. 31 standard sites; 2 with electric; dump station. 50 foot limit. Reservations accepted.

3. Bay View State Park, Mt. Vernon, WA 98273. Phone: (360) 757-0227. Located in northern WA, 7 miles west of Burlington off WA 20; I-5 exit 231, west to park. 46 standard sites; 1 full hook-up; 29 with electric, water. 60 foot limit.

4. Beacon Rock State Park, Skamania, WA 98648. Phone: (509) 427-8265. Located in southern WA, 35 miles east of Vancouver on WA 14. Also accessible from Oregon I-84 via Cascade Locks exit and toll bridge to WA 14. 34 standard sites; dump station. 40 foot limit.

5. Belfair State Park, Belfair, WA 98528. Phone: (360) 275-0668. Located in Hood Canal, 3 miles west of Belfair on WA 300. From I-5, exit in Tacoma onto WA 16, north to WA 3 in Bremerton then west to WA 300. 135 standard sites; 47 full hook-ups; dump station. 60 foot limit. Reservations accepted.

6. Birch Bay State Park, Blaine, WA 98230. Phone: (360) 371-2800. Located in northwestern WA, 8 miles south of Blaine on WA 58, near Canadian border; I-5 exits 260, 263 or 274 to WA 68. 146 standard sites; 4 full hook-ups; 18 with electric, water; dump station. 60 foot limit. Reservations accepted.

7. Bogachiel State Park, Forks, WA 98321. Phone: (360)374-6356. Located on Olympic Peninsula, 6 miles south of Forks on US 101. 36 standard sites; 6 with electric, water; dump station. 35 foot limit.

8. Bridgeport State Park, Bridgeport, WA 98813. Phone: (509) 686-7231. Located in central WA, 3 miles NE of Bridgeport near Chief Joseph Dam on the Columbia River; accessible from US 97 or WA 174. 14 standard sites; 20 with electric, water; dump station. 45 foot limit.

9. Brooks Memorial State Park, Goldendale, WA 98620. Phone: (509) 773-4611. Located in southern WA, 13 miles north of Goldendale on US 97; accessible from WA 14 or Oregon I-84 exit 104 to US 97. 22 standard sites; 23 full hook-ups; dump station. 30 foot limit.

10. Camano Island State Park, Camano Island, WA 98282. Phone: (360) 387-3031. Located in northwestern WA, 5 miles SW of Stanwood (I-5 exit 212) on WA 532. 87 standard sites; dump station. 45 foot limit.

11. Conconully State Park, Conconully, WA 98819. Phone: (509) 826-7408. Remote location in north-central WA, 22 miles NW of Omak, off US 97 on marked county roads. 84 standard sites; dump station. 60 foot limit

12. Curlew State Park, Republic, WA 99166. Phone: (509) 775-3592. Located in northeastern WA on WA 21, 20 miles NE of Republic via US 97 or WA 20. 57 standard sites; 18 full hook-ups; 7 with electric, water; dump station. 40 foot limit.

13. Daroga State Park, Orondo, WA 98843. Phone: (509) 664-6380. Located in central WA, 18 miles north of East Wenatchee on US Alt. 97. 1 full hook-up site; 27 with electric, water; dump station. 45 foot limit.

14. Dash Point State Park, Federal Way, WA 98023. Phone: (253) 661-4855. Located in western WA on Puget Sound, 5 miles NE of Tacoma on WA 509. From I-5 exit 143 west to 47th Avenue, follow signs. 107 standard sites; 29 with electric, water; dump station. 45 foot limit.

15. Deception Pass State Park, Oak Harbor, WA 98277. Phone: (360) 675-2417. Located in western WA on Whidbey Island (bridge access), 10 miles north of Oak Harbor on WA 20. 241 standard sites; dump station. 60 foot limit. Reservations accepted.

16. Dosewallips State Park, Brinnon, WA 98320. Phone: (360) 796-4415. Located on Olympic Peninsula, 1 mile south of Brinnon on US 101. Access from Olympia via I-5 exit 104, 50 miles north of US 101. 97 standard sites; 40 full hook-ups; dump station. 60 foot limit. Reservations accepted.

17. Fay-Bainbridge State Park, Bainbridge Island, WA 98110. Phone: (206) 842-3931. Located in Puget Sound, northeastern end of Bainbridge Island, near WA 305. *Not easily accessible; requires ferry from Seattle or via WA 104 from the north.* 26 standard sites; 13 primitive sites; dump station. 30 foot limit.

18. Fields Spring State Park, Anatone, WA 99401. Phone: (509) 256-3332. Located in southeastern WA, south of Lewiston, Idaho, on WA 129. 20 standard sites; dump station. 30 foot limit.

19. Cape Disappointment State Park, Ilwaco, WA 98640. Phone: (360) 642-3078. Located in southwestern WA near mouth of the Columbia River,

outside Ilwaco off US 101. 152 standard sites; 83 full hook-ups, 23 with electric, water; dump station. 45 foot limit. Reservations accepted. (Park was once called Fort Canby State Park.)

20. Fort Casey State Park, Coupeville, WA 98239. Phone: (360) 678-4519. Located in Puget Sound on Whidbey Island, (bridge access) 3 miles south of Coupeville on WA 20. 35 standard sites. 40 foot limit.

21. Fort Ebey State Park, Coupeville, WA 98239. Phone: (360) 678-4636. Located on Whidbey Island (bridge access), 8 miles south of Oak Harbor on WA 20. 50 standard sites; 4 with electric. 100 foot limit. Reservations accepted.

22. Fort Flagler State Park, Nordland, WA 98358. Phone: (360) 385-1259. Located on northeastern tip of Olympic Peninsula, 8 miles NE of Port Hadlock off WA 20. 101 standard sites; 15 with electric, water; dump station. 50 foot limit. Reservations accepted.

23. Fort Worden State Park, Nordland, WA 98358. Phone: (360) 344-4400. Located on northern end Olympic Peninsula, just north of Port Townsend off WA 20. 50 full hook-up sites; 30 with electric, water; dump station. 60 foot limit. Reservations accepted.

24. Grayland Beach State Park, Grayland, WA 98547. Phone: (360) 267-4301. Located on Washington coast, SW of Aberdeen on WA 105, 6 miles north of Wallapa Bay. 60 sites with electric, water. 40 foot limit. Reservations accepted.

25. Columbia Hills State Park, Dallasport, WA 98617. Phone: (509) 767-1159. Located in southern WA, 28 miles SW of Goldendale on WA 14. 4 standard sites; 8 with electric, water; dump station. 60 foot limit. (Once called Horsethief Lake State Park.)

26. Ike Kinswa State Park, Silver Creek, WA 98585. Phone: (360) 983-3402. Located 18 miles east of I-5 exit 68 via US 12 and WA 122. 30 standard sites; 71 full hook-ups; dump station. 60 foot limit.

27. Illahee State Park, Bremerton, WA 98310. Phone: (360) 478-6460. Located in Puget Sound, 9 miles north of Bremerton on WA 303, about 9 miles east of WA 16. 24 standard sites; 1 full hook-ups; dump station. 40 foot limit.

28. Kanaskat- Palmer State Park, Ravendale, WA 98051. Phone: (360) 886-0148. Located in western WA, SE of Seattle, 9 miles NE of Enumclaw.

From I-5 exit 143 to Auburn then WA 164 to Enumclaw, follow signs. 31 standard sites; 19 with electric; dump station. 50 foot limit. Reservations accepted.

29. Kitsap Memorial State Park, Poulsbo, WA 98370. Phone: (360) 779-3205. Located in western WA in Puget Sound, NW of Seattle, on WA 3 off WA 104, 4 miles south of Hood Canal Bridge. 25 standard sites; 18 with electric, water; dump station. 40 foot limit.

30. Kopachuck State Park, Gig Harbor, WA 98335. Phone: (253) 265-3606. Located in Puget Sound, NW of Tacoma on WA 16, 7 miles west of Gig Harbor. From I-5, exit at WA 16 in Tacoma, north on WA 16 to park. 41 standard sites; dump station. 35 foot limit.

31. Lake Chelan State Park, Chelan, WA 98816. Phone: (509) 687-3710. Located in central WA, 9 miles west of Chelan, off US 97 on WA 971. 109 standard sites; 17 full hook-ups; 18 with electric, water; dump station. 30 foot limit. Reservations accepted.

32. Lake Easton State Park, Easton, WA 98925. Phone: (509) 656-2230. Located in central WA near Easton, off I-90 exit 71. 92 standard sites; 45 full hook-ups; dump station. 60 foot limit. Reservations accepted.

33. Lake Sylvia State Park, Montesano, WA 98563. Phone: (360) 249-3621. Located in western WA, 1 mile north of Montesano, off US 12 between Olympia and Aberdeen. 35 standard sites; dump station. 30 foot limit.

34. Lake Wenatchee State Park, Leavenworth, WA 98826. Phone: (509) 763-3101. Located in central WA, 18 miles north of Leavenworth, off US 2 on WA 207. 197 standard sites; dump station. 60 foot limit. Reservations accepted.

35. Larrabee State Park, Bellingham, WA 98225. Phone: (360) 676-2093. Located in northwestern WA, 7 miles south of Bellingham off WA 11, next to I-5. 51 standard sites; 26 full hook-ups; dump station. 60 foot limit. Reservations accepted.

36. Lewis & Clark State Park, Winlock, WA 98596. Phone: (360) 864-2643. Located in southwestern WA, 12 miles SE of Chehalis on US 12, just off I-5 exit 68. 25 standard sites; 10 with water, sewer. 60 foot limit.

37. Lewis & Clark Trail State Park, Dayton, WA 99328. Phone: (509) 337-

6457. Located in southeastern WA, 24 miles NE of Walla Walla on US 12. 25 standard sites; dump station. 65 foot limit.

38. Lincoln Rock State Park, East Wenatchee, WA 98801. Phone: (509) 884-8702. Located in central WA, 6 miles north of East Wenatchee on US 2/97. 27 standard sites; 32 full hook-ups; 35 with electric, water; dump station. 65 foot limit. Reservations accepted.

39. Manchester State Park, Manchester, WA 98353. Phone: (360) 871-4065. Located on Olympic Peninsula, 6 miles NE of Port Orchard on WA 16. 35 standard sites; 15 with electric, water; dump station. 60 foot limit. Reservations accepted.

40. Maryhill State Park, Goldendale, WA 98620. Phone: (509) 723-5007. Located in southern WA on US 97, on the Columbia River, 12 miles south of Goldendale. 20 standard sites; 50 full hook-ups; dump station. 60 foot limit.

41. Millersylvania State Park, Olympia, WA 98512. Phone: (360) 753- 1519. Located in southwestern WA on WA 121 near I-5 exit 95. 120 standard sites; 48 with electric, water; dump station. 60 foot limit. Reservations accepted.

42. Mount Spokane State Park, Mead, WA 99021. Phone: (509) 238-4258. Remote location in eastern WA, 30 miles NE of Spokane off US 2 on county roads, follow signs. 12 standard sites. 30 foot limit.

43. Ocean City State Park, Ocean Shores, WA 98569. Phone: (360) 289-3553. Located on Washington coast at intersection of WA 109 & 115, 1.5 miles north of Ocean Shores. 149 standard sites; 29 full hook-ups; dump station. 50 foot limit. Reservations accepted.

44. Old Fort Townsend State Park, Port Townsend, WA 98368. Phone: (360) 344-4400. Located on northern Olympic Peninsula, 3 miles south of Port Townsend off WA 20. 40 standard sites; dump station. 38 foot limit.

45. Osoyoos Lake State Park, Oroville, WA 98844. Phone: (509) 476-3321. Located in north-central WA near Canadian border, outside Oroville on US 97. 80 standard sites; 1 with electric, water; dump station. 45 foot limit. Reservations accepted.

46. Pacific Beach State Park, Pacific Beach, WA 98571. Phone: (360) 276-

4297. Located on Washington coast, just south of Pacific Beach on WA 109. 20 standard sites; 42 with electric; dump station. 50 foot limit. Reservations accepted.

47. Paradise Point State Park, Ridgefield, WA 98642. Phone: (360) 263-2350. Located in southwestern WA, 5 miles south of Woodland, at I-5 exit 16. 69 standard sites; dump station. 40 foot limit. Reservations accepted.

48. Pearrygin Lake State Park, Winthrop, WA 98862. Phone: (509) 996-2370. Located in north-central WA outside Winthrop on WA 20. 53 standard sites; 30 full hook-ups; dump station. 60 foot limit. Reservations accepted.

49. Penrose Point State Park, Lakebay, WA 98349. Phone: (253) 884-2514. Located on Olympic Peninsula, 3 miles north of Longbranch on WA 302. 83 standard sites; dump station. 35 foot limit. Reservations accepted.

50. Potholes State Park, Othello, WA 99344. Phone: (509) 346-2759. Located in east-central WA, 25 miles SW of Moses Lake (I-90 exit 179) on WA 262, via WA 17. 60 full hook-up sites; dump station. 50 foot limit; Reservations accepted.

51. Potlatch State Park, Shelton, WA 98584. Phone: (360) 877-5361. Located on Olympic Peninsula NW of Olympia, 12 miles north of Shelton on US 101. 17 standard sites; 18 full hook-ups; dump station. 60 foot limit.

52. Rainbow Falls State Park, Chehalis, WA 98532. Phone: (360) 291-3767. Located in southwestern WA, 17 miles west of Chehalis off I-5 exit 77, on WA 6. 50 standard sites; dump station. 32 foot limit.

53. Rasar State Park, Concrete, WA 98237. Phone: (360) 826-3942. Located in northwestern WA, 17 miles east of Sedro Woolley (I-5 exit 229) on WA 20. 19 standard sites; 19 with electric, water; dump station. 40 foot limit. Reservations accepted.

54. Riverside State Park, Nine Mile Falls, WA 99026. Phone: (509) 465-5064. Located in eastern WA on Spokane River in NW Spokane, off Aubrey White Parkway. 22 standard sites; 17 with electric, water; dump station. 45 foot limit.

55. Rockport State Park, Rockport, WA 98283. Phone: (360) 853-8461. Located in northwestern WA, 40 miles east of Burlington (I-5 exit 229) on WA 20. 8 standard sites; 50 full hook-ups; dump station. 45 foot limit.

56. Saltwater State Park, Des Moines, WA 98198. Phone: (360) 830-5079. Located in northwestern WA south of Seattle on Puget Sound, 2 miles south of Des Moines (I-5 exit 149) on WA 509. 51 standard sites; dump station. 60 foot limit.

57. Scenic Beach State Park, Seabeck, WA 98380. Phone: (360) 830-5079. Located on the Olympic Peninsula, 12 miles NW of Bremerton on WA 300. 50 standard sites; dump station. 60 foot limit. Reservations accepted.

58. Schafer State Park, Elma, WA 98541. Phone: (360) 482-3852. Located on the Olympic Peninsula, 12 miles north of Elma off US 12, on WA 102. 34 standard sites; 6 with electric, water; dump station. 40 foot limit.

59. Seaquest State Park, Castle Rock, WA 98611. Phone: (360) 274-8633. Located in southwestern WA, 5 miles east of Castle Rock (I-5 exit 49). 58 standard sites; 16 full hook-ups; 18 with electric, water; dump station. 32 foot limit. Reservations accepted.

60. Sequim Bay State Park, Sequim, WA 98261. Phone: (360) 683-4235. Located on northern Olympic Peninsula, 4 miles east of Sequim on US 101. 60 standard sites; 16 full hook-ups; dump station. 30 foot limit. Reservations accepted.

61. South Whidbey State Park, Freeland, WA 98249. Phone: (360) 331-4559. Located on Puget Sound, on Whidbey Island (bridge access), 3 miles south of Greenbank on WA 525. 37 standard sites; 9 with electric, water; dump station. 50 foot limit. Reservations accepted.

62. Steamboat Rock State Park, Electric City, WA 99123. Phone: (509) 633-1304. Located in east-central WA, 12 miles SW of Grand Coulee on WA 155, on Banks Lake. 26 standard sites; 100 full hook-ups; dump station. 50 foot limit. Reservations accepted.

63. Sun Lakes-Dry Falls State Park, Coulee City, WA 99115. Phone: (509) 632-5583. Located in east-central WA, 7 miles SW of Coulee City on WA 17. 158 standard sites; 18 full hook-ups; dump station. 50 foot limit. Reservations accepted.

64. Twanoh State Park, Union, WA 98592. Phone: (360) 275-2222. Located on the Olympic Peninsula, 19 miles SW of Bremerton on WA 106, off WA 3. 17 standard sites; 9 full hook-ups; 13 with electric, water. 35 foot limit.

65. Twenty-five Mile Creek State Park, Chelan, WA 98816. Phone: (509) 687-3610. Remote location in central WA, 18 miles NW of Chelan via US 97A,

WA 971, and S Lakeshore Rd. 53 standard sites; 13 full hook-ups; 9 with electric, water; dump station. 30 foot limit. Reservations accepted.

66. Twin Harbors State Park, Westport, WA 98595. Phone: (360) 268-9717. Located in western WA, just south of Grays Harbor on central WA coast, 3 miles south of Westport on WA 105. 253 standard sites; 49 full hook-ups; dump station. 35 foot limit.

67. Wallace Falls State Park, Gold Bar, WA 98251. Phone: (360) 793-0420. Located in west-central WA on US 2 southeast of Everett, between Gold Bar and Index. 6 standard sites.

68. Wanapum State Park, Vantage, WA 98950. Phone: (509) 856-2700. Located in south-central WA , 3 miles south of Vantage (I-90 exit 136) on the Columbia River. 50 full hook-up sites. 60 foot limit. Reservations accepted.

69. Wenatchee Confluence State Park, Wenatchee, WA 98801. Phone: (509) 664-6373. Located in central WA, in Wenatchee on US 97/2. 18 standard sites; 51 full hook-ups; dump station. 65 foot limit. Reservations accepted.

70. Wenberg State Park, Stanwood, WA 98292. Phone: (360) 652-7417. Located in northwestern WA, 18 miles NW of Everett on Lake Goodwin, off I-5 exit 199 west, follow signs. 45 standard sites; 30 with electric, water; dump station. 50 foot limit.

71. Yakima Sportsman State Park, Yakima, WA 98901. Phone: (509) 575-2774. Located in south-central WA, 1 mile east of Yakima off I-82 exit 34. 28 standard sites; 37 full hook-ups; dump station. 60 foot limit. Reservations accepted.

72. Moran State Park, Olga, WA 98279. Phone: (360) 376-2326. Located on Orcas Island (San Juan Islands) near Eastsound. 136 standard sites; dump station. *Washington State ferry access.*

73. Spencer Spit State Park, Lopez Island, WA 98261. Phone: (360) 468-2251. Located on Lopez Island (San Juan Islands), south from ferry landing. 37 standard sites; dump station. *Washington State ferry access.*

West Virginia

West Virginia maintains 28 parks or wildlife management areas with RV facilities. These locations are well appointed with facilities but most are "off the beaten track" as far as access to major highways. Most of the parks are open only seasonally. Four locations (Canaan, Stonewall, Pipestem and Twin Falls) are resorts with exceptional amenities. Senior discounts are available with proof of age but you must request this discount. Pets are allowed on leases and alcohol is prohibited in some parks. Credit cards are accepted in most locations. All parks accept reservations, which require a 48-hour advance request. Campsites are listed as "Standard" (with some or full hook-ups) or "Rustic" (no site facilities). Unless noted in park listing, there are no rig size limitations. Rate groups: B and C depending on site facilities.

West Virginia Division of Tourism
1201 Washington St. East
Charleston, WV 25305
Information and Reservations: (800) 225-5982. For reservations, ask for particular park.
NOTE: Any park can be reached through the above central number during business hours.
Internet: www.wvstateparks.com

West Virginia Park Locator

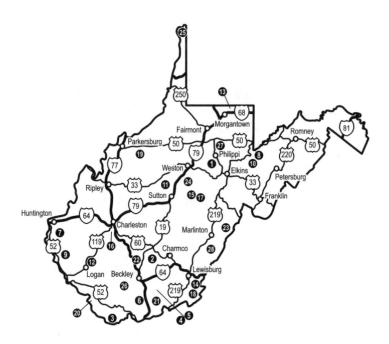

1. Audra State Park, Buckhannon, WV 26201. Phone: (304) 457-1162. Located NE of Buckhannon between US 119 & US 250. 65 sites; showers; laundry; dump station.

2. Babcock State Park, Clifftop, WV 25831. Phone: (304) 438-3004. Located NE of Beckley on WV 41 at Clifftop, 2 miles south of US 60. 52 sites; showers; laundry; dump station. No alcohol.

3. Berwind Lake Wildlife Management Area, War, WV 24894. Phone: (304) 875-2577. Located in southern WV, near VA state line, SW of War (west of Bluefield), off WV 16. 8 sites, 4 with electric.

4. Bluestone State Park, Hinton, WV 25951. Phone: (304) 466-2805. Located 4 miles south of Hinton on WV 20. 32 sites, 22 with electric; 45 rustic sites; showers; dump station.

5. Bluestone Wildlife Management Area, Indian Mills, WV 24935. Phone: (304) 466-3398. Located near Bluestone State Park, SE of Hinton on Bluestone Lake. Follow signs from Hinton. 315 rustic sites.

6. Camp Creek State Park, 2390 Camp Creek Rd., Camp Creek, WV 25820. Phone: (304) 425-9481. Located off I-77 exit 20 in southern WV. 38 sites (2 areas), 26 with electric, 14 rustic; showers; laundry.

7. Beech Fork State Park, 5601 Long Branch Rd., Barboursville, WV 25504. Phone: (304) 528-5794. Located in western WV, south of Huntington, off WV 152 (I-64 exit 11). 275 full hook-up sites, (some 50-amp); showers; laundry.

8. Blackwater Falls State Park, Davis, WV 26260. Phone: (304)259-5216. Located near Davis in eastern WV off US 219. 65 sites, 30 with electric; showers; laundry; dump station.

9. Cabwaylingo State Forest, Dunlow, WV 25511. Phone: (304) 385-4255. Remote location 27 miles south of Huntington, off WV 152, near KY state line. 31 sites, 6 with electric; showers.

10. Canaan Valley Resort State Park, Davis, WV 26260. Phone: (304) 866-4121 or (800) 622-4121. Located SW of Davis on WV 72, off US 219 in northern WV. 34 sites with full hook-ups; showers.

11. Cedar Creek State Park, Glenville, WV 26351. Phone: (304) 462-8517. Located 25 miles west of I-79 exit 79 in central WV, south of Glenville off US 33. 47 sites, 10 with electric; showers; laundry.

12. Chief Logan State Park, Route 10, Logan, WV 25601. Phone: (304) 792-7125. Located in southwestern WV, 4 miles north of Logan on WV 10. 24 sites, 14 with full hook-ups; 10 with electric; showers.

13. Coopers Rock State Forest, Bruceton Mills, WV 26525. Phone: (304) 594-1561. Located in northern WV, NE of Morgantown, off I-64 exit 23; follow signs. 25 sites with electric; showers.

14. Greenbrier State Forest, Caldwell, WV 24925. Phone: (304) 536-1944. Located near White Sulphur Springs in southeastern WV at I-64 exit 175. 16 sites with electric; showers.

15. Holly River State Park, Hacker Valley, WV 26222. Phone: (304) 493-6353. Remote location in central WV, 22 miles east of I-79 exit 67, on WV 20. 88 sites with electric; showers; laundry; dump station.

16. Kanawha State Forest, Charleston, WV 24314. Phone: (304) 558-3500. Located 7 miles south of Charleston. From I-64 exit 58A, follow signs. 46 sites with electric; showers; laundry; dump station.

17. Kumbrabow State Forest, Huttonsville, WV 26273. Phone: (304) 335-2219. Remote location in central WV, 26 miles south of Buckhannon off WV 55. 13 rustic sites; showers; laundry. 20 foot limit.

18. Moncove Lake State Park, Gap Mills, WV 24941. Phone: (304) 772-3450.

Located in southeastern WV, SW of White Sulphur Springs, off US 219 at Union, follow signs. 48 sites, 25 with electric; showers; dump station.

19. North Bend State Park, Cairo, WV 26337. Phone: (304) 643-2931. Located SE of Parkersburg, off US 50 on WV 31, SE of Cairo. 49 sites, 26 with electric.

20. Panther State Forest, Panther Creek Road, Panther, WV 24872. Phone: (304) 938-2252. Located in southwestern WV, near VA/KY state line, off US 52 at Iaeger, follow signs. 6 sites with electric.

21. Pipestem Resort State Park, Pipestem, WV 25979. Phone: (304) 466-1800. Located in southern WV, 15 miles south of Hinton on WV 20. 82 full hook-up sites; showers; laundry.

22. Plum Orchard Wildlife Management Area, Scarbro, WV 25917. Phone: (304) 469-9905. Located off I-77 exits 54 or 60, near Moss and Pax, on CR 23. 42 rustic sites; water available.

23. Seneca State Forest, Dunmore, WV 24934. Phone: (304) 799-6213. Remote location in eastern WV in Monongahela National Forest, east of WV 28. 10 rustic sites; showers (nearby); laundry.

24. Stonewall Jackson Lake State Park, (Resort) 149 State Park Trail, Roanoke, WV 26447. Phone: (304) 269-0523. Located in central WV off US 19 at I-79 exit 91; follow signs. 35 full hook-up sites; showers.

25. Tomlinson Run State Park, New Manchester, WV 26056. Phone: (304) 564-3651. Located in WV "Panhandle," north of Weirton off WV 8, on Ohio River. 54 sites, 39 with electric; showers; laundry; dump station.

26. Twin Falls Resort State Park, Mullens, WV 25882. Phone: (304) 294-4000. Located in southwestern WV, SW of Beckley on WV 97, off I-77 exits 28 or 43; follow signs. 50 sites, 25 with electric; showers; laundry; dump station.

27. Tygart Lake State Park, Grafton, WV 26354. Phone: (304) 265-6148. Located in northern WV, south of Grafton (17 miles east of Clarksburg) on US 250. 40 sites, 14 with electric; showers; water available; dump station.

28. Watoga State Park, Marlinton, WV 24954. Phone: (304) 799-4087. Located in southeastern WV, 14 miles south of Marlinton on WV 28, off US 219. Two campgrounds with 88 sites, 31 with electric; showers; laundry.

Wisconsin

There are 34 Wisconsin state parks with RV facilities. Some of the parks are seasonal (Spring/Summer) and are noted in the listings. No parks offer site water; however water is available at all parks. Most have dump stations and limited electric hook-up sites. The State reservation system requires 48 hours advance contact. You should contact the particular state on the day of an intended stay to verify available space. No park can hold space except through the state-wide system. Each park charges a daily admission fee in addition to the campground fee. Non-residents pay more for camping fees than Wisconsin residents. Sunday-Thursday and off season rates are less. Rate group: A, plus entrance fee.

Wisconsin Dept. of Natural Resources
101 South Webster St.
Box 7921
Madison, WI 53707
Information: (608) 266-2181 or (800) 432-8747
Reservations: (888) 947-2757
Internet: www.wiparks.net

Wisconsin Park Locator

Wisconsin Park Locator (*cont.*)

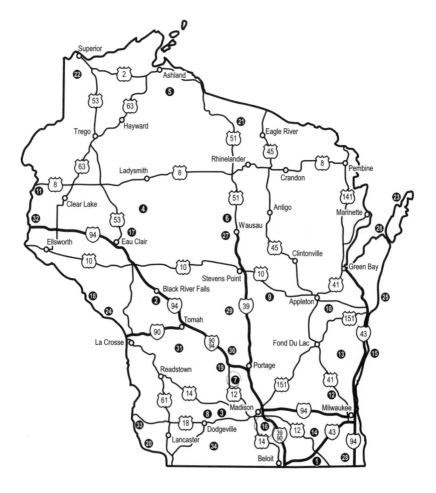

1. Big Foot Beach State Park, 1452 County Hwy (Lakeshore Dr.) Lake Geneva, WI 53147. Phone: (262) 248-2528. Located off WI 120 south of Lake Geneva. Seasonal; 100 sites; showers; dump station.

2. Black River State Forest, State Route 54, Black River Falls, WI 54615. Phone: (715) 284-4103. Located on WI 54, I-94 exit 116, east about 12 miles. 98 sites, 5 with electric; showers; dump station.

3. Blue Mound State Park, 4350 Mounds Park Rd., Blue Mounds, WI 53517. Phone: (608) 437-5711. Located about 25 miles west of Madison, off US 18 at CR K. 78 sites, 16 with electric; showers; dump station.

4. Brunet Island State Park, 23125 255th St., Cornell, WI 54732. Phone: (715) 239-6888. Located near Cornell (WI 27 & 64) about 25 miles east of US 53. Seasonal. 69 sites, 24 with electric; showers; dump station.

5. Copper Falls State Park, Mellen, WI 54546. Phone: (715) 274-5123. Located 3 miles north of Mellen, off WI 169. 55 sites, 13 with electric; showers; dump station.

6. Council Grounds State Park, Council Grounds Dr., Merrill, WI 54452. Phone: (715) 536-8773. Located 4 miles west of Merrill via WI 64 and WI 107. Seasonal. 55 sites, 19 with electric; showers; dump station.

7. Devil's Lake State Park, Park Rd., Baraboo, WI 53913. Phone: (608) 356-8301. Located about 5 miles south of Baraboo, east of US 12. 407 sites, 121 with electric; showers; dump station.

8. Governor Dodge State Park, 4175 Hwy 23 N, Dodgeville, WI 53533. Phone: (608) 935-2315. Located about 4 miles north of Dodgeville (US 18 & WI 23) on WI 23. 270 sites, 79 with electric; showers; dump station.

9. Hartman Creek State Park, Hartman Creek Rd., Waupaca, WI 54981. Phone: (715) 258-2372. Located about 4 miles SW of Waupaca on WI 22 (off US 10). 101 sites; showers; dump station.

10. High Cliff State Park, State Park Rd., Sherwood, WI 54169. Phone: (920) 989-1106. Located on Lake Winnebago on WI 55. 112 sites, 32 with electric; showers; dump station.

11. Interstate State Park, Hwy 35, St. Croix Falls, WI 54024. Phone: (715) 483-3747. Located on St. Croix Waterway, on WI 87, south of US 8. Seasonal. 85 sites; showers; dump station.

12. Kettle Moraine State Forest-Pike Lake Unit, 3544 Kettle Moraine Rd., Hartford, WI 53027. Phone: (262) 670-3400. Located about 45 miles east

of Hartford, off WI 60 at US 41. Seasonal. 32 sites; showers; dump station.

13. Kettle Moraine State Forest-Northern Unit, CR G, Campbellsport, WI 53010. Phone: 262-626-2116. Located near junction of US 45 & WI 67. 135 sites, 52 with electric; showers; dump station.

14. Kettle Moraine State Forest-Southern Unit, State Route 59, Eagle, WI 53119. Phone: (262) 670-3400 Located about 4 miles west of Eagle on WI 59. 265 sites, 49 electric; showers; dump station.

15. Kohler-Andrae State Park, 1020 Beach Park Lane, Sheboygan, WI 53081. Phone: (920) 451-4080. Located on Lake Michigan about 6 miles south of Sheboygan, off I-43 exit 120. 106 sites, 49 with electric; showers; dump station.

16. Lake Kegonsa State Park, 2405 Door Creek Rd., Stoughton, WI 53589. Phone: (608) 873-9695. Located on Lake Kegonsa off US 51, SE of Madison. Seasonal. 80 sites; showers; dump station.

17. Lake Wissota State Park, 18127 County Hwy O, Chippewa Falls, WI 54729. Phone: (715) 382-4574. Located on Lake Wissota off WI 178, NE of Eau Claire. Seasonal. 81 sites, 17 with electric; showers; dump station.

18. Merrick State Park, State Rd. 35, Fountain City, WI 54629. Phone: (608) 687-4936. Located 7 miles south of Cochrane along WI 35. Seasonal. 67 sites, 22 with electric; showers; dump station.

19. Mirror Lake State Park, Fern Dell Rd., Baraboo, WI 53913. Phone: (608) 254-2333. Located on WI 33, NW of Baraboo, off I-90/94 exit 89. 151 sites, 30 with electric; showers; dump station.

20. Nelson Dewey State Park, 12190 County Rd. VV, Cassville WI 53806. Phone: (608) 725-5374. Located 3 miles northwest of Cassville off WI 133, along CR W. 46 sites, 18 with electric; showers; dump station.

21. Northern Highland/American Legion State Forest, 4125 County Rd. M, Boulder Junction, WI 54512. Phone: (715) 385-2727. This is a 225,000-acre state forest in northern Wisconsin along US 51. 871 sites; showers; dump station.

22. Pattison State Park, 6294 S State Rd. 35, Superior, WI 54880. Phone: (715) 399-3111. Located on WI 35 about 15 miles south of Superior. 62 sites, 18 with electric; showers; dump station.

23. Peninsula State Park, 9462 Shore Rd., Fish Creek, WI 54212. Phone: (920) 868-3258. Located in WI Upper Peninsula between Fish Creek and

Ephraim along WI 42. 472 sites, 102 with electric; showers.

24. Perrot State Park, Sullivan Rd., Trempealeau, WI 54661. Phone: (608) 534-6409. Located on the Mississippi River off WI 93, northwest of I-90 at La Crosse. 98 sites, 36 with electric; showers; dump station.

25. Point Beach State Forest, 9400 County Rd. O, Two Rivers, WI 54241. Phone: (920) 794-7480. Located on Lake Michigan between Two Rivers and Kewaunee on WI 42. 127 sites, 70 with electric; showers; dump station.

26. Potawatomi State Park, 3740 County Hwy PD, Sturgeon Bay, WI 54235. Phone: (920) 746-2890. Located in Upper Peninsula off WI 57 near Sturgeon Bay. 123 sites, 25 with electric; showers; dump station.

27. Rib Mountain State Park, 4200 Park Rd., Wausau, WI 54401. Phone: (715) 842-2522. Located 5 miles west of Wausau, off WI 29. Seasonal. 30 sites, 3 with electric; showers.

28. Richard Bong State Recreation Area, 26313 Burlington Rd., Kansasville, WI 53139. Phone: (262) 878-5600. Located 9 miles east of Burlington on WI 142. 217 sites, 54 with electric; showers; dump station.

29. Roche-A-Cri State Park, 1767 Hwy 13, Friendship, WI 53934. Phone: (608) 339-6881. Located on WI 13 in Friendship about 19 miles west of I-39 exit 124. Seasonal. 44 sites, 1 electric; showers; dump station.

30. Rocky Arbor State Park, State Hwy 16, Wisconsin Dells, WI 53965. Phone: (608) 254-8001. Located near junction of US 12 and WI 16. Seasonal. 89 sites, 18 with electric; showers; dump station.

31. Wildcat Mountain State Park, State Hwy 33, Ontario, WI 54651. Phone: (608) 337-4775. Located about 38 miles SE of La Crosse, near Ontario, on WI 33. 30 sites; showers; dump station.

32. Willow River State Park, 1934 County Rd. A, Hudson, WI 54016. Phone: (715) 386-5931. Located northeast of Hudson about 4 miles north of I-94 exit 4 via US 12 and CR A. 78 sites, 25 with electric; showers; dump station.

33. Wyalusing State Park, 13081 State Park Ln., Bagley, WI 53801. Phone: (608) 996-2261. Located on the Mississippi River, off US 18, west of Bridgeport. 109 sites, 34 with electric; showers; dump station.

34. Yellowstone Lake State Park, 8495 Lake Rd., Blandchardville, WI 53516. Phone: (608) 523-4427. Located west of Blandchardville off WI 78, SW of Madison. 128 sites, 36 with electric; showers; dump station.

Wyoming

Eleven of Wyoming's State Parks or Recreation Areas have RV parking spaces. However, four of these locations have camping areas with no specific sites identified. These four parks do not accept reservations so the RV spaces are "open" and available on a first-come basis. While the other seven parks do have designated sites, there are no facilities at the sites; they are "dry camping" sites. These locations do accept reservations. All the parks offer drinking water and most have dump stations. There are no shower facilities in any park. Three parks have RV size limitations (see below). Rate group: A

Wyoming State Parks & Historic Sites
2301 Central Ave.
Barrett Bldg. - 4th Floor
Cheyenne, WY 82002
Information: (800) 225- 5996 / Reservations: (877) 996-7275
Internet: www.wyobest.org

Wyoming Park Locator

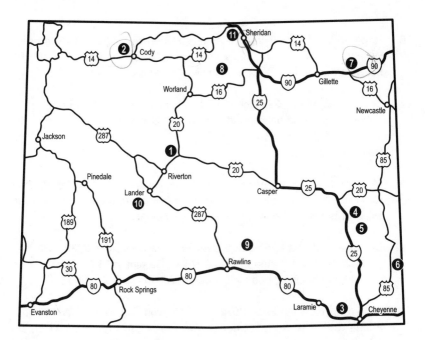

1. Boysen State Park, Boysen Route, Shoshoni, WY 82649. Phone: (307) 876-2796. Located 13 miles north of Shoshoni on US 20; also accessible from US 26. 200+ sites; dump station. Reservable.

2. Buffalo Bill State Park, 47 Lakeside Rd., Cody, WY 82414. Phone: (307) 876-2796. Located 9 miles west of Cody on US 14. 88 sites; 44 foot limit; dump station. Reservable.

3. Curt Gowdy State Park, 1351 Hynds Lodge Rd., Cheyenne, WY 82009. Phone: (307) 632-7946. Located between Cheyenne and Laramie on WY 210, just north of I-80. 150 sites; dump station. Reservable.

4. Glendo State Park, Glendo, WY 82213. Phone: (307) 735-4433. Located outside of Glendo, off I-25 exit 104. 300 sites; dump station. Reservable.

5. Guernsey State Park, Guernsey, WY 82214. Phone: (307) 836-2334. Located off US 26 outside of Guernsey. 142 sites; dump station. Reservable.

6. Hawk Springs State Recreation Area, c/o Guernsey State Park, Guernsey, WY 82214. Phone: (307) 836-2334. Located in southeastern WY, off US 85, south of Torrington. Open campsites. Water available.

7. Keyhole State Park, 353 McKean Rd., Moorcroft, WY 82721. Phone: (307) 756-3596. Located between Moorcroft and Sundance, off I-90 exits 165 or 153/154; north to US 14 and WY 113. 170+ sites; dump station. Reservable.

8. Medicine Lodge State Archaeological Site, Hyattville, WY 82428. Phone: (307) 469-2234. Located 6 miles NE of Hyattville, off WY 31 on west slope of Big Horn Mountains. 25 sites. Reservable.

9. Seminoe State Park, Seminoe Dam Road, Sinclair, WY 82334. Phone: (307) 320-3013. Located 40 miles NE of Rawlins off I-80 exits 219 or 221. 3 campgrounds, open sites; dump station. 32 foot limit.

10. Sinks Canyon State Park, 3079 Sinks Canyon Rd., Lander, WY 82520. Phone: (307) 332-3077. Located 6 miles SW of Lander on WY 131. Open campsites. 40 foot limit.

11. Cannor Battlefield State Historic Site, c/o Fort Phil Kearny SHS, Story, WY 82842. Phone: (307) 684-7629. Located in Ranchester in northern Wyoming, just off US 14. Open campsites.